Booker T. Washington
Rediscovered

Booker T. Washington
Rediscovered

Edited by Michael Scott Bieze and Marybeth Gasman

The Johns Hopkins University Press   Baltimore

© 2012 The Johns Hopkins University Press
All rights reserved. Published 2012
Printed in the United States of America on acid-free paper
9 8 7 6 5 4 3 2 1

The Johns Hopkins University Press
2715 North Charles Street
Baltimore, Maryland 21218-4363
www.press.jhu.edu

Library of Congress Cataloging-in-Publication Data

Booker T. Washington rediscovered / edited by Michael Scott Bieze and
Marybeth Gasman.
    p. cm.
  Includes bibliographical references and index.
  ISBN-13: 978-1-4214-0470-7 (hdbk. : acid-free paper)
  ISBN-13: 978-1-4214-0471-4 (pbk. : acid-free paper)
  ISBN-13: 978-1-4214-0552-0 (electronic)
  ISBN-10: 1-4214-0470-2 (hdbk. : acid-free paper)
  ISBN-10: 1-4214-0471-0 (pbk. : acid-free paper)
  ISBN-10: 1-4214-0552-0 (electronic)
    1. Washington, Booker T., 1856–1915.   2. Washington, Booker T.,
1856–1915—Political and social views.   3. African American authors.
4. African Americans—Biography.   5. Educators—United States—Biogra-
phy.   I. Bieze, Michael, 1956–   II. Gasman, Marybeth.
    E185.97.W4B673 2012
    370.92—dc23   2011034756
    [B]

A catalog record for this book is available from the British Library.

*Special discounts are available for bulk purchases of this book. For
more information, please contact Special Sales at 410-516-6936 or
specialsales@press.jhu.edu.*

The Johns Hopkins University Press uses environmentally friendly book
materials, including recycled text paper that is composed of at least 30
percent post-consumer waste, whenever possible.

Contents

Preface

Historical accounts are only as good as the primary sources on which they are based. In the case of Booker T. Washington, the primary sources are very good indeed. Louis R. Harlan and Raymond W. Smock oversaw the selection and organization of materials known as the *Booker T. Washington Papers*. This selection of writings from the Library of Congress collection provides readers with an enormous number of letters and articles by Washington, a context for Washington's letters (by reproducing many letters from other men and women), and a bibliography of many of his books and articles. Moreover, the *Papers* offer brief biographies of many of those whom Washington knew and with whom he exchanged letters over the years.

The *Papers* may be accessed online at the University of Illinois Press website. This site offers a helpful search option that makes even the location of words and phrases possible. Since their publication and online launch, the *Papers* have remained the starting point for nearly every historian conducting research on Washington. Harlan used them to create his Pulitzer Prize–winning biography of Washington. Robert Norrell analyzed selections from the *Papers* from a different perspective to write his recently published response to Harlan, *Up from History*. Like so many other projects, the *Papers* provided the starting point for this book.

We hope that readers will see our book as an important extension of the *Papers* in several ways. First, the *Papers'* bibliography is incomplete. It does not contain all of Washington's books; many of Washington's contributions to other books and many journal articles are omitted, as are a great number of newspaper articles. Undoubtedly, new works by Washington will be discovered in the future. In other words, the *Papers'* bibliography is essential but not definitive. For example, an 1897 letter in the *Papers* references a Washington article in the Boston journal *Golden Rule* (1897) but does not include it in the bibliography (fig. P.1). This article in Amos Wells's Christian journal points toward a body of Washington works destined to be discovered to expand our knowledge of him. Second, many of Washington's letters and speeches were not stored at Tuskegee University and therefore did not enter the Library of Congress collection Harlan and his team organized when they created the *Papers*. Many of Washington's letters, notes, and speeches remain in private hands and in institutions. We include a few examples of these so that, again, readers know that Washington's writings extend far beyond the *Papers*. Third, the *Papers* do not reproduce Washington's writings in their original form. A significant number of Washington's works were created using photographs he selected and in layouts that he directed. As one of the first modern media masters, Washington crafted his thoughts in words and pictures. Without pictures and the original layout of the words, readers miss both the aura of the intent and original work. *Booker T. Washington Rediscovered* extends the known works, offers a thematic context for his writings, reproduces them in their original format as readers first encountered them, clarifies that he changed his mind on many subjects, and reminds the researcher that sources survive or gain importance for complex reasons.

This book would not have been possible without my dear friend Marybeth Gasman who has made so many things possible for me; the companionship and trust of Margaret Washington Clifford; Gerald Norwood's wisdom and friendship on this journey; the beautiful mind of Vida Avery; Phil Hutcheson, my mentor at Georgia State University; Lester Sullivan at Xavier University; Dana Chandler for all his generous help and guidance in the Tuskegee University Archives; Catherine Glass and Juanita Roberts in the Ford Motor Library at Tuskegee University; Mellie Kerins at the Augusta State University Reese Library; Vernon Courtney and Donzella Maupin at the Hampton University Museum and Archives; Jason Guzman; and the many insightful suggestions from Greg Nicholl, Andre Barnett, and Ashleigh McKown at the Johns Hopkins University Press. In addition, I am thankful for the research assistance of Meg Brooks, Carson Evans, and Marc Rosenkoetter; for my former students at Marist School; for the friendship and support of my Marist colleagues, Louisa Moffit, Gigi Muirhuid, and Stefanie and Sergio Stadler; and for most of all, my Laura, my Henry, and my Will, who are the center of my world.

Michael S. Bieze

I am grateful to Michael Bieze who has one of the most beautiful minds I have ever encountered. It has been a pleasure to work with him for years on this book. In addition to those individuals noted above by Michael, I am thankful for the support of my research assistants who read earlier drafts of this manuscript: Thai-Huy Nguyen, Christopher Tudico, and Stephen Garlington. And last, I am grateful to my very good friend and colleague, Nelson Bowman III, and, my sweet daughter, Chloe Sarah Epstein.

Marybeth Gasman

GOLDEN RULE

FRANCIS E. CLARK, EDITOR

MANAGING EDITOR,
AMOS R. WELLS

CONTRIBUTING EDITORS,
"PANSY" (Mrs G. R. ALDEN),
Mrs F. E. CLARK

Copyright, 1897, by The Golden Rule Company.

Boston and Chicago

August 26, 1897

made sacred by the death of so many thousands of patriots. Remembering the history of Boston Common, what more appropriate use for these gates could be devised?

"To raise the standard, encourage study, and reward true merit." This is the commendable purpose of an Ohio college that has established a post-graduate course for the degree of D. D. The new departure is said to meet with favor; and why should it not? Anything that shall add to the efficiency of our ministers, whether or not they have affixed to their names a "reward for true merit," ought to meet with favor.

* * *

Sensible Fears.—Queen Victoria is so much afraid of fire that she has established the most elaborate system of protection against the dread element in all her palaces, and instant dismission from her service is the penalty if any one—no matter who—neglects to observe these rules. Her Majesty is right, as usual. What a world-wide calamity it would be if Windsor Palace, for instance, should burn down! We should like to see some of the persons responsible for the preservation of our own important historical buildings and records afflicted with a nervousness like the Queen's.

* * *

What Was Gained?—The newspapers give us extensive accounts of a duel fought on the other side of the sea by the representatives of two European nations, men of royal blood. The cause lay in a criticism of the Italian army made by the Duke of Orleans, a member of the family that once ruled in France. This led to a challenge from the nephew of the king of Italy. Such trivial causes have brought about duels before, and even war, but conflict fails utterly to make matters right. Both men were but slightly wounded. Both doubtless cherish the same feeling as before. It is boyish to rush in and "fight it out," but duelling will never be a manly way for differences to be settled.

* * *

An Instructive Contest.—For some time a vigorous discussion has been going on as to the teaching of English in our colleges and universities, many wishing to see our native tongue given greater prominence, and desiring that a more practical training in the use of English be furnished to our young men and women. A competition announced by the *Century* magazine will do much to disclose the real situation. The magazine offers three prizes of $250 each, one to be given for the best piece of metrical writing of not fewer than fifty lines, another for the

come as gifts, but Commander Booth-Tucker feels that from such an investment a return of five per cent can be assured. The settlers will not be pauperized, but will be expected to repay any loans made to them. Managed in the businesslike way characteristic of the Salvation Army, the proposed colony may well become "the poor man's paradise" that it has already been called, and may offer some real help in lessening the problems of the modern city.

* * *

The Gem of the Jubilee.—Apparently nothing connected with the jubilee of England's loved queen has found a more ready response in the hearts of men than Mr. Kipling's poem that came at its close. There has been wide-spread comment and some surprise expressed because the poem is so thoroughly religious, but the fact that men have been moved by the "Recessional" is conclusive proof that men are still swayed by the deep, true notes of the religious life. There is true recognition of the sovereign God in these noble lines.

> "God of our fathers, known of old;
>   Lord of our far-flung battle line,
> Beneath whose awful hand we hold
>   Dominion over palm and pine;
> Lord God of hosts, be with us yet,
> Lest we forget—lest we forget!
>
> "The tumult and the shouting dies;
>   The captains and the kings depart;
> Still stands thine ancient sacrifice,
>   An humble and a contrite heart.
> Lord God of hosts, be with us yet,
> Lest we forget—lest we forget!"

* * *

Tuskegee and Its President.—No man has a better right to speak on the progress of the negro race than has Booker T. Washington, who contributes an article on the following page. In his own career he furnishes an example of the spirit that is back of all progress of black and white alike. Having himself struggled successfully, he is giving his life to trying to lift others of his race, and grandly is he succeeding. There is always promise for the rising generation, and Tuskegee is doing a great work in training it. But not all the youth can go to school, and it is always a question what can be done for those beyond the age for schools. The needs of these are considered as well, and through the Tuskegee conferences Booker Washington is giving powerful help to this class. The conference brings together hundreds of people from the surrounding country; they present their problems and tell of their successes, gain new ideas and courage, and go back to better work. All the discussions are skilfully guided by President Washington, and his wise words thus reach many hearers, to be repeated by them to others on their return, and thus to have a great influence in moulding the future of his people and so of the country.

* * *

A Heroic Woman.—Miss Alice Fletcher, who will read a paper at the next meeting of the American Association for the Advancement of Science, is said to be the

T. THOMAS FORTUNE,
Editor of *The New York Age*, the leading African paper
of the country.

HON. B. K. BRUCE,
For six years United States Senator from Missouri and
afterwards Register of the U. S. Treasury.

The Progress of the Negro Race.

By President Booker T. Washington,

Superintendent of Tuskegee Institute, Tuskegee, Ala.

YOU ask me to send you a few lines bearing upon the progress of the negro race. In considering the progress of my race, it is well to consider the starting-point of the race, in order to be able to determine its progress. As the late Hon. Frederick Douglass expressed it, the negro is to be judged not so much by the heights to which he has climbed as by the depths from which he has come.

One of the criticisms most often heard against the negro is the one to the effect that he does not save his earnings, does not plan for the future. In order to decide whether the negro is making progress along this line it is well to bear in mind that he had no reason to think of saving or providing for the future during the days of slavery; that his training for 250 years in this country rather taught how *not* to save, how *not* to provide for the future; and that the habit and ability to provide for the future are the sign and test of the highest civilization.

Is the negro beginning to save, to provide for the future? He is. The best evidence of this is to be found on the outer edges of any city or town in the South. If one will make a careful investigation, he will find that in many of the cities and towns in the South the colored people own a large proportion of the houses that they occupy. Thousands who do not own their houses at present are gradually buying on small monthly or yearly payments. Such progress speaks volumes for a people that thirty-five years ago did not own their own bodies.

Too often persons of the white race, both North and South, misjudge the progress of the negro race, because they see only those negroes who are to be found upon the street-corners, at the barrooms and railroad stations. This is not fair. A race is judged by its best, not by its worst. Boston is judged by its Edward Everett Hale, not by its John L. Sullivan. When one wants to study the progress of the negro, he should carefully follow him from his rented one-room cabin into his little cottage with two or three rooms, where often will be found evidences of growth, such as books, pictures, newspapers, and carpets.

Perhaps the most interesting hour in connection with the Tuskegee Negro Conference—which meets each year at the Tuskegee Institute in February, and brings together about eight hundred people from the Black Belt—is when the people are permitted to tell about their struggles in acquiring a small home. In these conferences the people tell how in many cases they go without food and clothing that they may begin the purchase of a small home. A race that can make such sacrifices is making progress.

One of the happiest men I ever met was a colored man I saw a short time ago, who told me that he had just

PRESIDENT BOOKER T. WASHINGTON.

made his first payment on a lot. I asked him how much he had paid, and he replied, "Fifty cents."

Note to Reader

The reader will soon discover that this book begins in a printed format but extends into a digital component at a website (www.press.jhu.edu/BTW). The reasons are both conceptual and practical. As a conceptual matter, this book is being published during a period of revolutionary change in how the written word is communicated. The Janus-headed format speaks to this moment in time by recognizing the importance of the physical object in conducting archival work and, at the same time, the reality of digital archives and the future of research in digital forms. The future will require researchers to still hunt through the physical holdings of archives.

Beyond the aura of the original, one needs to see it to ascertain the content and completeness of the digital copy; letters are cropped, their backs not photocopied; embossments are lost; context is incomplete until verified; and, as Erik Larson discovered while writing about a killer in *The Devil in the White City*, seeing the killer's handwriting on a postcard and imagining the pressure of the pencil into the paper were viscerally exciting and yielded information beyond a mouse click. At the same time, access to primary sources online is also an essential part of academic inquiry. The cost of reproducing high-resolution copies of the originals in a printed version is often prohibitive in a book but not on a website. We hope that in this book researchers will find material to consider both the strengths and the limitations of encountering text in print and online.

Booker T. Washington
Rediscovered

Introduction

Understanding Booker T. Washington continues to challenge anyone seriously studying twentieth-century American history. Washington remains a subject worthy of investigating because so many of the monumental debates on race in America—including the themes of African American identity, politics, philanthropy, art, religion, social class, education, and leadership—are knotted into Washington's writings and actions. That he is simultaneously well known and completely unknown should raise questions about how we have judged him. Today, few people remember why he is famous, and he suffers the unenviable fate of being spoken for by a long list of detractors who cherry-pick from a mountain of writings, a line that fits a now-established historical narrative with a tragic plot. As a result, Washington largely exists as an abstraction, reduced to a World's Fair speech and a feel-good, up-by-one's-bootstraps autobiography.

Yet he keeps reappearing in our national consciousness, resisting such easy conceptualization. Nearly everything one may examine concerning Washington and Tuskegee Industrial and Normal Institute is riddled with complexities. As a school, Tuskegee was not easily labeled; it was neither a high school nor a college. Washington was referred to as both the principal and the president of Tuskegee, further complicating matters. Was Washington a hero of the downtrodden or a manipulative little man behind the curtain of a Black Oz? Was he the simple countryman that he professed to be in words and pictures, or was he the cultured man who delivered speeches with the rolled *r*'s of a Boston sophisticate? Was he an integrationist or a separatist? He always claimed to be working for an America of inclusiveness and opportunity, yet he only hired Black teachers and workers for Tuskegee—the Black Arcadian campus he designed in Alabama. Was his plan to teach agricultural skills and to promote community investment simply backward looking?[1] Finally, how do we decide whether he was successful? What criteria are used to make that determination? His detractors would look at low graduation rates and the lack of social equality under his period of leadership. Washington answered his critics with a book, *Tuskegee and Its People*, arguing that the mission of the school was ultimately community development, networking, and fighting against the perception of Black inferiority at a time when racism was institutional and supported by science.

His death in 1915, on the eve of America's plunge into the Great War and the Great Migration, buried for nearly a century his many complexities, his furtive actions, and his many writings, speeches, and images that made him the most famous Black man in the world. After the war, Black America moved to a new beat whose center was in Harlem. Washington, who symbolized the Old Time Negro, was now a reminder of the many things that needed to be forgotten. The first step in his erasure from history was to bind him into an equation as the counterpart to the Black scholar, author, and editor W. E. B. Du Bois, effectively limiting his contributions. Du Bois grew to represent the direction of the New Negro: civil rights advocacy opposing all forms of accommodationism and political conservativism.[2] Although there is much to be gained from seeing Washington in opposition to Du Bois, there are other more illuminating ways to study the Wizard of Tuskegee. Lost in such a simple formula are Washington's many other roles as a celebrity, a college president, and a cultured thinker who mingled with leading progressives. Instead, Washington was cast in bronze, as a nineteenth-century relic of a bygone era. For those who continued to uphold him as a champion of the poor, he remained a folk legend, a Moses of his people, a Black Prometheus who stole from the White philanthropy gods to give fire to the forgotten sharecroppers. For those who vilified him, he quickly came to symbolize the worst kind of Negro, a traitor to the race and an Uncle Tom who sold out on civil rights for meager material gains.

Unsatisfied with either portrait, scholars continue to try to understand Washington, sensing that these abstractions are politically motivated distortions. Every few years, new books and articles are written to attempt to explain Booker T. Washington's elusive nature. Solving the many riddles of his character and philosophies has perplexed many great minds. It took Louis R. Harlan, Washington's biographer of a two-volume biography, several articles, and a fourteen-volume edited set of papers to arrive at the conclusion that "Washington had no quintessence."[3] If that were true, less research would have been required. Writers often point to the description of the Booker T. Washington statue on the Tuskegee campus in Ralph Ellison's *Invisible Man* as best symbolizing the ambiguity of Washington's leadership and philosophy. The invisible man sees in his mind's eye the Washington sculpture, the Tuskegee founder, holding a billowing curtain over a crouching man, "unable to decide whether the veil is really being lifted, or lowered more firmly in place."[4] Overlooked in the query is, What in the world is a brilliant high-art statue by one of America's leading White sculptors of the early twentieth century doing on the campus of a Black, southern trade school? Only by looking closely at Washington and his writings does the answer emerge. In addition to his better-known agendas, Washington, a man with a rich aesthetic and a friend to many artists, was also deeply involved in the advancement of Black art in America.

Four reasons explain the value and sustainability of reexamining Washington in his own words and in his own pictures. First, a thematic approach to Washington's writings allows readers to see his diversity of topics. Furthermore, by focusing on themes, this book shows that, over time, Washington changed as a thinker and that he addressed different audiences with different messages. In keeping with our notion of a nontraditional book on Booker T. Washington, we have incorporated new technology to make various texts and images available with the highest resolution possible on an accompanying website (www.press.jhu.edu/BTW). On a practical level, the website provides readers with additional materials that would have been too unwieldy in book form.

Washington has not been studied this way before because few of his writings are readily available. This leads to the second reason for this book: accessibility of materials. The definitive works on Booker T. Washington are Louis R. Harlan's two-volume biography and the fourteen-volume edited papers. Washington wrote, depending on one's count, thirteen books, at least two hundred articles, many speeches, thousands of letters, and a variety of reports to various Tuskegee constituencies. In part, this book supplements Harlan's by reproducing works found in the *Booker T. Washington Papers*.[5] In addition, this book reproduces Washington's works in their original formats and by theme rather than by chronology. Except for *Up from Slavery*, which has never gone out of print, Washington's works are otherwise difficult to locate in their original form.

The original formats are, in fact, critical and provide the third reason for this new volume. Our book raises specific questions of historiography regarding the form of Washington's publications. Most of the works were created with visual support, most often photographs by artists Washington hired. Consequently, scholars researching Washington, even those using primary sources such as the *Booker T. Washington Papers*, have missed the rebus nature of the writings. The photographers he hired included some of the most prominent artists from both Black and White America, and therefore, he should be recognized as playing a critical role in developing the "New Negro cultural movement," which should not be confused with the later use of the phrase *New Negro* during the Harlem Renaissance.

Reproducing Washington's writings in their original layout with images challenges the traditional notions of primary sources and even questions the nature of Harlan's edited *Papers* as a primary source since they alter layout, omit or displace photographs, and misappropriate writings from their original context.

Context, or what Roland Barthes describes as the site of the text, is extremely important in Washington's writings because he is often miscast as a far-right conservative. In this book, readers will see Washington's writings with original layout, fonts, pictures, and design work so that the author's audiences and intentions may be properly examined. For example, in this introduction, an article by Washington published in *The Nautilus* is reproduced.[6] The article shows how Washington's richly illustrated articles were published in a variety of leading journals of the day and even graced the cover of *The Nautilus*, which advanced the religious ideas of the New Thought Movement.

The other historiographic issue raised in this book concerns the holdings of archives. Researching African American figures such as Washington is not fully possible without an awareness of vast private holdings within Black families and among collectors of African American ephemera. This book provides some of those materials to illustrate that much of the primary materials needed to tell the whole story remain outside the reach of most researchers.

The great hidden archives in Black families raise the fourth issue of this book: Who gets to tell the story of a historical figure? Washington was the first to tell his story. He authored at least three autobiographies. This is the subject of chapter 1. After he completed performing in a complex Jim Crow masque, academic historians began to tell their own Washington story. However, a third voice has always existed in telling Washington's story—his family's. Families have often played a crucial part in promoting and in guarding the depiction of their role in history. Wary of having their viewpoint erased, African American families have always been strong storytellers, ensuring that their family legacies endure and inspire. Since Washington's death, the Washington family has been active in telling the story of its patriarch's vision. Until her death in 2009, Margaret Washington Clifford, Booker T. Washington's granddaughter and oldest-living relative, traveled the country celebrating his legacy, promoting his philosophy, and arguing with anyone who judged him without consulting Washington's actual writings. She carried on the work of her father, Davidson (Booker T. Washington's youngest son), who kept the legacy alive with publications of Washington's speeches and philosophy. Mrs. Clifford's bookshelves were filled with Washington's original books, photographs, pamphlets, and letters. Many of these are one-of-a-kind items, maintained by the family to use in their speaking engagements. Her treasure trove of materials, some of which appear in this book, are a starting point for discussing the complex roles families play in preserving and creating history.

THE BOOKER WASHINGTON NUMBER

The NAUTILUS

WE have hard problems, it is true, but instead of despairing in the face of the difficulties we should as a race, thank God that we have a problem. As an individual I would rather belong to a race that has a great and difficult task to perform, than be a part of a race whose pathway is strewn with flowers. It is only by meeting and manfully facing hard, stubborn and difficult problems that races, like individuals, are, in the highest degree, made strong.

—*Booker T. Washington.*

FEBRUARY, 1912   PRICE 10 CTS.

THE OFFICE BUILDING, IN WHICH ARE LOCATED THE ADMINISTRATIVE OFFICES OF THE SCHOOL, THE INSTITUTE BANK, AND THE INSTITUTE POST OFFICE.

The Story of Tuskegee Institute.

By BOOKER T. WASHINGTON.

Founder and Principal.

The Tuskegee Normal and Industrial Institute was established by the Legislature of Alabama in 1880, when the Legislature appropriated $2,000 to be used to pay the salaries of teachers. The school was opened July 4, 1881, in a shanty church with 30 pupils and one teacher. No provision was made by the Legislature for the buildings.

Thrown upon its own resources, the school has grown by its own necessities. Whatever it was necessary to do the students have done under the direction of their teachers, thus one by one the different industries were organized and made part of the training and teaching of the school; this in addition, of course, to the studies in the books.

As it was necessary to have food for the students, farming was the first definite industry established. This was started on a small scale in 1883. Previous to that students simply did chores. One hundred acres of land with three small buildings had been secured during the first session of the school, through the aid of Northern friends. As the school grew, however, there was need of more land to sup-port it, and more land was obtained. Students, under the direction of the teachers, did the work now as before, and the means for carrying it on were supplied by those who believed in that kind of education.

The school has grown until at the present time the population of the school community, including 180 teachers and officers and employes, amounts to nearly 2,000 persons. The total enrollment in 1911 was 1702. From its foundation up to the present, about 9,000 men and women have gone out from the school and are doing good work, mostly as teachers and industrial workers.

The educational plant consists at present of 2,345 acres of land, 103 buildings large and small, including dwellings, dormitories, class rooms, shops, barns, which, together with the equipment, stock in trade, live stock and personal property is valued at $1,279,248.45.

The school's truck garden of 80 acres supplies the school's dining hall and the town market with vegetables. Eighty acres more are devoted to orchard and small fruits, 848 acres to general farming.

The dairy herd consists of 277 head of cattle,

THE NAUTILUS.

45

TOMPKIN'S MEMORIAL HALL.

breeders, yearlings and calves. The creamery in the year 1910 received 6 ,949 gallons of milk and manufactured 15,718 pounds of butter. The swine herd consists of 562 head of hogs. In the poultry yard there are over 2,000 fowls.

The work of the farm was carried on in 1910 by 228 students, about 40 hired men, and 18 instructors. The leading crops were 632 tons of ensilage, 12,000 bushels of sweet potatoes, 3,500 bushels of corn, 3,650 bushels of oats.

The orchard contains about 12,500 peach trees, 140,000 strawberry plants, 3,850 grape vines and 185 fig trees.

Next to food it was necessary to have houses to live in and buildings in which to carry on the work of the school, therefore the second industry established was that of bricklaying and plastering. The first bricks were made in a ravine which is now part of the school campus, in the year 1883. The first bricks were made by hand. At the present time the two machines in use have a daily capacity of 25,000 each. The bricks used in all the buildings on the campus were made by the students and teachers on the grounds.

About this same time a blacksmith shop was started in a little frame building 12x16. The present blacksmith shop contains 10 forges, and in 1910 did work to the value of $3,158. This included the work on 64 new vehicles constructed in the school, and the shoeing of 1,248 horses and mules.

Carpentry was introduced in a small way in 1884. Most of the carpenter work on the 103 buildings upon the grounds has been performed by the students. In 1910 work to the value of $43,787 was done by the students in this division, under the direction of their teachers.

Printing was started in 1885. At the present time two papers are published in the interest of the school and its work, the Tuskegee Student and the Southern Letter, and besides that a negro country paper, The Messenger, four monthly periodicals and a considerable amount of printing for business firms and for other schools is done in the Tuskegee Institute Printing Office. The value of the work of the office in 1910 averaged $1,750 per month.

The school's saw mill was started in 1886. At that time the school owned a large tract of heavily timbered land and it was found that it could be manufactured into lumber at a considerable saving. During 1910, 78,000 feet of lumber were sawed, 153,500 feet of lumber dressed and 105,000 laths and 100 cords of wood were sawed.

The first wagon was made on the grounds in 1887, by an untutored colored man who was working at that time in the saw mill. The school was in need of a wagon, but did not have money enough to buy it. This man said that if the school would purchase the hubs and enough iron he would build the wagon. This wagon was built under an oak tree on the campus, and was the direct cause of the establishment of the wheelwright shop in 1888.

In 1891, as the blacksmith shop began to build buggies and carriages, it was found necessary to establish a new trade, namely that of carriage trimming.

CLASS IN OUTDOOR GEOGRAPHY.

In 1890 it was found that the bill for tinware had grown so large that it had become profitable to establish a tin shop on the grounds. Lewis Adams, a colored man, who was largely responsible for the securing of the location of the Institute at Tuskegee, was at that time doing the work. It was found that he could be employed to do the work on the school grounds and give instruction to the students for less than the school was paying him during the year for odd jobs. Mr. Adams was also a harnessmaker and shoemaker, and did a large part of the repairing for the school. He was employed, and for a time taught all three of these trades. About 3,000 pieces of tinware, including dozens of wash pans, slop cans, etc., are made every year by the tin shop for the use of the school. Nearly all the roofing for the larger buildings on the grounds has been made and put upon the buildings by the students of the tin shop. The value of the work in this division for 1910 was $11,067. In the shoe shop 61 pairs of shoes were made by students during the year, and 1,070 pairs repaired. In the harness shop in 1910 were made 43 sets of harness, 500 pairs of harness, and 27 vehicles were trimmed and other work done for the school to the value of $4,087.

An abandoned cupola which was presented to J. H. Washington, brother of the Principal, by the authorities of the Auburn Agricultural and Mechanical School for whites at Auburn, brought about the establishment of a foundry and machine shop. For sometime Mr. Washington, who was in charge of the industries,

had been looking forward to the setting up of a machine shop. To do such work as he desired, however, it was necessary to have a foundry. About this time the authorities of the Auburn school had decided to take out the small cupola they had been using and put in a large one. When they learned that the Tuskegee Institute was in need of something of this kind, they decided to give them the old cupola. The Tuskegee Institute was so poor at that time that it did not feel able to pay the freight. Mr. Washington finally sent a three-yoke ox team after the cupola and pulled it fifteen miles over an Alabama country road. Since that time the school has made its own castings. The foundry manufactures boiler grates, cast iron bed locks and sash weights of different sizes, machine castings and various miscellaneous castings. The value of the work in 1910 was $1,633. The machine shop inclusive of the foundry, now occupies an area in the Trades Building of 2,370 square feet. There are now installed at different points on the grounds 17 steam boilers with a total capacity of 861 horse power. The total value of the business in the machine shop in 1910 was $24,017.

Plumbing and steam fitting, which was at first part of the work of the machine shop, have since been organized as separate industries. Under the charge of this division there have been installed 9,595 feet of steam and 30,937 feet of water line, carrying steam and water to all of the large buildings on the grounds.

The first electric dynamo was purchased in

ARCHITECTURAL DRAWING DIVISION.

1898 and the first electric lights were used in the new Chapel, completed in that year. Over six thousand electric lights are used at the present time in lighting the buildings and grounds of the school. Over 26 miles of wiring have been installed and are now maintained by the students in this division.

In addition to these industries already mentioned, there is the tailor shop in which the students' uniforms are made and repaired, and a department of architectural and mechanical drawing in which the drawings and specifications for all the mechanical work and building on the grounds are made.

Before there was farming at Tuskegee there was cooking, and that is still, with plain sewing, the chief industry in which girls are instructed. In 1901 the girls' trades were centered in a building which is now known as Dorothy Hall. This building contains the laundry, cooking, sewing, dressmaking and millinery shops. In this building baskets, mattresses, brooms and soap are made. In the year 1910, 2,779 articles were made. In the ladies' tailoring division, 1,072 shirt waists, collars, cuffs, and aprons were made.

In 1887 a mattress factory was started in connection with the cooking and sewing. The girls made in 1910, 1,449 brooms, 125 mattresses, 70 mats, 484 curtains, 193 table cloths, 263 bed ticks, 2,011 pillow cases, 123 window shades and 99 screens, in all articles valued at $2,279.

All the laundry work for the school is done by the girls in a building which is now fully equipped with all the appliances of a modern steam laundry. Reports show that 1,432,023 pieces were laundered in this department during the year 1910.

In 1892 the Phelps Hall Bible Training School was established and made a part of the work of the Tuskegee Institute. The purpose of this school is to fit students for work as preachers, and missionaries under the actual conditions now existing among colored people. Much of the work of the school is carried on among the Macon County ministers. There is, for instance, a night Bible class which gives opportunity to the ministers in the town and surrounding country, who are not able to attend the school during the day, to learn something at night of the Bible and its history. There is also a Macon County Ministers' Association which meets four times a year at the school and brings the Bible students in touch with the ministers of the county and with the practical problems of community work. Since it was founded, 611 men and 29 women have studied at the Bible Training School; of this number 84 men and 6 women have graduated.

The actual work of Tuskegee has for a number of years grown beyond the limits of the school grounds. Every year sees the amount of the so-called "Extension Work" increasing. In the year 1891 Principal Booker T. Washington sent out invitations to about 75 representative negroes in Macon County and invited them to come to the school and spend a day in talking over the interests of the negroes in their county. About 400 men, mostly farmers, responded. This was the beginning of the An-

48   THE NAUTILUS.

nual Negro Conference which now draws together every year from all parts of the South negro farmers and teachers and all the plain and simple people who are interested or practically engaged in the welfare of the race. A

BOOKER T. WASHINGTON

Conference Agent is employed during the year to organize local conferences in the different parts of Alabama and adjoining states, in order to keep up the interest and encourage further work in the different localities, along the lines suggested by the Annual Conference. At the last gathering there were 105 of these local organizations.

In 1897 a farmers' institute was established and has held monthly meetings, winter and summer, in the Agricultural Building ever since that time. At these meetings farmers hear simple lectures on agriculture and give their own experiences in attempting to apply these methods.

In 1904 a "Short Course" in agriculture was started which attempted to give farmers in the surrounding country, at the season when most of them are idle, the advantage of two weeks' study and observation of the work of the school farm. The first year there were 11 students and most of them older men. In 1911 this number had been increased to 1,900, and more than a thousand of them were young men and women.

In 1905 the Jesup Wagon, a sort of agricultural school on wheels, designed and built by the students at the Institute, was sent out into the surrounding country to take the instruction of the school directly to the farmers. Two

years later, under the direction of the Agricultural Department at Washington, the experiment of demonstration farming was started for colored people in Macon County. At the present time similar work is being done in Wilcox and Lee counties, Alabama, and in Bolivar county, Mississippi, under the direction of Tuskegee graduates.

For a number of years a negro county fair has been held every year in connection with the farmers' institute of the county near the school. In 1906 a permanent fair ground was erected on the school grounds.

In 1906 through the aid of funds furnished the school, the work of building up the country schools in Macon and surrounding counties was begun. Through the encouragement given them by this school fund negro farmers in Macon County, where Tuskegee Institute is located, have themselves contributed over $20,-000 to the building of school houses and the lengthening of school terms. A model country school has been established just beyond the limits of the Institute farm. This model school, which is a combined school and dwelling house, is taught by two Tuskegee graduates, a man and his wife. The house contains five rooms, sitting room, bed room, kitchen, dining room and class room. There is also a barn and horse, cow, pigs and chickens. Regular class room work is carried on in this as in any other public rural school except that, instead of spending all the time in the class room, the pupils are divided in sections and given instruction in the ordinary industries of a farming community. While some pupils cook, others clean the house, others work in the garden and others receive their book training.

In addition to the other extension work, "mothers' meetings" have been established in the town of Tuskegee by Mrs. Booker T. Washington, and these have extended their influence to other communities. More than 20 such communities in the county and elsewhere now maintain weekly meetings of this kind. In all, about 2,000 women on the farms are reached in this way.

Through the influence of Tuskegee and its graduates, a considerable number of other schools, similar in character to that of Tuskegee, have been established in different parts of the country. The most important of these schools are, the Snow Hill Normal and Industrial Institute at Snow Hill, Alabama, founded by William J. Edwards, the Mt. Meigs Institute at Waugh, Alabama, founded by Miss Cornelia Bowen, the Robert Hungerford Industrial School at Eatonville, Florida, founded by R. C. Calhoun, the Utica Normal and Industrial Institute at Utica, Mississippi, founded by William H. Holtzclaw, the Voorhees Normal and Industrial School at Denmark, S. C., founded by the late Elizabeth Wright Menafee, and the Topeka Industrial and Educational Institute at Topeka, Kansas, under the direction of W. R. Carter.

Tuskegee now has, in addition to its other property, an endowment fund which amounts to $1,401,926. The first sums raised to perpetuate the work of the school were raised by Tuskegee graduates. What was known as the Olivia Davidson Fund was started in 1890. It was not until 1900, ten years later, that the small amounts which students and graduates were contributing reached the amount of $1,000. Meanwhile the endowment had been increasing from various sources, the largest donation, $50,000 coming from Collis P. Huntington. The largest increase in the endowment was in 1903 when Andrew Carnegie gave the school the sum of $600,000. In the year of the quarter centennial, 1905, the endowment fund was increased by the sum of $150,000 contributed by the friends of William H. Baldwin, Jr. That same year the Tuskegee Alumni contributed $1,000.

The largest amount contributed to the perpetuation of the school by any negro was a bequest of $38,000 from the estate of Mrs. Mary E. Shaw, a colored woman of New York.

WHY I MADE TUSKEGEE AN INDUSTRIAL SCHOOL.

Tuskegee Institute was started, in a small way in the summer of 1881. At that time the negro had lost practically all political control in the South. As early as 1885 there were scarcely any members of my race in the National Congress or state legislatures, and long before this date they had ceased to hold state offices. This was true, notwithstanding the protests and fervent oratory of such strong race leaders as Frederick Douglass, B. K. Bruce, P. B. S. Pinchback, and John M. Langston, with a host of others. When Frederick Douglass, the greatest man that the negro has produced, died in 1895, it is safe to say that the negro in the Southern States, with here and there a few exceptions, had practically no political control or political influence, except in sending delegates to national conventions, or in holding a few Federal positions by appointment.

It became evident to many thoughtful negroes that the members of the race could no longer look to political agitation and the opportunity of holding office as a means of gaining a reputation or winning success. In short they must look to something more tangible and substantial upon which to base their future. It was at this period in the negro's development, when the distance between the races was greatest and the spirit and ambition of the colored people most depressed, that the idea of industrial or business development was introduced and began to be made prominent.

It did not take the more level-headed members of the race long to see that while the negro in the South was surrounded by many difficulties, there was practically no line drawn and little discrimination in the world of commerce, banking, storekeeping, manufacturing, the skilled trades, and in agriculture; and in this lay his great opportunity. They understood that, while the whites might object to a negro's being postmaster, they would not object to his being president of a bank, and in the latter occupation they would give him assistance and encouragement. The colored people were quick to see that while the negro would not be invited to attend the white man's prayer meeting, he would be invited every time to attend the stockholders' meetings of a business concern in which he had an interest, and that he could buy property in practically any portion of the South where the white man could buy it.

The white citizens were all the more willing to encourage the negro in this economic or industrial development, because they saw that the prosperity of the negro meant also the prosperity of the white man. They saw, too, that when a negro became the owner of a home and was a taxpayer having a regular trade or other occupation, he at once became a conservative and safe citizen and voter; one who would consider the interests of his whole community before casting his ballot; and, further, one whose ballot could not be purchased.

It was at this time that I set out to start an industrial school for the members of my race at the little town of Tuskegee, in what is known as the Black Belt of Alabama.

The first thing I did, as soon as I arrived at the place for establishing the new college, as it was called, was to study the actual needs of the people around it. For this purpose I spent several weeks traveling about in different parts of the county, visiting the colored people in their homes and talking to them in their churches. At the same time I felt compelled to take account of the attitude and disposition of the white people in regard to the new school. I did this because the legislature was furnishing the funds for starting the school and because I saw clearly that there was no hope of putting negro education on a firm basis in the South, unless it was possible to secure the interest and sympathy of the white people. I saw that, if the school I proposed to establish was to be successful, it must find a common ground somewhere between the races. Thus it was that I set out at the very start to secure the support and interest of both white people and black people.

Many people, especially in the North, have a wrong conception of the attitude of the Southern white people towards negro education. It has been very generally thought that what is termed "higher education" of the negro has from the first been opposed by the white South. This opinion is far from correct. I remember that, when I began work at Tuskegee, practically all of the white people who talked to me on the subject took it for granted that instruction in Greek, Latin and modern languages, would make up the greater part of the curriculum. No one opposed this course of study. In fact, there are many white people in the South today who do not know that instruction in the dead languages is not given at Tuskegee Institute.

The truth is that a large part of the people in the South had little faith in any kind of education for the negro. They were indifferent, but not openly opposed to it. On the other hand, there has always been an influential group of white people in the Southern States who have stood out prominently and courageously for the education of all the people, regardless of race. This group of people has thus far been successful in shaping and directing public opinion, and I think that it will continue to do so more and more. This statement must not be taken to mean that there is as yet an equitable division of the school funds between the two races in all sections of the South, although the Southern States deserve much credit for what has been done.

I wish, however, to emphasize the fact that, while there was open antagonism or indifference in certain directions it was the introduction of industrial training in the negro's education that furnished the first basis for anything like a common interest and united action between the two races in the South, and between the whites in the North and those in the South. Aside from its direct benefit to the black race, industrial education has furnished a basis for mutual confidence and co-operation. And this has meant more to the South, and to the work of education, than has been realized.

From its inception the white people of the South were favorable to industrial education for the negro because they had noted, what was not unnatural, that a large portion of the colored people were disposed immediately after emancipation to interpret freedom to mean freedom from work with the hands. The white people saw in the setting up of schools to teach the negro youth that labor with the hands was honorable, something that would lead the negro into his new life of freedom gradually and prevent him from flying from one extreme of life to the other.

Besides that industrial education appealed directly to the interest of the individual white man and to the community. They saw at once that intelligence, coupled with skill, would add wealth to the community and to the state. Crude labor, in the days of slavery, had been made profitable to a certain extent. The ignorant and unskilled labor, in a state of freedom, could not be made so. Practically every white man in the South was interested directly or indirectly in agriculture or in some other business or trade which employed manual labor. Every white man was interested in all that related to the home life, the cooking and serving of food, laundrying, dairying, poultry raising and housekeeping generally, so there was a general recognition of the fact that the education of the black people, who had hitherto performed this kind of work, was of vital interest to every white man in the South.

If the black man became a lawyer, a doctor, a minister or a teacher his professional duty did not under ordinary circumstances bring him into contact, in any direct and vital way, with the life of the white people of the community. The result was that as long as the education of the negro was of a purely literary or professional character it had little interest or significance to the average white man. There was a confused idea that such kind of education might bring about a higher and better type of negro manhood, but that seemed remote and doubtful.

The minute, however, it appeared that as a result of industrial education the negro would not only, for example, study chemistry but apply that chemistry to the enrichment of the soil and the production of crops; apply it to

THE NAUTILUS.   51

cooking, to dairying and to other practical matters; the minute it was seen that in the new industrial school the negro was not only learning geometry and physics but applying his knowledge to blacksmithing, brickmaking, house building and what not; at that moment there began for the first time to be a common bond between the two races and an opportunity for co-operation between the North and the South in the matter of negro education.

It was not so easy to convince the masses of the colored people that there was any virtue in a school that taught their children to work with their hands. They argued, not unnaturally, that they and their people had been worked for 250 years in slavery and now they thought they ought to have a little rest. At any rate, it seemed to them, that a school was the last place on earth where work ought to be so much as mentioned.

I said to them, in reply to these arguments, that it was true that they *had been worked* in slavery; but that now I proposed to teach them *to work.* I said to them that there was a great deal of difference between working and being worked. I said that a man who was worked was a slave but that a man who worked was a free man. I tried to make clear to them that as long as it was necessary to have some one over them to direct, superintend and follow them up in everything which they did they would remain slaves, but as soon as they learned to work independently, to put skill and intelligence and conscience into their labor then, and not till then, would they become free. It was not easy at first, because of the prejudice that had grown up in slavery against working with the hands, to make the mass of the people see and believe that there was any advantage in having their sons taught

to plow and their daughters to cook. They said these things they had done at home and now they wanted them to go to school and learn something new and different.

Nevertheless, the Tuskegee Institute has gone forward year after year, preaching the gospel of the beauty and the dignity of labor and putting it in practice in the shops, in the kitchen and on the farm. Year by year the number of students has grown as the facilities of the school have increased. Still hundreds of students are turned away every year because we have not room for them in the school grounds. In the meantime, I am glad to say the sentiment with regard to work has completely changed inside the school. Today our students are just as eager to perform the work allotted to them on the farm or in the shop as they are ready to go to a lesson in history, geography or arithmetic.

At the same time the sentiment towards work has changed among the masses of the colored people outside of the school. In fact I have always believed that the most important service which the Tuskegee Institute has performed, during its thirty years of existence, has been in the direction of changing the sentiment of the masses of the negro people in the South towards the subject of labor with the hands.

FOOT NOTE.—*In Tompkin's Memorial Hall, pictured at the first of this article, students during the school term take their meals three times daily. The building also contains an assembly room, with a seating capacity of 2500, a teachers' dining room, kitchens for teachers and students, and a large bakery, which supplies the needs of the school and of the institute community. The building cost approximately $175,000 and is the largest building on the institute grounds.*

DR. BOOKER T. WASHINGTON IN HIS GARDEN.

1

Autobiography

Throughout Booker T. Washington's professional life, autobiography played a crucial role in marketing himself and his ideals. Only a few years after founding Tuskegee Institute in 1881, the stalwart Black leader learned that people wanted to know his story. He met their curiosity with his moving Black Horatio Alger tale. His amazing journey from a Virginia slave cabin to the White House, of rising from a fatherless, dirt-poor houseboy to the most famous man of African descent in the world captivated audiences worldwide. Like Benjamin Franklin, another great American rags-to-riches autobiographer, Washington learned how to perform as a celebrity to gain power and money. Unlike Franklin or later nineteenth-century celebrities who crafted their life stories, Washington was a Black man rising to power under the darkening shadow of Jim Crow laws and policies that flared after the Reconstruction collapsed. His articles, speeches, and life stories took on different tones, depending on their audiences. For White audiences, he crafted an image of Victorian grace to appeal to those in a position to fund Tuskegee. For Black audiences, he increasingly dropped the passive mask and appeared more as an activist.

Many people are familiar with his autobiography *Up from Slavery*; however, Washington's life story in print underwent constant editing—beginning years before that book was published. By 1895, his celebrity rose after the Atlanta Cotton States and International Exposition speech boosted him onto the national stage. Immediately, requests poured in for his life story. He consented to have it first published as a pamphlet, *A Joshua in the Camp*, which remains an obscure work.[1] It is reprinted here because it contains the essential elements of Washington's later autobiographies. Meanwhile, his speeches from the same period subtly outlined the first drafts of an autobiography. Eventually, Washington would write three autobiographical books and a few autobiographical sketches.

Readers confront three issues in Washington's autobiographies.[2] The first is authorship. Perhaps it is best to understand his books as collaborations because a different ghostwriter with a distinct writing assisted with each book.[3] The second concern for readers is recognizing how each autobiography was written for a particular audience. Washington's first autobiography, *The Story of My Life and Work*, was primarily intended for a Black audience.[4] It had a Black ghostwriter and included numerous photographs most likely taken by the Black photographer Harry Shepherd.[5] A page from a salesman's copy is included here for the reader to see how the book, which was only sold by subscription with different cover options, was marketed.

Washington's follow-up work, *Up from Slavery*, was ghostwritten by a White journalist and contained a frontispiece by Gertrude Kasebier, the famous White photographer whom the White audiences buying the book would have surely known.[6] The excerpts from *The Story of My Life and Work* and *Up from Slavery* are accounts of Washington's speech delivered in the vast, lavish Auditorium Building at the Chicago Peace Jubilee as part of the victory celebration of the Spanish American War. The subtle differences in the texts serve as examples of Washington's awareness of different audiences.

Washington recorded the Chicago speech in his first two biographies in very different ways. In his first full autobiography, *The Story of My Life and Work*, a book heavily marketed toward a Black audience, Washington included the entire text of the speech, part of it recounted by him and part described by the *Chicago Times Herald*.[7] This strategy of having prominent sources recount his words became a constant rhetorical technique, lending increased significance to his words. In this book, Washington repeated his statement that "a cancer" was growing in America.[8] He added, "This is not a threat, but a warning, and one which the White race should give heed. The only solution of the 'Negro Problem' which will remove all menace to the tranquility and interest of the country, is a universal recognition of the Negro's rights."[9] The northern press paid minimal attention to the speech. The *Chicago Tribune* only noted that the president of Tuskegee arrived late, received cheers, and General Nelson A. Miles, heroic leader of the Civil War, Indian Wars, and Spanish-American War, was the star attraction.[10] However, southern Whites fiercely criticized this testing of the social and political waters, and Washington chose not to speak out again for many years. He backpedaled by writing that the southern press had misunderstood him as asking for social equality, but this does not negate the fact that he included the whole speech in the book.

A few months later, in his White-directed autobiography *Up from Slavery*, Washington recorded a highly edited version of the speech that avoided any controversial statements.[11] In *Up from Slavery*, he wrote that the southern press had "misunderstood" him, retreating through a muddy discussion of how he never meant to raise the question of "social recognition" and how there are always "cranks" in the crowd.[12] After the Chicago Peace Jubilee, Washington fully retreated into a private world, redoubling his efforts to stay clear of public controversy. He allowed the newly formed Tuskegee Machine to project identities and protect Tuskegee the school by creating a mechanism to ferret out enemies, raise money, and covertly work for social issues independently from Tuskegee the school.

The third concern for readers of Washington's autobiographies is that his autobiographies changed slightly over time. This becomes a historiographic issue when citing the texts. After the first printing of *The Story of My Life and Work* came two quick revisions that each added new materials. *Up from Slavery* was originally serialized and contained several photographs and drawings that were dropped in the book version. Washington's third autobiography, *My Larger Education* (serialized as *Chapters from My Experience*), was ghostwritten by the White sociologist Robert E. Park.[13] It is a patchwork of life vignettes that lack the dramatic plots of earlier autobiographies. *My Larger Education* dropped images, such as the sentimental, sunny south photographs by noted White photographer Julian Dimock, in the serialized version and replaced them with images of Black leaders.

Contents

"A Joshua in the Camp,"

or the life of

Booker T. Washington,

of Tuskegee, Alabama.

By H. RUFUS WHITE,

ATTORNEY-AT-LAW and Editor of THE SUBURBAN ENTERPRISE,

TOWSON, MARYLAND.

1895.

DEDICATION.

To the young manhood and womanhood of the Colored Race which Mr. Washington is laboring to promote, this work is respectfully dedicated

By the arthur.

A JOSHUA IN THE CAMP.

BY H. RUFUS WHITE.

INTRODUCTORY.

That there has never lived in this country a colored man so prominent, at least, as was the late lamented FREDERICK DOUGLASS goes withoutsaying, and there is no doubt that in many respects he was the greatest man the race in America has produced. Much of his greatness was, during his lifetime, partially obscured by the prejudice agaiust him on the one hand and jealousy on the other ; but, dispite this, Douglass was a great man even in the eyes of his enemies. He was a leader. While the ordinary mind was dealing with a single problem, Douglass' great mind, like that of the philosopher, was unraveling a chain of problems whose effects were universal. While the ordinary or private soldier was trying to climb a single craig, Douglass, like Napoleon, was planning the entire conquest and subjugation of Italy. A causual perusal of his life's works and utterances will show the truthfulness of these comparisons. It was Douglass who, when Lincoln was pondering over the advisability of using colored men to garrison forts and dig trenches, urged the placing into their hands the muskets and enrolling their names as regular full-paid soldiers, and the same extremes characterized his views on the questions of emancipation, suffrage, and the efforts of the colored man regarding his own advancement. It was these things which made Douglass the leader of his own people and the peer of the leaders of the white race. Having completed his work, we were not surprised to see him hand back to General Harrison the portfolio of the Haytian ministry and settle down in quietude among the cedars of Anacostia, from whence, like the exiled and regicide Colonel Goffe, he came out once in a while to do "one more good deed for God's people." Over his bier men will uncover and call him Douglass the leader, Douglass the great !

4

On the day following his demise it was said that there would probably never be again a concurance of the circumstances which made Douglass great, and I believe it is true.

Douglass was a creation of a certain age, it seems fitted and moulded in the moulds from which iconoclasts come, and designed to give to the world a living object lesson on the subject of man's Brotherhood. When this was done 'God touched him and he slept.''

Israel is still in the wilderness. Moses has been taken away, and some seem to think that there is not even a Joshua in the in the camp. The purpose of this pamplet is to show that there is a Joshua in the camp, and that he is receiving that ''good success'' which God promised.

Times have changed and with this change have come new measures and new problems which demand new men to deal with and solve them. The uniting of beligerent fragments into a German Empire required the hand of a Bismark, but the meeting and settling of questions pertaining to the devolopment of German manhood and resources requires a bold, jovial and fearless William. Colored men have their freedom (some have, possibly, too much of it) and citizenship for which Douglass labored, but they have not grasped the new ideas which these changes brought about, viz: the nobility of labor, the rigid application of theory to practic, and the judicial use of the almighty dollar, ''which alway elects its candidate,'' be he white or black. This is the condition which Douglass could not change, but which he left as a legacy to his successor when he ''handed back to his people the tiara of leadership;'' and it is upon the successful meeting of these issues that the future success of the colored man in this country depends.

The colored race at this time needs no iconoclast. What it needs is a leader and a teacher—a leader broad and liberal in his views, well versed in the relation which the races sustain to each other; a lovor of his own race, a respecter of what is noble and good in the other and a friend of both. A teacher who thoroughly understands both the subject and the pupils which he teaches simple in precept, profound in reason and gifted with the tact of impressing the truthfulness of his teaching upon the minds and hearts of his pupils. Such a man we have in our midst, and un-

5

consciously to himself the mantle of Douglass fell upon his shoulders, and he is wearing it with becoming dignity and grace. This man is Booker T. Washington, Principal of the Tuskegee, Alabama, Normal and Industrial Institution—a Joshua in the camp.

THE MAN.

Having made a lengthy introduction, we shall in this and the following divisions consider the man, his work and what others say of him, then we shall leave our readers to judge whether or not we have established our claim.

Booker T. Washington was born a slave at Hale's Ford, Va., April, 1858. The place of his birth and early childhood was the old conventional one room quarter-house with a dirt floor and a "potato hole" in the middle of the room where sweet potatoes were kept during the winter. He was the "chattel" of a family by the name of Burrows, but being young he experienced little of the rigors of slavery. Soon after the war he went with his step-mother to Malden, W. Va., where he worked in salt furances for nine months in the year and attended school for three months. After spending several years in this manner, young Washington secured work in the house of a kind but exacting New England lady where he remained until 1871, attending night school under a privaie tutor and picking up information in whatever way he could. At this time, having heard of the Hampton school, he resolved to go there and make his way as best he could; accordingly taking what little money he had been able to save from his wages ($6.00 per month), he started for Hampton. When he reached Richmond, Va., he found himself friendless, homeless, shelterless and penniless. After looking around he found a hole in the sidewalk and in this hole he spent his first night in the Confederate Capitol. As luck would have it, on the next morning when he awoke, he found himself near a vessel that was unloading pig iron. He made application to the captain for work and it was given him. Mr. Washington worked there until he had made money enought to pay his way to Hampton, and to use his own words, he reached Hampton with but 50 cents in his pocket and nothing in his head. He remained at Hampton until he graduated with the honors of his class, having worked his way through. After graduating he returned to his old home and

6

taught school for a while then further pursued his studies at Wayland Seminary, Washington, D. C. While at Wayland, Mr. Washington was invited to become a teacher at Hampton which he did. In this capacity he remained at Hampton two years, until 1881, when application was made to Gen. Armstrong by citizens of Tuskegee, Ala., for some one to start an institution at that place on the plan of Hampton. With hundreds from whom to select, Mr. Washington was the one selected. The wisdom of this choice will be seen by generations yet to come.

Mr. Washing is a teacher in all that that term implies He is not only a teacher when in his school room he is knocking the rough bark off a sapling cut from the forests of Alabama, but among the foremost educators of this country, Booker T. Washington is known and honored as an able and distinguished educator whose work has been the subject of articles published in some of the leading magazines both of this country and England.

In its issue of August 19, '93, the "Out-Look," formerly Christian Union (New York) paid a high tribute to the Negro race. The "Out Look" published the pictures of 28 of the leading college presidents of this country, and among them, by the side of President Eliot of Harvard, President Timothy Dwight of Yale, President Potter of Princeton, President Harper of Chicago University, was the picture of President Booker T. Washington of the Tuskegee Institution, (Tuskegee, Alabama), a young man who was born a slave 38 years ago, who worked his way thorough the Hampton Institute and now presides over the largest Negro Institution (where teachers and pupils are all colored) in the world.

In personal appearance, as we saw him eleven years ago, Mr. Washington is tall in statue, somewhat slim with a clean youthful, almost boyish face, high forehead, piercing eyes looking out from under heavy eye brows and firm lips which seldom relax into a smile, A stranger would take him for an Episcopalian minister instead of a teacher. A perfect gentleman, modest, unselfish too busy with his life's work to think of himself, Mr. Washington goes right on doing all the good he can for his unfortunate people. Mr. T. L. Mann says of him in the Indianopolis Freeman : "It seems a direct act of Providence that the field should be kept open until this Moses should come to lead his people out of the darkness of ignorance into the light of knowledge. The man was called, his mission came from on high, and should you

7

visit his great school, you would exclaim with the "Sage of Ana-costia" "I see a change, a great change. I can exclaim like John in the apocalatic vision, I see a new heaven and a new earth."

HIS WORKS.

There can be but one standard by which the claim of any man upon greatness and leadership can be successfully established, and that is through his works ahd their results. The prophet is known by his prophesies and their fulfillment. The great man must secure his title by deeds of greatness, and the leader by per-forming the functions of leadership. That Booker T. Washing-ton has secured both of these titles is an undisputed fact, and therefore admits no argument. But some dispute the exteut of his leadership; they said it is not universal as was that of the lamented Douglass; they say that, like T. Thomas Fortune, the gifted writer and editor of the NEW YORK AGE, he is a special-ist, and thus imply that the work which he is doing in his school and on the rostrum is not universal in its comprehension and far-reaching in its influnce. This we deny, and we think, with good reason, which we shall endeavor to show further on.

It is no our purpose to cut down any tree in the forest that ours may appear the more towering; but we can, with a single stroke of the pen, show the fallacy of the claims to leadership of all those great men whose names have come to us in connection with the position which Douglass so ably filled for more than a quarter of a century; yet we admire each man for those accomplishments which have redounded to the good of the race.

Now there is one Mr. Cuney, of Texas, who is simply a 19th century American politician--no stateman, no diplomate no schol-ar, no orator, simply a politician. Bishop Lee, a refined Chris-tain minister, honored by his church. Here his star descends. Hon. John Mercer Langston, a text-book oratorial egotist who has been honored by several administrations, and this is enough said, if you have read his book. And lastly, there is T. Thomas Fortune who without a doubt is the most gifted writer the race has produced since the war, but you known that the man who simply writes must be cold in death before this "sin cussed" world can properly appreciate his writing. Either of these gen-tlemen might die to-morrow and the loss would be local. Not

8

so with Booker T. Washington, for his is a work which effects not only his own race but alike the Cancasian, for its chief object is to show (which is admirably being done) that whatever vocation is honorable enough for an honest man to pursue in order to win his bread and butter, imposes upon the man the duty of dignifying that vocation. This is not only in keeping with the most advanced and practical ideas of to-day, but it reaches back to the duties imposed upon man when he was driven away from Edenic bliss.

Now we come to the plain questions of industrial and business education, both of which were touched upon by Mr. Douglass, the first when he asked his colored brethren if they got up as early to work for themselves as they had done to work for their masters, and the latter is shown in his purchase and improvement of property at Baltimore and Bay Ridge—the accomplishment of his letter-day dreams.

Mr. Washington's work comprises these two questions, and with them unites economy, the judicious use of money, the abolition of the mortgage system, a proper regard for hygenic laws, and suggests what to our minds is the only true solution to the race question--the possession by colored men of that which white men will respect. The man who is ignorant of these facts is indeed unqualified to hail any one as the leader of the race.

In all of these things the work of Mr. Washington is universal in that it effects the whole race. Everywhere reading men and women have read of his Farmer's Conferences, his plain common-sense utterances, and his noble work in his school.

According to nature's laws, the water of a stream can be no purer than the source from which it comes. The proper way to purify the water is to clean out the spring. Mr. Washington is doing more than this. In his conferences and on the rostrum he is purifying the homes of his people, while at his school he is putting the streams through filters of charcoal in order that the coming generations may trace their parentage to sources as pure and as clear as sunlight.

This is not the work of Douglass, the iconoclast. This is not the work of an orator "whose eloquence burst like a clap of thunder from a clear sky." But it is the work of the leader and the teacher that Mr. Washington is. It is the work of the man who first takes high ground himself, then by appealing to the under-

9

standing of his followers leads them step by step onward and upward to something nobler and better.

HIS SCHOOL.

In the heart what is known as the "Black Belt" of Alabama is
an institution at which nearly one thousand colored boy and girls
are being yearly led further and further away from ignorance,
idleness and vice, and whose minds are being impregnated with
nobler conceptions of what is truly great and good in life. This
institution--grand and magnificent in all its proportions--is a living, animated monument to the ability, genius, greatness and
leadership of its worthy principal and founder, Booker T. Washington.

No doubt Holmes had in mind such a man as Mr. Washington
when he said that no man who deserves a monument should ever
have one.

When Mother Nature shall have reclaimed Mr. Washington as
her own, what nobler monument could he desire to his memory
than Tuskegee with her various departments, her boys being
made intellectual men and skilled mechanics, and her girls cultivating every virtue and learning every detail necessary to the
development of the successful woman?

Aside from these, there have already taken their places in the
world men and women filled with the inspiration of Tuskegee
principles and teachings, who in years to come when the claim
of some man will be brought forth as the greatest of his race, will
rise up with voices pathetic and hearts filled with devotion, call
to memory Booker T. Washington, his works, his school, his con-
ferencee, and the testimony of others as to his greatness and
leadership.

The Nashville American, in its edition of March 12th, last,
speaking of industrial education, said among other things : "The
Tuskegee Institute was founded for the purpose of giving industrial training and education to colored pupils, and the entire State
of Alabama is now experiencing great benefits from the good
work done at the school."

General Armstrong, founder of the Hampton Institution, said
of Tuskegee : "The Norman and Industrial Institution, with its
six hundred students, $200,00c worth of land and buildings, six-

10

ty-two teachers, twenty-five of whom are graduates of Hampton, and an annual expense of $65,000, so far secured, is a wonderful growth, (about equal to that of this school in the same period), and is, I think, the grandest and noblest work of any colored man in the land. What compares with it in genuine power and value for good. It is on the Hampton plan, combining labor and study; commands high respect from both races: flies no denominational flag, but is thoroughly and earnestly Christian, is out of debt, well managed and organized. Mr. Washington deserves cordial assistance. Should not good people consider that he is made of flesh and blood, and unite to see him through, and fix forever a great light in the "Black Belt" of Alabama? Next to Frederick Douglass, Mr. Washington is the ablest negro in the country, and is doing the grandest and most successful work of any colored man in the land."

This last quotation is the expressed opinion of a man who devoted his life's labors to the education of black boys and girls, and the man to whom Mr. Washington is greatly indebted for what he is to-day. The recommendation of any institution or any man coming from such a source can be but beneficial and helpful.

Tuskegee, like Hampton, differs from so many institutions for colored boys and girls in that it impresses upon their minds the fact that they are preparing to lift burdens from the shoulders of their brethren, and in order to do this they must not be afraid to come in contract with those who are less fortunate than themselves. In short, Tuskegee teaches its pupils to speak, read and write English before they attempt Greek, Latin and Sanscrit; it puts common fractions in the young man's head before it puts Cæsar under his arm; it teaches him to hoe corn before it takes him into the region of stars; it teaches him the truthfulness of the maxim "*Labor omnia vincent.*"

Tuskegee fails wherein so many of our institutions succeed, that is in putting big heads on its students, thereby unfitting them for life's battles. Too often we have heard young men quote Cicero to uncultivated audiences when they ought to have been using those plain, common-sense expressions which have placed Mr. Washington among the formost orators of the day.

When the masses of our people shall have become thoroughly imformed as to the needs of to-day; when colored men shall have learned wherein their great strength lieth, then the work of Tus-

II

kegee will be more appreciated and the greatness and leadership of Booker T. Washington will be universally acknowledged and conceded.

HIS CONFERENCE AND SPEECHES.

Probably in no phase of Mr. Washington's work, not even in the building and management of the great institution, at whose head he stands shows his greatness and power of leadership more than the Annual Conferences which he holds at Tuskegee. These Conferences unlike political and other clans which are wonted to assemble having in view a single purpose, are shorn of politics in its narrow sense, but attempt to make men better citizens in the fullest sense of the word. They are broad in their conceptions for while the invitation is addressed to the colored men as the class most needing their help, white men are extended a cordial welcome, and many have expressed themselves as having been benefitted by their attendance. This phase of Mr. Washington's work shows his greatness and leadership because in this he has not only successfully called together large bodies of men of various minds and circumstances, but he has succesfully shaped a policy or course of action for them which has far removed them from their former condition. To substantiate this last statement we need but cite a quotation from a letter written by Miss Alice M. Bacon, a teacher at Hampton and published in the ''Congregationalist,'' and used by Mr. Albert Shaw, in a letter to the *''Review of Reviews''* on ''Negro Progress on the Tuskegee Plan.'' This estimable lady who attended the last Conference and wrote : ''It was interesting to notice during the discussion how many changes were said to have taken place since the last Conference or since the first Conference. The Tuskegee Farmers' Conference evidently furnishing an incentive to whole communties, and a date from which events were to be reckoned. Many had been putting up school houses since the last conference. So great a change in the matter of one-room cabins was noted as dating from the Conference, that the original fraction used in the declaration that four-fifths of the people were still living in one-room cabins, was changed after the discussion to two-thirds as nearer the present state of affairs.''

12

Here, then is an institution "furnishing an incentive to whole communities," and like the Olympiad, "a date from which events were to be reckoned, and a continual decrease in the value of the fraction representing the destitution of space necessary to the possession by every home of the privacy necessary to its highest and purest moral atmosphere. Such an accomplishment as this alone would be calculated to make Mr. Washington a leader, but this, as all who have followed my week and imperfect presentation of the subject so far will recognize, constitutes only a portion of the excellent work which this grand leader has done and is doing.

Aside from all this Mr. Washington is an orator of the first magnitude. His is not the thundering voice of Douglass as aimed at the bulwarks of slavery, which had enslaved all black men of the South and were fast making the white men of the North the sleuth hounds of Southern slave-drivers, but it is the calm, gentle voice of Lincoln at Gettysburg which arouses patriotism and inspires pride; it is the voice of the great Hollander counseling his people not to invade the sacred and vested rights of others, but to force back the ocean from their own shores and thus, by overcoming nature, increase their domain. Want of space prevents us from saying more in this connection. So we will close this part by quoting from a letter from Mr. Henry McFarland, to the "Philadelphia Record," in which he says: "Booker T. Washington delivered in the hall of the Colored Y. M. C. Association, Washington, D. C., the most sensible and practical talk on how his race should work out its own material salvation which I ever heard or read. * * * Washington is indeed a remarkable man, intellectually, in several different ways, but not even his executive ability, marked as it is, is so extraordinary as his common-sense. This was so evident in his talk the other night that he carried his audience with him from beginning to end, and even men like Douglass and Langston were forced to applaud utterances, which, when they did not run counter to what they themselves had said, put them to blush by contrast. He indulged in no flights of rhetoric, but his cold facts, with homely but striking illustrations, were more convincing than eloquence."

13

WHAT OTHERS SAY OF HIM.

That I am not alone in the opinion that to-day Booker T. Washington is a great man and the leader of his race, is, I think, well attested in the qoutations below, may of which were written while the blood still circulated through the veins of the "sage of Anacostia." The Washington News said of Mr. Washington: "The colored man who can persuade any number of his fellows that there is as much dignity in munual work as in preaching a sermon or being an attorney-at-law is a real benefactor not only to his own race, but to the whites."

"Providence seems to have put Mr. Washington in a place of leadership, and furnished him with an opportunity for pointing to his people the way upward, which makes him a factor of the first importance in the progress of his race," says the Chicago Advance. Prof. Wm. Patterson says: "This man is to the Negroes of American what Arnold was to the Brittish." "The entire State of Alabama is now experiencing great benefits from the good work done at his (Tuskegee) school." The Nashville American: "Surely, if we take into account his great work, it is not going too far to place Mr. Washington among the foremost men of his country and time." says the Boston Courant.

"There is no man in this whole country that has done more for our people than Prof. Booker T. Washington, of the Tuskegee, (Ala.) Institute." Daily Herald, Quincy, Ill.

"Earnestness, simplicity and common-sence characterized the man and his addresses at the Congregational Church January 20th. Very large congregations greeted him both morning and evening, and no one could have more attentive listeners. He speaks with great rapidity, with much emphasis, but weaves in his humor so that it is never wearisome. His stories were full of wit and always to the point. Some passages we exceedingly eloquent, especially one last evening where he described the contrast between the negro when he entered slavery and when he came out. He interested every one greatly on the subject. Mr. Washington goes from here to Chicago, where he speaks in Dr. Gunsaulus' and Dr. McPherson's churches."

The Boston Daily Globe in an editorial in its issue of Aug. 24th, last, says: "The directors of the Atlanta Exposition have done the right thing at the right time. They have invited that

14

able representative of "the colored South," Booker T. Washington, of the Tuskegee Normal and Industrial, to deliver one of the special addresses on the occasion of the opening of the great Fair.

In the development of the resources of the South, the negro is destined to take no small or unimportant part. He is in America to stay, and the more encouragement he receives from the white man in his efforts to advance, the better it will be for both races and for the whole south.

The wise action of the Atlanta directors ought to be a potent factor in allaying race suspicions and jealousies throughout the south, and thus bringing about an era of good feeling between white and black througout Dixie land."

These are only a few of the compliments and appreciative expressions which Mr. Washington's work and character have drawn out, and which we think, justify us in taking the position we have taken.

Prof. Scarborough, who, by the way, can lay some claim to greatness himself, under the caption, "Hunting for a Moses," says in the New York Age of May last:

"There is no Douglass living. This generation has not furnished one, and the generation to come may not furnish one. Perhaps never again shall we see quite so wonderful, so unique a figure among us. But there may be one who can do what the present requires. It may call for some qualities not demanded by the past, during Douglass' lifetime and in his work, for to some extent different methods must prevail. Still the one who is to occupy the place made vacant so recently must be no demagogue, no extremist, no mere office-seeker, not one thirsting for power, possessed of ambition that seeks only self-aggrandizement not one on the sole track of wealth, not one whose destructive powers are superior to his constructive—one who would build barriers by fanning the flames of prejudice even in his own race.

"On the contrary, the leader must, first of all posses elements of true manhood, his integrity must be unquestioned, he must have breadth of views, be open to conviction and have the courage of the conviction he holds. He must be discreet and farseeing with such confidence in movement that he can afford to face criticism calmly, secure in the well-grounded belief that the course of events will in due time prove the wisdom of his action. He must be one who knows when to lead and when to follow,

15

and with all he must be able to command the recognition of his position on the of other races of men.''

You have very neatly drawn the picture, Professor, now take the subject, not as I have imperfectly presented it, but in its perfection of detail, place it by the picture you have drawn, examine and compare them, note that the subject is no demagogue no office-seeker, no extremist, has no thirst for power, no self ambition, no covetousness for wealth, is no destroyer, no build er of barriers, but one who on the other hand, possesses all of those noble qualities and convictions which you claim for your ideal, and you will agree with me that in Booker T. Washington, the race has *A Joshua in the camp*.''

BOOKER T. WASHINGTON

Drawn from life for The Outlook by Alfred Houghton Clark.

UP FROM SLAVERY[1]
An Autobiography
BY BOOKER T. WASHINGTON

Chapter I.—A Slave Among Slaves

I WAS born a slave on a plantation in Franklin County, Virginia. I am not quite sure of the exact place or exact date of my birth, but at any rate I suspect I must have been born somewhere and at some time. As nearly as I have been able to learn, I was born near a cross-roads post-office called Hale's Ford, and the year was 1858 or 1859. I do not know the month or the day. The earliest impressions I can now recall are of the plantation and the slave quarters—the latter being the part of the plantation where the slaves had their cabins.

My life had its beginning in the midst of the most miserable, desolate, and discouraging surroundings. This was so, however, not because my owners were especially cruel, for they were not, as compared with many others. I was born in a typical log cabin, about fourteen by sixteen feet square. In this cabin I lived with my mother and a brother and sister till after the Civil War, when we were all declared free.

Of my ancestry I know almost nothing. In the slave quarters, and even later, I heard whispered conversations among the colored people of the tortures which the slaves, including, no doubt, my ancestors on my mother's side, suffered in the middle passage of the slave ship while being conveyed from Africa to America. I have been unsuccessful in securing any information that would throw any accurate light upon the history of my family beyond my mother. She, I remember, had a half-brother and a half-sister. In the days of slavery not very much attention was given to family history and family records—that is, black family records. My mother, I suppose, attracted the attention of a purchaser who was afterward my owner and hers. Her addition to the slave family attracted about as much attention as the purchase of a new horse or cow. Of my father I know even less than of my mother. I do not even know his name. I have heard reports to the effect that he was a white man who lived on one of the near-by plantations. Whoever he was, I never heard of his taking the least interest in me or providing in any way for my rearing. But I do not find especial fault with him. He was simply another unfortunate victim of the institution which the Nation unhappily had engrafted upon it at that time.

The cabin was not only our living-place, but was also used as the kitchen for the plantation. My mother was the plantation cook. The cabin was without glass windows; it had only openings in the side which let in the light, and also the cold, chilly air of winter. There was a door to the cabin—that is, something that was called a door—but the uncertain hinges by which it was hung, and the large cracks in it, to say nothing of the fact that it was too small, made the room a very uncomfortable one. In addition to these openings there was, in the lower right-hand corner of the room, the "cat-hole," a contrivance which almost every mansion or cabin in Virginia possessed during the ante-bellum period. The "cat-hole" was a square opening, about seven by eight inches, provided for the purpose of letting the cat pass in and out of the house at will during the night. In the case of our particular cabin I could never understand the necessity for this convenience, since there were at least a half-dozen other places in the cabin that would have accommodated the cats. There was no wooden floor in our cabin, the naked earth being used as a floor. In the center of the earthen floor there was a large, deep opening covered with boards, which was

556   The Outlook

used as a place in which to store sweet potatoes during the winter. An impression of this potato-hole is very distinctly engraved upon my memory, because I recall that during the process of putting the potatoes in or taking them out I would often come into possession of one or two, which I roasted and thoroughly enjoyed. There was no cooking-stove on our plantation, and all the cooking for the whites and slaves my mother had to do over an open fireplace, mostly in pots and "skillets." While the poorly built cabin caused us to suffer with cold in the winter, the heat from the open fireplace in summer was equally trying.

The early years of my life, which were spent in the little cabin, were not very different from those of thousands of other slaves. My mother, of course, had little time in which to give attention to the training of her children during the day. She snatched a few moments for our care in the early morning before her work began, and at night after the day's work was done. One of my earliest recollections is that of my mother cooking a chicken late at night, and awakening her children for the purpose of feeding them. How or where she got it I do not know. I presume, however, it was procured from our owner's farm. Some people may call this

theft. If such a thing were to happen now, I should condemn it as theft myself. But taking place at the time it did, and for the reason that it did, no one could ever make me believe that my mother was guilty of thieving. She was simply a victim of the system of slavery. I cannot remember having slept in a bed until after our family was declared free by the Emancipation Proclamation. Three children—John, my older brother, Amanda, my sister, and myself—had a pallet on the dirt floor, or, to be more correct, we slept in and on a bundle of filthy rags laid upon the dirt floor.

I was asked not long ago to tell something about the sports and pastimes that I engaged in during my youth. Until that question was asked it had never occurred to me that there was no period of my life that was devoted to play. From the time that I can remember anything, almost every day of my life has been occupied in some kind of labor; though I think I would now be a more useful man if I had had time for sports. During the period that I spent in slavery I was not large enough to be of much service, still I was occupied most of the time in cleaning the yards, carrying water to the men in the fields, or going to the mill, to which I used to take the corn, once a week, to be

THE CABIN IN VIRGINIA IN WHICH MR. WASHINGTON, UNTIL RECENTLY, THOUGHT HE WAS BORN

THE LOG CABIN IN WHICH MR. WASHINGTON NOW THINKS HE WAS BORN

ground. The mill was about three miles from the plantation. This work I always dreaded. The heavy bag of corn would be thrown across the back of the horse, and the corn divided about evenly on each side; but in some way, almost without exception, on these trips, the corn would so shift as to become unbalanced and would fall off the horse, and often I would fall with it. As I was not strong enough to reload the corn upon the horse, I would have to wait, sometimes for many hours, till a chance passer-by came along who would help me out of my trouble. The hours while waiting for some one were usually spent in crying. The time consumed in this way made me late in reaching the mill, and by the time I got my corn ground and reached home it would be far into the night. The road was a lonely one, and often led through dense forests. I was always frightened. The woods were said to be full of soldiers who had deserted from the army, and I had been told that the first thing a deserter did to a negro boy when he found him alone was to cut off his ears. Besides, when I was late in getting home I knew I would always get a severe scolding or a flogging.

I had no schooling whatever while I was a slave, though I remember on several occasions I went as far as the school-house door with one of my young mistresses to carry her books. The picture of several dozen boys and girls in a school-room engaged in study made a deep impression upon me, and I had the feeling that to get into a school-house and study in this way would be about the same as getting into paradise.

So far as I can now recall, the first knowledge that I got of the fact that we were slaves and that freedom of the slaves was being discussed was early one morning before day, when I was awakened by my mother kneeling over her children and fervently praying that Lincoln and his armies might be successful, and that one day she and her children might be free. In this connection I have never been able to understand how the slaves throughout the South, completely ignorant as were the masses so far as books or newspapers were concerned, were able to keep themselves so accurately and completely informed about the great National questions that were agitating the country. From the time that Garrison, Lovejoy, and others began to agitate for freedom, the slaves throughout the South kept in close touch

THE HOME FROM WHICH BOOKER WASHINGTON WENT TO HAMPTON

Up from Slavery   559

with the progress of the movement. Though I was a mere child during the preparation for the Civil War and during the war itself, I now recall the many late-at-night whispered discussions that I heard my mother and the other slaves on the plantation indulge in. These discussions showed that they understood the situation, and that they kept themselves informed of events by what was termed the " grape-vine " telegraph.

During the campaign when Lincoln was first a candidate for the Presidency, the slaves on our far-off plantation, miles from any railroad or large city or daily newspaper, knew what the issues involved were. When war was begun between the North and the South, every slave on our plantation felt and knew that, though other issues were discussed, the primal one was that of slavery. Even the most ignorant members of my race on the remote plantations felt in their hearts, with a certainty that admitted of no doubt, that the freedom of the slaves would be the one great result of the war, if the Northern armies conquered. Every success of the Federal armies and every defeat of the Confederate forces was watched with the keenest and most intense interest. Often the slaves got knowledge of the results of great battles before the white people received it. This news was usually gotten from the colored man who was sent to the post-office for the mail. In our case the post-office was about three miles from the plantation, and the mail came once or twice a week. The man who was sent to the office would linger about the office long enough to get the drift of the conversation from the group of white people who naturally congregated there after receiving their mail to discuss the latest news. The mail-carrier on his way back to our master's house would as naturally retail the news that he had secured among the slaves, and in this way they often heard of important events before the white people at the " big house," as the master's house was called.

I cannot remember a single instance during my childhood or early boyhood when our entire family sat down to the table together, and God's blessing was asked, and the family ate a meal in a civilized manner. On the plantation in Virginia, and even later, meals were gotten by the children very much as dumb animals get theirs. It was a piece of bread here and a scrap of meat there. It was a cup of milk at one time and some potatoes at another. Sometimes a portion of our family would eat out of the skillet or pot, while some one else would eat from a tin plate held on the knees, and often using nothing but the hands with which to hold the food. When I had grown to sufficient size, I was required to go to the " big house " at meal-times to fan the flies from the table by means of a large set of paper fans operated by a pulley. Naturally much of the conversation of the white people turned upon the subject of freedom and the war, and I absorbed a good deal of it. I remember that at one time I saw two of my young mistresses and some lady visitors eating ginger-cakes in the yard. At that time those cakes seemed to me to be absolutely the most tempting and desirable things that I had ever seen, and I then and there resolved that, if I ever got free, the height of my ambition would be reached if I could get to the point where I could secure and eat ginger-cakes in the way that I saw those ladies doing.

Of course as the war was prolonged the white people, in many cases, often found it difficult to secure food for themselves. I think the slaves felt the deprivation less than the whites, because the usual diet for the slaves was corn bread and pork, and these could be raised on the plantation; but coffee, tea, sugar, and other articles which the whites had been accustomed to use could not be raised on the plantation, and the conditions brought about by the war frequently made it impossible to secure these things. The whites were often in great straits. Parched corn was used for coffee, and a kind of black molasses was used instead of sugar. Many times nothing was used to sweeten the so-called tea and coffee.

The first pair of shoes that I recall wearing were wooden ones. They had rough leather on the top, but the bottoms, which were about an inch thick, were of wood. When I walked they made a fearful noise, and besides this they were very inconvenient, since there was no yielding to the natural pressure of the foot. In wearing them one presented an exceedingly awkward appearance. The most

560   The Outlook

trying ordeal that I was forced to endure as a slave boy, however, was the wearing of a flax shirt. In the portion of Virginia where I lived it was common to use flax as part of the clothing for the slaves. That part of the flax from which our clothing was made was largely the refuse, which of course was the cheapest and roughest part. I can scarcely imagine any torture, except, perhaps, the pulling of a tooth, that is equal to that caused by putting on a new flax shirt for the first time. It is almost equal to the feeling that one would experience if he had a dozen or more chestnut burrs, or a hundred small pin-points, in contact with his flesh. Even to this day I can recall accurately the tortures that I underwent when putting on one of these garments. The fact that my flesh was soft and tender added to the pain. But I had no choice. I had to wear the flax shirt or none, and had it been left to me to choose, I should have chosen to wear no covering. In connection with the flax shirt, my brother John, who is several years older than I am, performed one of the most generous acts that

I ever heard of one slave relative doing for another. On several occasions when I was being forced to wear a new flax shirt, he generously agreed to put it on in my stead and wear it for several days, till it was " broken in." Until I had grown to be quite a youth this single garment was all that I wore.

One may get the idea, from what I have said, that there was bitter feeling towards the white people on the part of my race, because of the fact that most of the white population was away fighting in a war which would result in keeping the negro in slavery if the South was successful. In the case of the slaves on our place this was not true, and it was not true of any large proportion of the slave population in the South where the negro was treated with anything like decency. During the Civil War one of my young masters was killed, and two were severely wounded. I recall the feeling of sorrow which existed among the slaves when they heard of the death of " Mars' Billy." It was no sham sorrow, but real. Some of the slaves had nursed " Mars' Billy ;" others had played

RUINS OF THE SALT FURNACE IN KANAWHA VALLEY WHERE BOOKER WASHINGTON
WORKED AS A BOY
Drawn by G. Alden Peirson.

ENTRANCE TO COAL-MINE IN WHICH BOOKER WASHINGTON WORKED AS A BOY
Drawn by G. Alden Peirson.

with him when he was a child. "Mars' Billy" had begged for mercy in the case of others when the overseer or master was thrashing them. The sorrow in the slave quarter was only second to that in the "big house." When the two young masters were brought home wounded, the sympathy of the slaves was shown in many ways. They were just as anxious to assist in the nursing as the family relatives of the wounded. Some of the slaves would even beg for the privilege of sitting up at night to nurse their wounded masters. This tenderness and sympathy on the part of those held in bondage was a result of their kindly and generous nature. In order to defend and protect the women and children who were left on the plantations when the white males went to war, the slaves would have laid down their lives. The slave who was selected to sleep in the "big house" during the absence of the males was considered to have the place of honor. Any one attempting to harm "young Mistress" or "old Mistress" during the night would have had to cross the dead body of the slave to do so. I do not know how many have noticed it, but I think that it will be found to be true that there are few instances, either in slavery or freedom, in which a member of my race has been known to betray a specific trust.

As a rule, not only did the members of my race entertain no feelings of bitterness against the whites before and during the war, but there are many instances of negroes tenderly caring for their former masters and mistresses who for some reason have become poor and dependent since the war. I know of instances where the former masters of slaves have for years been supplied with money by their former slaves to keep them from suffering. I have known of still other cases in which the former slaves have assisted in the education of the descendants of their former owners. I know of a case on a large plantation in the South in which a young white man, the son of the former owner of the estate, has become so reduced in purse and self-control by reason of drink that he is a pitiable creature, and yet, notwithstanding the poverty of the colored people themselves on this plantation, they have for years supplied this young white man with the necessities of life. One sends him a little coffee or

HOUSE IN MALDEN IN WHICH MR. WASHINGTON, AFTER LEAVING HAMPTON, TAUGHT HIS
FIRST SCHOOL

Drawn by G. Alden Peirson.

sugar, another a little meat, and so on. Nothing that the colored people possess is too good for the son of "old Mars' Tom," who will perhaps never be permitted to suffer while any remain on the place who knew directly or indirectly of "old Mars' Tom."

I have said that there are few instances of a member of my race betraying a specific trust. One of the best illustrations of this which I know of is in the case of an ex-slave from Virginia whom I met not long ago in a little town in the State of Ohio. I found that this man had made a contract with his master, two or three years previous to the Emancipation Proclamation, to the effect that the slave was to be permitted to buy himself, by paying so much per year for his body, and while he was paying for himself he was to be permitted to labor where and for whom he pleased. Finding that he could secure better wages in Ohio, he went there. When freedom came, he was still in debt to his master some three hundred dollars. Notwithstanding that the Emancipation

Proclamation freed him from any obligation to his master, this black man walked the greater portion of the distance back to where his old master lived in Virginia, and placed the last dollar, with interest, in his hands. In talking to me about this, the man told me that he knew that he did not have to pay the debt, but that he had given his word to his master, and his word he had never broken. He felt that he could not enjoy his freedom till he had fulfilled his promise.

From some things that I have said one may get the idea that some of the slaves did not want freedom. This is not true. I have never seen one who did not want to be free, or one who would return to slavery.

I pity from the bottom of my heart any nation or body of people that is so unfortunate as to get entangled in the net of slavery. I have long since ceased to cherish any spirit of bitterness against the Southern white people on account of the enslavement of my race. No one section of our country was wholly respon-

Up from Slavery 563

sible for its introduction, and, besides, it was recognized and protected for years by the General Government. Having once got its tentacles fastened on to the economic and social life of the Republic, it was no easy matter for the country to relieve itself of the institution. Then, when we rid ourselves of prejudice, or racial feeling, and look facts in the face, we must acknowledge that, notwithstand-

as missionaries to enlighten those who remained in the fatherland. This I say, not to justify slavery—on the other hand, I condemn it as an institution, as we all know that in America it was established for selfish and financial reasons, and not from a missionary motive—but to call attention to a fact, and to show how Providence so often uses men and institutions to accomplish a purpose. When persons

MR. WASHINGTON AT THE RUFFNER HOME, MALDEN, IN 1899

ing the cruelty and moral wrong of slavery, the ten million negroes inhabiting this country, who themselves or whose ancestors went through the school of American slavery, are in a stronger and more hopeful condition, materially, intellectually, morally, and religiously, than is true of an equal number of black people in any other portion of the globe. This is so to such an extent that negroes in this country, who themselves or whose forefathers went through the school of slavery, are constantly returning to Africa

ask me in these days how, in the midst of what sometimes seem hopelessly discouraging conditions, I can have such faith in the future of my race in this country, I remind them of the wilderness through which, and out of which, a good Providence has already led us.

Ever since I have been old enough to think for myself, I have entertained the idea that, notwithstanding the cruel wrongs inflicted upon us, the black man got nearly as much out of slavery as the white man did. The hurtful influences of the insti-

564   The Outlook

tution were not by any means confined to the negro. This was fully illustrated by the life upon our own plantation. The whole machinery of slavery was so constructed as to cause labor, as a rule, to be looked upon as a badge of degradation, of inferiority. Hence labor was something that both races on the slave plantation sought to escape. The slave system on our place, in a large measure, took the spirit of self-reliance and self-help out of the white people. My old master had many boys and girls, but not one, so far as I know, ever mastered a single trade or special line of productive industry. The girls were not taught to cook, sew, or to take care of the house. All of this was left to the slaves. The slaves, of course, had little personal interest in the life of the plantation, and their ignorance prevented them from learning how to do things in the most improved and thorough manner. As a result of the system, fences were out of repair, gates were hanging half off the hinges, doors creaked, window-panes were out, plastering had fallen but was not replaced, weeds grew in the yard. As a rule, there was food for whites and blacks, but inside the house, and on the dining-room table, there was wanting that delicacy and refinement of touch and finish which can make a home the most convenient, comfortable, and attractive place in the world. Withal

there was a waste of food and other materials which was sad. When freedom came, the slaves were almost as well fitted to begin life anew as the master, except in the matter of book-learning and ownership of property. The slave-owner and his sons had mastered no special industry. They unconsciously had imbibed the feeling that manual labor was not the proper thing for them. On the other hand, the slaves, in many cases, had mastered some handicraft, and none were ashamed, and few unwilling, to labor.

Finally the war closed, and the day of freedom came. It was a momentous and eventful day to all upon our plantation. We had been expecting it. Freedom was in the air, and had been for months. Deserting soldiers returning to their homes were to be seen every day. Others who had been discharged, or whose regiments had been paroled, were constantly passing near our place. The "grape-vine telegraph" was kept busy night and day. The news and mutterings of great events were swiftly carried from one plantation to another. In the fear of "Yankee" invasions, the silverware and other valuables were taken from the "big house," buried in the woods, and guarded by trusted slaves. Woe be to any one who would have attempted to disturb the buried treasure. The slaves would give the Yankee soldiers food, drink, clothing—anything but that

MR. WASHINGTON AND THE TEACHERS OF TUSKEGEE

THE YARD AT TUSKEGEE.   A CLASS IN HORTICULTURE

which had been specifically intrusted to their care and honor. As the great day drew nearer, there was more singing in the slave quarters than usual. It was bolder, had more ring, and lasted later into the night. Most of the verses of the plantation songs had some reference to freedom. True, they had sung those same verses before, but they had been careful to explain that the "freedom" in these songs referred to the next world, and had no connection with life in this world. Now they gradually threw off the mask, and were not afraid to let it be known that the "freedom" in their songs meant freedom of the body in this world. The night before the eventful day, word was sent to the slave quarters to the effect that something unusual was going to take place at the "big house" the next morning. There was little, if any, sleep that night. All was excitement and expectancy. Early the next morning word was sent to all the slaves, old and young, to gather at the house. In company with my mother, brother, and sister, and a large number of other slaves, I went to the master's house. All of our master's family were either standing or seated on the veranda of the house, where they could see what was to take place and hear what was said. There was a feeling of deep interest, or perhaps sadness, on their faces, but not bitterness. As I now recall the impression they made upon me, they did not at the moment seem to be sad because of the loss of property, but rather because of parting with those whom they had reared and who were in many ways very close to them. The most distinct thing that I now recall in connection with the scene was that some man who seemed to be a stranger, a United States officer, I presume, made a little speech and then read a rather long paper—the Emancipation Proclamation, I think. After the reading we were told that we were all free, and could go when and where we pleased. My mother, who was standing by my side, leaned over and kissed her children, while tears of joy ran down her cheeks. She explained to us what it all meant, that this was the day for which she had been so long praying, but fearing that she would never live to see.

For some minutes there was great rejoicing, and thanksgiving, and wild scenes of ecstasy. But there was no feeling of bitterness. In fact, there was pity among the slaves for our former owners. The wild rejoicing on the part of the emancipated colored people lasted but for a brief period, for I noticed that by the time they returned to their cabins there was a change in their feelings. The great responsibility of being free, of having charge of themselves, of having to think and plan for themselves and their children, seemed to take possession of them. It was very much like suddenly turning a youth of ten or twelve years out into the world to provide for himself. In a few hours the great questions with which the Anglo-Saxon race had been grappling for centuries had been thrown upon these people to be solved. These were the questions of a home, a living, the rearing of children, education, citizenship, and the establishment and support of churches. Was it any wonder that within a few hours the wild rejoicing ceased and a feeling of deep gloom seemed to pervade the slave quarters? To some it seemed that, now that they were in actual possession of it, freedom was a more serious thing than they had expected to find it. Some of the slaves were seventy or eighty years old; their best days were gone. They had no strength with which to earn a living in a strange place and among strange people, even if they had been sure where to find a new place of abode. To this class the problem seemed especially hard. Besides, deep down in their hearts there was a strange and peculiar attachment to "old Marster" and "old Missus," and to their children, which they found it hard to think of breaking off. With these they had spent in some cases nearly a half-century, and it was no light thing to think of parting. Gradually, one by one, stealthily at first, the older slaves began to wander from the slave quarters back to the "big house" to have a whispered conversation with their former owners as to the future.

Booker T. Washington

By Paul Laurence Dunbar

[From the "New England Magazine"]

The word is writ that he who runs may read.
What is the passing breath of earthly fame?
But to snatch glory from the hands of blame,—
That is to be, to live, to strive indeed.
A poor Virginia cabin gave the seed,
And from its dark and lowly door there came
A peer of princes in the world's acclaim,
A master spirit for the nation's need.
Strong, silent, purposeful beyond his kind,
The mark of rugged force on brow and lip,
Straight on he goes, nor turns to look behind
Where hot the hounds come baying at his hip;
With one idea foremost in his mind,
Like the keen prow of some on-forging ship.

THE SATURDAY EVENING POST

An Illustrated Weekly Magazine
Founded Aᵒ Dⁱ 1728 by Benj. Franklin

Volume 172, No. 8   Philadelphia, August 19, 1899   5 Cents the Copy; $2.50 the Year

The ECCENTRICITIES of GENIUS

PAPER Nᵒ 1
Famous Orators I Have Known
By
Major J. B. POND

THE great triumvirate of lecture kings consisted of Gough, Beecher and Wendell Phillips. Other men for a season, and sometimes for a few years, were as popular as any of them, but theirs was a calcium-light popularity, whereas the popularity of the "Big Three" endured for their entire lives.

Now that Phillips and Garrison and the era in which they flourished have passed into history, it is common for writers who treat on that period to talk of these two champions of freedom as if they were equals, or of Phillips, even, as if he were Garrison's inferior.

Those who knew both men smile at such absurdities.

Phillips and Garrison were equals in one respect only—in moral courage and unselfish devotion to the slave. Garrison was a commonplace man in respect to intellectual ability, whereas Phillips was a man of genius of the rarest culture. Garrison was a strong platform speaker. Phillips was one of the greatest orators of the century. Only three men of his time could contest the palm of eloquence with him: Webster, Clay and Beecher.

HOW WENDELL PHILLIPS MASTERED THE MOB

Phillips was a terrible radical, with a polish about his performance that took away from it, for the average outdoor audience, the effect of the deadly earnestness with which his reputation was associated. Mr. Phillips spoke as quietly as though talking in his own parlor, and almost entirely without gesture, though he had a greater power over all kinds of audiences than any man we have ever known. Often called before a howling mob who went to the halls to shout and sing and prevent his being heard, he never failed to subdue them in a short time. These were instances when such men as Garrison and Parker were as powerless as children.

A mob had congregated in Faneuil Hall determined that he should not be heard. There was a crowd of reporters in front. Mr. Phillips bent down and was seen talking to these reporters. Very soon the mob became quiet, and stopped to listen to what he was saying to the reporters. Phillips looked up at them quietly and said: "Go on, gentlemen, go on; I do not need your ears. With these pencils I am addressing fifty millions of people." That mob had found its master.

There never was a more benevolent face than William Lloyd Garrison's. He had a kindly eye, a winning smile, a gentleness of way, a crisp, straightforward way of talking, and a merciless movement in straight lines of thought.

Mr. Garrison visited England after the war was over and the emancipation of the slaves was accomplished, and received unusual courtesies. At a dinner given him by the British Anti-Slavery Society he was presented with a gold watch. As he took it in his hand he said:

"Well, gentlemen, if this had been a rotten egg I should have known what to do with it, but as it is a gold watch, I have nothing to say."

THE GREATNESS OF HENRY WARD BEECHER

John Bright told me that Henry Ward Beecher was the greatest orator who spoke the English tongue. When Beecher came to Plymouth Church, in 1844, he was thirty-four years of age, strong and rugged in health, unconventional in manners, but never ungentlemanly. His free, brusque address and direct approach was different from more polished clergymen, and everything he said and did was made the subject of remark. I suppose no man ever lived more directly under the public gaze than did Mr. Beecher for forty years; his life was seen and read by all men—his public life—but few have known of his domestic gentleness and invariable sweetness of nature.

He was the centre of loving hearts. Strong and powerful as he knew he was, to those he loved he was as gentle as a mother. As to enmities, he had none, and he hardly knew he had enemies. He was the most joyous, radiantly happy man that was ever known.

I remember one day I had seen him walking arm in arm with a man who had injured him, who had been abusing him. I said to Mr. Beecher: "I think you are carrying the doctrine of Christian love too far."

He said: "Pond, can we go further than to bless those who curse us, and pray for those who despitefully use us? Ah, there is so little known of the spirit of Christ in the world that when a man is trying feebly and afar off to follow Him, even Christians do not understand it."

No answer could be made to such reasoning as this.

His friends knew and learned from him what was meant by being a Christian. His theory was that as the son of God and in unison with his

113

2

Speeches

Booker T. Washington was one of the Progressive Age's most popular speakers on both sides of the color line. His public-speaking gift first received acclaim when a *New York Times* reporter mentioned the young Washington's skill in an article, after hearing Washington speak at his 1875 Hampton Institute graduation. Debating and public speaking became his passion. Eventually, intellectuals from William James to W. E. B. Du Bois praised his speeches. In 1899, the aging Major James Burton Pond, one of the era's great lecture series managers, said of Washington: "He has fire and magnetism and gifts of oratory which few of our Northern orators possess, whether they be Black or White. He speaks with force and conviction, and leaves an indelible impression that whatever he says, right or wrong, he believes it to be right."[1] In his capacity to impress such diverse audiences, Washington stood alone in his time. Unlike any other American of his day, he crisscrossed the country speaking at both Black and White churches, Black and White colleges, and Black and White towns to sell his message and to raise money. Washington was as big a hit on the northern Chautauqua circuit as he was on whistle-stop tours of the Deep South. Standing on the stage with his handwritten word list outlining a speech, Washington delivered a repertoire of homey sayings, anecdotes, and jokes that expectant audiences came to hear. He mastered the art of shifting his speaking voice from crisp New England diction to Black vernacular. He was so proud of his public speaking that he included a chapter on it in *Up from Slavery* and had his ghostwriter, Max Bennett Thrasher, submit an article to *The Ram's Horn* extolling his mastery of the art of storytelling.[2]

Washington and Du Bois represent two very different understandings of the term *reformer*. Washington was a pragmatic, Christian businessman reformer whose activism rarely surfaced publicly. His approach, to use the term applied by Howard University professor Kelly Miller, was as a *statesman*. He cautiously moved public opinion toward change by gathering, synthesizing, and refining the wisdom in the air.[3] Readers familiar with Booker T. Washington's famous speech delivered at the Cotton States Exposition on September 18, 1895, better-known today as the Atlanta Compromise speech, are probably not aware that the speech was crafted over many years. It followed Washington's method of cautious advancement as he carefully tested the murky waters of Jim Crow for reaction. Washington collected ideas and key phrases familiar in this speech through keen listening. He knew the sound of a winning phrase. When his speeches were printed, Washington typically validated his thoughts by using the effusive praise of prominent people and sources.

Years before the Atlanta speech, Washington had laid down his basic message and approach in what would be his first national address. It took place in 1884 (three years after the founding of Tuskegee Institute) at the National Educational Association's meeting in Madison, Wisconsin. The speech established his stance on pursuing change through education and economic empowerment rather than political means: "Brains, property, and character for the Negro will settle the question of civil rights. The best course to pursue in regard to the civil rights bill in the South is to let it alone; let it alone and it will settle itself [referring to the 1883 overturning of the Civil Rights Act of 1875]." Washington's Madison speech also established his method of speaking to White audiences by artfully telling them that racial uplift was ultimately in their best interest and his habit of offering fulsome praise to southern Whites. It was in Madison that Washington voiced his soon-to-be favorite phrase, "the dignity of labor," which summarized his belief that work was inextricably bound with character, knowledge, service, aesthetics, and religion.

For a brief time in the late 1880s, Washington tried out a different voice. When he addressed the Alabama State Teachers' Association on April 11, 1888, he adopted a loftier voice, peppering his speech with "hitherto" and "verily." Bold name-dropping replaced local characters as Washington called on Pestalozzi, Josiah Strong, Newton, Aristotle, and Thomas Edison to bolster his message. No doubt, the language and references were the influence of his second wife, Olivia, the beneficiary of a New England education, whom he had married in 1885.[4] In all likelihood, the handwritten notes included in this book are Olivia's. She died in 1889, the year Washington's third wife, the Fisk University–trained English teacher Margaret Murray, arrived on campus. They married in 1892.

The road to the development of Washington's oft-quoted (and misunderstood) phrase "cast down your buckets" and a turning point in Washington's public speaking life occurred in Atlanta, two years before the famous Atlanta Cotton States Exposition speech. In *Up from Slavery*, Washington described how, in November 1893, after traveling "two thousand miles" from Boston, he gave a five-minute speech before an international gathering of the Christian Workers in Atlanta. He knew this was a decisive moment in his career. Washington, who had perfected his fund-raising speeches for northern White audiences, now learned to craft another voice for a southern White audience. For this latter audience, whom Washington did not see as donors, he directed an economic message based on the familiar theme of the dignity of labor, industrial education, the cultivation of abandoned lands, and a self-help program that avoided not blaming southerners for Blacks' current condition. Washington's Christian Workers speech was enthusiastically supported by the *Atlanta Journal*, providing Washington with the security to proceed.[5] In fact, Washington would use such endorsements from White newspapers as an important strategy to legitimize the Tuskegee plan of industrial education.

The road to the Atlanta Cotton States speech went through Montgomery and Fisk University. As final dry runs for his big day, Washington delivered two final drafts of the famous speech. The first was delivered as the Emancipation Day Address in Montgomery, Alabama, on January 1, 1895. The Black newspaper *The Indianapolis Freeman* reported that Professor B. T. Washington told "how a vessel not far off, saying help, save us or we perish for water, and the captain of the other vessel's reply was, cast down your buckets where you are."[6] No known text of the speech survives. A few months later, in the spring of 1895, Washington delivered a speech at Fisk University on industrial education.[7] It was the "simplicity" of his speech, the dignity of labor theme, and the advocation of social changes through economic rather than political pressure that won over the "large number of educated and representative colored people" audience. The local press (and papers across the South) gave the speech its blessings.[8] In May 1895, Washington delivered a speech at Knoxville College, another Black institution. Notes from this speech are included on the corresponding website of this book so that readers may see the outline format Washington used when speaking. He was ready for Atlanta.

Booker T. Washington delivered a speech at the Atlanta Cotton States Exposition that was ten years in the making.[9] It served as the final blueprint for Washington's ideas, combining religion, politics, civil rights, and aesthetics into one grand vision. Its rich complexities make it much more than a simple accommodationist speech. First, its social Darwinist acceptance of a racial hierarchy proposed only temporary suspension of social equality for economic security. Second, aesthetics frame the entire work. Washington understood how his Victorian audience perceived higher culture as a sign of civility. Throughout the speech, he told the audience, "there is as much dignity in tilling a field as in writing a poem." Washington suggested that people see the books and paintings in the Negro building, and that for the moment it's more important "to earn a dollar in a factory" than "to spend a dollar in an opera house" (i.e., amid talking about common laborers, he found a way of speaking about art as well). Third, he subtly mixed Black and White references in the speech. The famous "separate as five fingers" line was borrowed from former president Rutherford B. Hayes.[10] The equally famous line "cast down your buckets," which Washington had used in an earlier journal article, was borrowed from the Black educator Hugh Browne.[11] This speech launched Washington into the national spotlight and solidified his role as the leader of the majority of his people.

Washington's later speeches either cashed in on the Atlanta success by retelling familiar stories and themes or moved toward increasingly data-driven analysis. Retold speeches were presented to Chautauqua crowds and fund-raising venues, when celebrity mattered more than substance. Data-filled speeches aimed at audiences he wanted to inspire and challenge politically, such as the National Negro Business League, represent a strong departure from his early speeches. Included here is a speech from August 1915, only months before he died. It was delivered to a Boston crowd comprising members of the league, an organization he founded and led until his death. Washington's muses of this later period were such men as Robert Park and Monroe Work, social science thinkers who could provide scientific evidence to bolster his agenda.

Individuals throughout the learned world admired the craft of Washington's oratory skills and speechwriting. In 1913, for instance, Arthur Charles Fox Davis published a five-volume series entitled *The Book of Public Speaking* that included Winston Churchill, Charles Dickens, Mark Twain, Theodore Roosevelt, and Booker T. Washington.[12] Through this exposure, G. Douglas Wardrop, a Scottish journalist interested in aviation, contacted Washington about his public-speaking skills. Washington's response to Wardrop was his clearest and most concise description and account of his public speaking development.[13] This book includes examples of Washington's handwritten notes that he read from when he spoke to audiences. Readers can see both those aspects of the speech that Washington highlighted as well as compare the notes to the text of the published speech.[14]

Contents

Report

OF THE

Board of Commissioners

Representing the State of New York

AT THE

Cotton States

AND

International Exposition

HELD AT

Atlanta, Georgia

1895

WYNKOOP HALLENBECK CRAWFORD CO
STATE PRINTERS
ALBANY AND NEW YORK
1896

Address of Booker T. Washington,

Principal Tuskegee Normal and Industrial Institute, Tuskegee, Ala.,

At the Opening of the Exposition

————————★————————

Mr President and Gentlemen of the Board of Directors and Citizens

One-third of the population of the South is of the negro race. No enterprise seeking the material, civil or moral welfare of this section, can disregard this element of our population and reach the highest success. I but convey to you, Mr President and Directors, the sentiment of the masses of my race, when I say that in no way have the value and manhood of the American negro been more fittingly and generously recognized than by the managers of this magnificent Exposition at every stage of its progress. It is a recognition that will do more to cement the friendship of the two races than any occurrence since the dawn of our freedom.

Not only this, but the opportunity here afforded will awaken among us a new era of industrial progress. Ignorant and inexperienced, it is not strange that in the first years of our new life we began at the top instead of at the bottom, that a seat in Congress or the State Legislature was more sought than real estate or industrial skill, that the political convention or stump speaking had more attractions than starting a dairy farm or truck garden.

A ship lost at sea for many days suddenly sighted a friendly vessel. From the mast of the unfortunate vessel was seen the signal "Water, water, we die of thirst." The answer from the friendly vessel at once came back "Cast down your bucket where you are." A second time the signal, "Water, water, send us water' ran up from the distressed vessel, and was answered, "Cast down your bucket

190

where you are.' And a third and fourth signal for water was answered "Cast down your bucket where you are. The captain of the distressed vessel, at last heeding the injunction, cast down his bucket, and it came up full of fresh sparkling water from the mouth of the Amazon river To those of my race who depend on bettering their condition in a foreign land, or who underestimate the importance of cultivating friendly relations with the Southern white man, who is their next-door neighbor, I would say, "Cast down your bucket where you are,"—cast it down in making friends in every manly way of the people of all races by whom we are surrounded.

Cast it down in agriculture, mechanics, in commerce, in domestic service, and in the professions. And in this connection it is well to bear in mind that, whatever other sins the South may be called to bear, when it comes to business, pure and simple, it is in the South that the negro is given a man's chance in the commercial world, and in nothing is this Exposition more eloquent than in emphasizing this chance. Our greatest danger is that, in the great leap from slavery to freedom, we may overlook the fact that the masses of us are to live by the productions of our hands, and fail to keep in mind that we shall prosper in proportion as we learn to dignify and glorify common labor and put brains and skill into common occupations of life, shall prosper in proportion as we learn to draw the line between the superficial and the substantial, the ornamental gewgaws of life and the useful. No race can prosper until it learns that there is as much dignity in tilling a field as in writing a poem. It is at the bottom of life we must begin, and not at the top. Nor should we permit our grievances to overshadow our opportunities.

To those of the white race who look to the incoming of those of foreign birth and strange tongue and habits for the prosperity of the South, were I permitted, I would repeat what I say to my own race: "Cast down your bucket where you are Cast it down among the 8,000,000 negroes whose habits you know, whose fidelity and love you have tested in days when to have proved treacherous meant the ruin of your firesides. Cast down your bucket among these people, who have, without strikes and labor wars, tilled your fields, cleared your forests, builded your railroads and cities, and brought forth treasures from the bowels of the earth and helped make possible this magnificent representation of the progress of the South. Casting down your bucket among my people, helping them and encouraging them, as you are doing on these grounds, and to education of head, hand and heart, you will find that they will buy your surplus land, make blossom the waste places in your fields and run your factories. While doing this, you can be sure in the future, as in the past, that you and your families will be surrounded by the most patient, faithful, law abiding and unresentful people that the world has seen As we have proved our loyalty to you in the past, in nursing your children, watching by the sick bed of your mothers and fathers, and often following them with tear-dimmed eyes to their graves, so in the future, in our humble way, we shall stand by you with a devotion that no foreigner can approach, ready to lay down our lives, if need be, in defense of yours, interlacing our industrial, commercial, civil and religious life with yours in a way that shall make the interests of both races one. In all things that are purely social, we can be as separate as the fingers, yet one as the hand in all things essential to mutual progress.

There is no defense of security for any of us except in the highest intelligence and development of all. If anywhere there are efforts tending to curtail the fullest growth of the negro, let these efforts be turned into stimulating, encouraging and making him the most useful and intelligent citizen. Effort or means so invested will pay a thousand per cent. interest. These efforts will be twice-blessed —"blessing him that gives and him that takes.

There is no escape, through law of God, from the inevitable

> " The laws of changeless justice bind,
> Oppressor with oppressed ,
> And close as sin and suffering joined,
> We march to fate abreast."

Nearly sixteen millions of hands will aid you in pulling the load upward, or they will pull against you the load downward. We shall constitute one-third, and more, of the ignorance and crime of the South, or one-third its intelligence and progress, we shall contribute one-third to the business or industrial prosperity of the South, or we shall prove a veritable body of death, stagnating, depressing, retarding every effort to advance the body politic.

Gentlemen of the Exposition, as we present to you our humble effort at an exhibition of our progress, you must not expect over much. Starting thirty years ago with ownership here and there in a few quilts and pumpkins and chickens (gathered from miscellaneous sources) remember the path that has led from these to the inventions and production of agricultural implements, buggies, steam engines, newspapers, books, statuary, carving, paintings, the management of drug stores and banks, has not been trodden with out contact with thorns and thistles. While we take pride in what we exhibit as a result of our independent efforts, we do not for a moment forget that our part in this Exhibition would fall far short of your expectations but for the constant help that has come to our educational life, not only from the Southern States, but especially from Northern philanthropists, who have made their gifts a constant stream of blessing and encouragement.

The wisest among my race understand that the agitation of questions of social equality is the extremest folly, and that progress in the enjoyment of all the privileges that will come to us must be the result of severe and constant struggle rather than of artificial forcing No race that has anything to contribute to the markets of the world is long in any degree ostracized. It is important and right that all the privileges of the law be ours, but it is vastly more important that we be prepared for the exercise of these privileges. The opportunity to earn a dollar in a factory, just now, is worth infinitely more than the opportunity to spend a dollar in an opera house.

13

194   *NEW YORK AT THE COTTON STATES*

In conclusion, may I repeat that nothing in thirty years has given us more hope and encouragement, and drawn us so near to you of the white race as this opportunity offered by the Exposition, and here bending, as it were, over the altar that represents the results of the struggles of your race and mine, both starting practically empty handed three decades ago, I pledge that in your effort to work out the great and intricate problem which God has laid at the doors of the South, you shall have at all times, the patient sympathetic help of my race, only let this be constantly in mind, that, while from representations in these buildings of the product of field, of forest, of mine, of factory, letters and art, much good will come, yet far above and beyond material benefits will be that higher good, that, let us pray God, will come in a blotting out of sectional differences and racial animosities and suspicions, in a determination to administer absolute justice, in a willing obedience among all classes to the mandates of the law This, this, coupled with our material prosperity, will bring into our beloved South a new Heaven and a new earth.

NEGRO BUILDING.

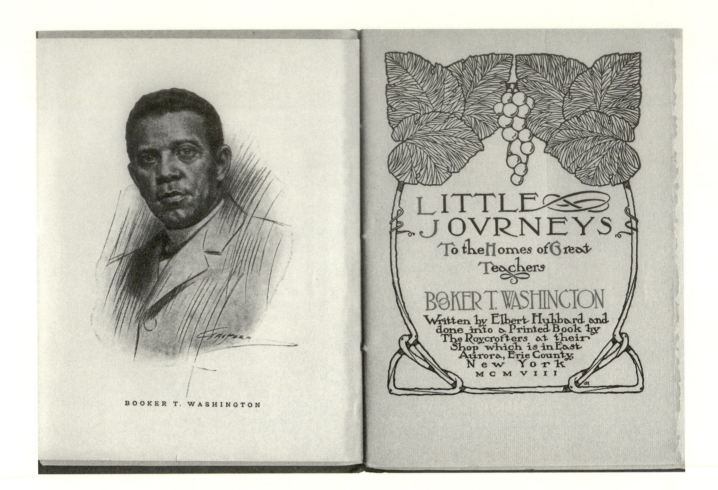

BOOKER T. WASHINGTON

LITTLE JOVRNEYS
To the Homes of Great
Teachers

BOOKER T. WASHINGTON
Written by Elbert Hubbard and
done into a Printed Book by
The Roycrofters at their
Shop which is in East
Aurora, Erie County,
New York
MCMVIII

3

Education

Although he was known for supporting only industrial education, Booker T. Washington's education plan went far beyond training students to master basic agricultural and trade skills. As outlined in his essay "Twenty-Five Years of Tuskegee," Tuskegee Normal and Industrial Institute also supported other forms of education and economic development, such as providing night school courses and an adult education program, teaching courses in the local town of Tuskegee, and establishing a laboratory grade school; professional meetings (e.g., annual farmer conferences, ministers and teachers meetings); promoting investment in the community through fund-raising for a local primary school, organizing a local Negro Business League group, and creating loan associations for farmers; and promoting both regional and worldwide development by sponsoring a health conference and sending students to Togo, Africa, to develop farming programs.[1] Washington even developed early forms of work study so that aspiring students could attend school while learning a trade.[2] Because of the influence of his third wife, Margaret Murray Washington, support grew for "settlement" or "clubwoman's work" with women's causes and for expanding the curriculum for female students, the latter of which he outlined in his book *Working with the Hands*.[3] However, it is the formal schooling at Tuskegee, consisting of three areas, that scholarship usually refers to when discussing Washington's curriculum. These areas included an Academic Department, the Phelps Hall Bible School, and certainly best known, the Industrial Department. Some of the country's elite Black intellectuals could be found among the Academic Department faculty, which included courses in the sciences and liberal arts.[4] Academic theory was not advanced as an end but to provide concepts to apply in real-life situations in various trades. Washington called this practice *dovetailing*, or *correlation*.

Moral teachings linked these disparate offerings. "Early in my educational work, I discovered that what offers the greatest difficulty to the progress of an individual or race is not the material, but the spiritual, surrounding conditions."[5] Viewed holistically, Washington ran Tuskegee on the belief that change started at the bottom and that education led to both independence and racial uplift by contributing to the community.

Despite his occasional claims to the contrary, Washington crafted a full educational philosophy that cannot be separated from his views on race and politics. This philosophy is not always easy to discern; for the wary, Washington told his audiences what he thought they wanted to hear. Early in his career, he stopped name-dropping such educational thinkers as Johann Heinrich Pestalozzi or Friedrich Froebel. Instead, Washington wanted others to believe that his educational philosophy was as natural as the Alabama countryside, free of the artifices of fancy theories. He believed his ideas grew, like cotton and plantation songs, directly from the red soil of Macon County. In this respect, his thoughts parallel those of his contemporary John Dewey; both believed that education should develop inductively from the ever-changing social environment. Like Dewey, Washington saw education as tightly woven into the social and political American democratic fabric. Unlike Dewey, Washington wove race into the tapestry. Washington saw his educational mission as one of both uplifting the rural, southern Black and White communities. Regarding Blacks, he believed that his students needed to learn the basic skills to gain employment, to be self-sufficient, and to teach to their own community. Regarding Whites, Washington saw education as the most effective means of political and social advancement. He held little faith in legislative change offering much hope. In 1884, he told the national teachers convention, "Brains, property, and character for the Negro will settle the question of civil rights."[6] Fifteen years later, as stated in an annual report, the solution to "many of our present political and sociological difficulties" remained the same: "Wherever our graduates and ex-students go they teach by precept and example, the wider lesson of thrift, economy and property-getting, and friendship between the races."[7] This theme, which continued throughout the 1890s, grew to contain veiled threats to Whites. For example, he warned them, in an 1898 *New England Magazine* article, that their assistance was ultimately self-serving since a country of eight million African Americans has the potential of becoming "a nation within a nation, that will be a burden, a menace to your civilization."[8]

His version of industrial education, therefore, contained a quiet activism in which an initial transformation took place within a Black community as citizens became self-sufficient, hard-working Christians whose character was beyond reproach. Soon the local White community, he imagined, would be transformed as they grew to need goods and services Blacks provided. Eventually, this change would rise to the highest levels and racial tensions would fade away. It was a grand vision wherein the premise of accommodationist activism, which saw mixed results, was as knotted as the times.

Washington frequently summarized this philosophy as "head, heart, and hand," a phrase meant to capture a spirit of applied knowledge built on a frame of Christian character. Although he first heard the phrase during his school days at Hampton Institute under the direction of his mentor General Samuel Armstrong Chapman, the words were in the air even at Black schools with higher-education programs.[9] They could be heard from many quarters, ranging from Arts and Crafts promoter Elbert Hubbard to the National Educational Association leadership.[10] One of the best summations of Washington's education philosophy is found in his speech at Armstrong's memorial service in 1893.[11] In richly aesthetic language, he honored his mentor by placing Tuskegee as the rose on his grave, telling those gathered that the philosophy of head, heart, and hand was the Hampton founder's great idea. In the speech, the reader finds the essence of Washington's thoughts on the subject of education: Christian-based self-sufficiency laying the groundwork for transforming both the Black and White communities and eventually for the higher, liberal education of Blacks.

Although this philosophy enjoyed wide appeal, its realization was far from straightforward. The operation of Tuskegee served as a symbol of the paradoxes of Jim Crow progressivism. Although Tuskegee was publicly supported by the state of Alabama and the federal land grant, the college never received adequate government support and had to depend on private donors. Washington was always proud that Tuskegee operated its own post office, which required a federally appointed Black postmaster, yet this office functioned in large part to keep the students from going to town and "getting into trouble."

The realities of Tuskegee were conflicted indeed, right down to its architecture. Its buildings were classical and medieval revival structures but housed vocational classes. Perhaps this contradiction reflected Washington's own mixed views on liberal education: Although he admitted the importance of higher learning, he did so with reluctance and frequent derision. He spoke frequently of the need for balance, yet he diverted the lion's share of philanthropic support toward schools implementing the Tuskegee model of education. Not wanting to force social and political change head on, Washington used the campus and his curriculum as the means. This resulted, in the end, with Washington wanting both a mecca of high culture and taste to demonstrate indirectly intellectual equality and a large series of learning laboratories aimed at teaching farming, dressmaking, and brick making. The hard-working, thrifty, industrious Tuskegee students were contrasted with images of dandies. Liberal education was often derided as useless abstraction that lacked grounding in application. He told the elite White audience reading *Cosmopolitan*, "Instead of writing an essay about something in the air," Tuskegee students used their "dove-tailed" academic teaching to write about "the growing of potatoes."[12]

One clear example of his suspicions of liberal education and his belief in simple Christian uplift is found in a speech delivered at Hampton. Notably, it was reprinted in Elbert Hubbard's *The Fra* in 1909, showing the widespread appeal of the message among a certain White liberal audience. Washington told the Black audience at Hampton to avoid big words, fancy clothes, and impressive titles—all signs of a liberal education. These "affectations" he contrasted with the "naturalness" of his plan. Instead, he contended, go home and "make yourself part of the life of the people . . . Go home and be the most humble and simple, but the most helpful one among them . . . Go into the community and make yourself a natural part of it for good service."[13] Yet it would be wrong to see Washington as determined to see only racial uplift as resulting from Little Tuskegees, for he worked just as hard to raise funds as a Howard University trustee. Despite his occasional snipes at liberal education, he knew precisely where his faculty received their training. Such are the complexities of the Wizard of Tuskegee.

Contents

The World's Work

WALTER H. PAGE, Editor

CONTENTS FOR APRIL, 1906

TERMS: $3.00 a year; single copies, 25 cents. Published monthly. Copyright, 1906, by Doubleday, Page & Company. All rights reserved. Entered at the Post-office at New York, N. Y., as second-class mail matter.

COUNTRY LIFE
IN AMERICA

DOUBLEDAY PAGE & CO
133-135 & 137 EAST 16TH ST.—NEW YORK

THE GARDEN
MAGAZINE

TWENTY-FIVE YEARS OF TUSKEGEE

THE BUILDING UP OF THE NEGRO, AS SHOWN BY THE GROWTH AND WORK OF THIS SCHOOL MANAGED WHOLLY BY NEGROES—THE RECORD OF ITS GRADUATES

BY

BOOKER T. WASHINGTON

FOUNDER AND PRINCIPAL OF TUSKEGEE INSTITUTE

EARLY in my educational work, I discovered that what offers the greatest difficulty to the progress of an individual or a race is not the material, but the spiritual, surrounding conditions. It is comparatively easy to build up a worn-out soil and make it productive. It is infinitely harder to change a state of mind. It is possible with sufficient capital to erect buildings and set up machinery; but to change ingrained habits and customs of a community or a people is a task requiring time and patience

Before the school at Tuskegee was started I spent a month traveling about the country getting acquainted with the people. What I discovered, discouraging as it appeared at the time, was after all what might have been expected. Some of the people I met were living practically in the same places where they, or their fathers and mothers, had formerly been slaves. The change which freedom had brought to them, important as it was for them potentially, had made very little practical difference in their lives. Their methods of work, their customs and habits of thought, had remained to all intents and purposes what they had been before emancipation. In some cases where they had used their freedom to get something better, the results were often at once ludicrous and pathetic.

In the plantation districts, I found large families, including the visitors when any appeared, living and sleeping in a single room. I found them living on fat pork and corn bread, and yet not infrequently I discovered in these cabins sewing-machines which no one knew how to use, which had cost as much as $60, or showy clocks which had cost as much as $10 or $12, but which never told the time. I remember a cabin where there was but one fork on the table for the use of the five members of the family and myself, while in the opposite corner was an organ for which the family was paying $60 in monthly instalments. The truth that forced itself upon me was, that these people needed not only book-learning, but knowledge of how to live; they needed to know how to cultivate the soil, to husband their resources, to buy land and build houses, and make the most of their opportunities.

The same thing was true of the students who applied for entrance at the school. Many had themselves been teachers. Others had picked up various scraps of learning here and there, of which they were, of course, very proud. Some had studied many books. But their knowledge was, in many cases, regarded as a toy or an ornament.

That is to say, they perceived only a slight connection between education and work. Education was rather a device for escaping work. Among the institutions in which some had been trained, a feeling prevailed that it was beneath the dignity of an institution of learning to give time and attention to the industries. I remember cases where students who were thinking of entering the school at Tuskegee were warned that it would disgrace them to enter a "working school," or a school for "poor boys and girls." During the first two or three years of the school, I received constant requests from parents, and from the students themselves, that only book studies be given, and there were not a few students who, if they did work, preferred not to be seen working.

In 1881, when the Tuskegee Normal and Industrial Institute was opened at Tuskegee, there was practically no school in Alabama, Mississippi, Georgia, Florida, Louisiana, South Carolina, or Texas that gave attention to industrial education. Now there is not a single institution of note that does not give manual or industrial training of some sort. Not only this, but the demand for industrial schools all over the South, and the North, too, not merely for colored students but for white students also, has grown to such an extent that it may be said that a permanent change in the prevailing ideas of popular education has been brought about. Industrial education for Negroes was first introduced thirty-seven years ago at Hampton Institute, Virginia. The Tuskegee Institute grew out of Hampton.

During the first ten years of its existence, a large part of the time and energy of the Tuskegee school was spent in convincing the students, their parents, and the white and colored population of the North and South, of the value of industrial education, and explaining its methods. It is only since then that the school has been able to do much to change the conditions of the farming class in the district around the school and in the other Negro communities to which the school extends its influence.

The Institute will complete this year the first twenty-five years of its existence. It was opened July 4, 1881, with one teacher and thirty pupils. At that time it had neither land nor buildings, nothing but the $2,000 a year granted by the Alabama legislature. Even the dilapidated shanty and the old church in which its first sessions were conducted were lent by the colored people of the village.

It was not long, however, before the school acquired a small tract of land. The first piece of live-stock of which it became possessed was an old blind mule, the gift of a white man in the neighborhood. This represented the capital of the school.

At the close of the school year last May it owned 2,000 acres of land, 83 buildings, large and small, used as dwellings, dormitories, class-rooms, shops, and barns, which, together with the equipment, live-stock, stock in trade, and other personal property, were valued at about $831,895.32. This does not include 22,000 acres of public land remaining unsold from the 25,000 granted by Congress valued at $135,000, nor the endowment fund, which amounted January 1, 1906, to $1,275,664. During the year 1904-5, there were enrolled in the regular normal and industrial departments, 1,504 students—1,000 young men and 504 young women—with an average attendance of 1,224. This number does not include the 194 in the training-school, or children's house, nor the 56 in the night schools of

the village of Greenwood and of the town of Tuskegee, nor the 25 in the night school Bible classes, nor the 11 in the afternoon cooking classes in the town of Tuskegee. If these latter were included, the total number of students during the year would be 1,790.

Last year there were thirty-seven industries in operation in which students were given training. It will give some idea of the character and extent of this training if I quote a passage from the last annual report:

"During 1904, mainly by student labor, we cultivated 900 acres of land. Our sweet potato crop alone amounted to 6,500 bushels. Our dairy herd, which has been cared for by the students, contains 171 milch cows, and 16,332 pounds of butter were made during the year. In the machinery division 124 students received instruction. One new 7-horse-power engine was built for school use; 6 steam engines were repaired and 163 iron bedsteads built. In the tailor shop, 250 full suits of clothes and 563 pairs of overalls were made, besides a large amount of jobs done. During the year 1,412 articles were made in the millinery division, 1,309 in the dressmaking division, 2,505 in the plain sewing division, 5,118 in the mattress-making division, 1,367 in the broommaking and basketry divisions, and 498,076 pieces were laundered during the year. In the harness shop 36 sets of new harness were made in addition to the repair work done on all the harness belonging to the school and for outside parties. In the electrical division, the interior wiring of the academic building, Emery Dormitory No. 2, and three cottages, was done by students, besides extending the electric light system on the outside of the buildings. In the brickmasonry division 548,000 bricks have been laid, 224,800 laths have been put on, and 9,018 square yards of plastering completed. In the brickyard 970,000 bricks have been manufactured.

"The value of the products manufactured and sold from the mechanical departments of the school amounted to $100,295. The sales of the products of the industries carried on exclusively by women amounted to $5,709. The value of the farm products sold was $56,188. This did not include $220 credited to poultry and bees, nor $645 for the sale of flowers by the school florist. The sales in the commissary department amounted to $75,596. Putting these items together, they give the grand total of $236,655 as the amount of business done by the school last year in the sale of its own products, and of the food, clothing, etc., used by teachers and students."

It has been the constant purpose of the school to turn out not merely trained mechanics and farmers, but also leaders and

TUSKEGEE INSTITUTE TWENTY-FIVE YEARS AGO

THE ENTRANCE TO THE TUSKEGEE LIBRARY

teachers who will give character to the people, scatter abroad the spirit of industry, enforce the dignity of labor, and improve the condition of the masses so as to make them useful to themselves, their race, and their country. The measure in which the institution at Tuskegee has done this is the measure of its success.

In 1891, the first Negro Farmers' Conference was established. It was a sort of experience-meeting. The farmers from the surrounding county and from all over the state of Alabama and the adjoining states, were invited to come to make known their difficulties and to tell what they had done or what their neighbors had done to overcome them. The conference soon became very popular, and, as a result of it, local Negro conferences were established in different parts of the state. In a small way, these were schools of self-help. Their purpose was to discover what the farmers could do to improve their condition. In connection with the local conferences, farmers' institutes were established. At their meetings some member of the faculty of the school, or the local school-teacher, if a graduate of Tuskegee, told the farmers the best methods of cultivating the soil and discussed other matters of interest. Since 1897, monthly meetings of the

farmers of Macon county, in which Tuskegee is located, have been held at the Institute. Farmers have been invited to bring in their products and exhibit them. In November of every year a Negro farmers' county-fair has been held and prizes offered to those who exhibit the best specimens and the largest variety of farm products. There has been steady progress in the variety of subjects discussed and in the character of the discussions, showing that the farmers who attend are steadily gaining in understanding of those simple scientific principles of agriculture which these institutes seek to enforce. In the early years of this institute, much was formerly said about the effect of the moon upon the crops, but the discussions usually brought out the point that deep ploughing was more important in agriculture than the moon; and lunar theories of agriculture have long since been discarded by those farmers who have attended the meetings.

From 1890 to 1900, the number of farms in Macon county increased from 2,766 to 3,824, and the total area of improved land increased from 116,429 to 142,568 acres. The value of farms and buildings increased from $1,157,250 in 1890 to $1,953,197 in 1900. During the same time the value of the farm implements increased from $46,619 to $108,810,

AN UNSKILLED LABORER

As shiftless and improvident as he is good-natured; his physical and mental powers wasted for lack of training

TWENTY-FIVE YEARS OF TUSKEGEE   7437

A SKILLED STUDENT IN THE TUSKEGEE SHOE SHOP
Thorough training will make him a valuable and productive member of the community

and the value of live-stock increased from $369,570 to $496,820.

An earnest effort was made during the first twenty years of the Institute to inculcate better methods of farming, to improve the schools, to encourage thrift and industry, and to stimulate a desire for better life and conduct among the Negro farmers. Now a further experiment is being made in Macon county, Ala. Under the direction of Mr. E. J. Penny, head of the Bible Training School, the preachers and pastors of Macon county have formed an organization, which holds quarterly meetings at Phelps Hall Bible Training School to discuss the moral and social conditions of the communities in which they live, and to devise means for their im-

provement. At the last meeting of the ministers' organization, the subject of discussion was "The Difficulties and Dangers for the Negro in City Life." The subject for discussion at the next meeting is "The Camp-meeting: Its Influence for Good and Evil."

These meetings tend to divert the attention of the churches from the discussion of doctrines which divide them, to bring living issues into the pulpit, and to unite the religious forces in the work of building up the moral and social life of the people. A similar organization has been formed at Tuskegee, among the school teachers of the county. This organization brings the school teachers of the county together at stated periods to discuss the aims and methods of the Negro county school.

7438   TWENTY-FIVE YEARS OF TUSKEGEE

Improvement in the primary schools in Macon county has been greatly stimulated recently by the work of C. J. Calloway, who has had charge of the distribution of a small fund placed in my hands to encourage the schools, supplementing the public school fund. Largely through his work, something like $2,500 has been raised since October by contributions from Negro farmers to increase the school term and to improve the school buildings. With these sums raised by the Negro farmers themselves, supplemented by aid from the primary school fund, twenty-five

ciation, which levies voluntary taxes upon persons and property, the proceeds of which it employs in maintaining the streets and sidewalks, in furnishing light for the streets, and in making necessary improvements.

There has recently been organized in Tuskegee and neighboring communities a local Negro Business League also to encourage Negro business enterprises here and elsewhere in the county. For a number of years one of the best-conducted and most successful grocery stores in the village of Tuskegee has been that of A. J. Wilborn, a Tuskegee grad-

A NEGRO FISHERMAN

Living in rags and contentment through the summer months on the proceeds of intermittent fishing

school-houses are now building, and the school term in nearly every school in the county will be extended this year from four months to seven or eight months.

For some years an effort has been made to build up in the neighborhood of the school a model community. During the last few years this community has increased rapidly, until now, including the students and officers of the schools, we have a village of 2,100 inhabitants. Although this community is not incorporated, it maintains an unofficial government through a village improvement asso-

uate. More recently a stock company has been organized to conduct a general store in the village. The National Negro Business League, of which the local league is a member, had its origin in Tuskegee, where the practical necessity of it in "community building" had already been demonstrated. Now there are more than 200 local business leagues in different parts of the country, all encouraging Negro business enterprise and stimulating the interest of the masses of the people in the economic development of the race.

TWENTY-FIVE YEARS OF TUSKEGEE   7439

Another enterprise is that conducted by the Southern Improvement Company, on a tract of some 4,000 acres about five miles from the school, under the direction of William V. Chambliss, a graduate of Tuskegee. This tract has been divided into small tracts provided with model cottages, and thus far

Among the other agencies for the upbuilding and regeneration of the farming community is the Tuskegee Building and Loan Association, which, with the Dizier Fund, has furnished the capital for the building of nearly all the cottages in the community adjoining the school and throughout the county; the

IN THE HARNESS SHOP AT TUSKEGEE
A boy learning a trade which will give him steady, profitable employment

about fifty families have taken up land on long-term payments. This enterprise has stimulated the Negro farmers to own land and to compel better accommodations for the farmers on neighboring plantations. The late Alexander Purves, of the Hampton Institute, started this enterprise.

mothers' weekly meetings conducted by Mrs. Washington; the night school in the village; and the plantation settlement-work established by Mrs. Washington and carried on by Miss Anna Davis. To these should be added the work of the Farmers' Institute, the shorter course in agriculture given every year for

7440 TWENTY-FIVE YEARS OF TUSKEGEE

the farmers, and the work of the members of the Bible Training School among the churches and Sunday-schools of the county at large.

A Negro farmers' newspaper, established a few months ago, already has a wide circulation. This is probably the first local news-

ity or the purchase of a mule by some individual in that community is an item of general interest.

Six thousand students have come for a longer or shorter time under the influence of the institution during the twenty-five years of its existence. So far as I have been able to

AN OLD PLOW-HAND
His abilities are confined to doing only very simple tasks in a most elementary way

paper devoting itself exclusively to the affairs of a single locality ever printed and published in the interest of a Negro farming community. It aims to take account of every effort for progress and improvement made by an individual or a community in the county. The building of a new school-house by a commun-

ascertain, not one of the graduates has been convicted of a crime and less than 10 per cent. are failures in the occupations which they have adopted. There is an increasing demand all over the South for their services. One great reason why so many of the students who enter fail to finish their course is that

TWENTY-FIVE YEARS OF TUSKEGEE

their earning capacity is increased to such an extent—on an average, 300 per cent. at the end of the full course—by a few months' or years at study, that they yield to the temptation to go to work at the increased salary and do not return to complete their course at the school.

Take for an example the case of a young man who came to us recently from Mobile, where he had been earning fifty cents a day as a common laborer. At the end of nine months, he returned home and found his ser-

spirit and tradition of the school. We have sought to impress upon them the importance of making themselves an example for the other members of their race. We have tried to teach them that they should constantly seek, by their personal influence, their example and counsel, to extend to other members of their race the influence of the teachings they imbibed at Tuskegee.

One evidence of the extent to which the school has been successful in this effort is the

A STUDENT RUNNING THE HIGH SPEED ENGINE AT TUSKEGEE
Trained to do a high grade of intelligent work

vices in demand as a brick-layer at two dollars a day. The consequence was that he did not return at the close of his vacation. He did not feel that he could give up his job. Careful estimates make it appear that every student who finishes his course at Tuskegee increases thereby his capacity for earning money, on an average, about 300 per cent.

On the other hand, we have sought by every means possible to keep alive in the students who have gone from Tuskegee the

number of institutions doing, in a modified form, work similar to that at Tuskegee, that have been established by Tuskegee graduates or reorganized under their direction and influence, in different parts of the South. Here is an incomplete list of them:

Snow Hill Institute, Ala. Started by William J. Edwards, of the class of 1893, in a one-room cabin; now has 160 acres of land, buildings valued at $30,000, an income of $20,000, a faculty of 20 teachers, most of them former students of Tus-

7442   TWENTY-FIVE YEARS OF TUSKEGEE

ADDICTED TO SHIFTLESSNESS AND THE SNUFF HABIT

kegee, and 400 students who are taught seven different trades.

Ruhton, La. Started by Charles P. Adams, with
3 teachers (all Tuskegee graduates). It has 110 students and is receiving cordial encouragement from
the white people of Ruhton.

Utica, Miss., Normal and Industrial Institute.
Started by W. H. Holtzclaw and wife (both graduates of Tuskegee), with 7 teachers (all from Tuskegee) and more than 200 students.

Harriman Industrial Institute, Tenn. Founded

by J. W. Obeltrea and wife (both from Tuskegee)
with 4 teachers and 100 students.

Robert Hungerford Institute, Eatonville, Fla.
Founded by R. C. Calhoun of the class of 1896 and
his wife; has 140 students and 3 teachers (all from
Tuskegee).

The Voorhees Industrial School, Denmark, S. C.
Founded by Elizabeth E. Wright of the class of 1894;
has 300 acres of land, all paid for, and several buildings designed and erected by Tuskegee students; 300
pupils and 3 Tuskegee graduates as her assistants.

TWENTY-FIVE YEARS OF TUSKEGEE   7443

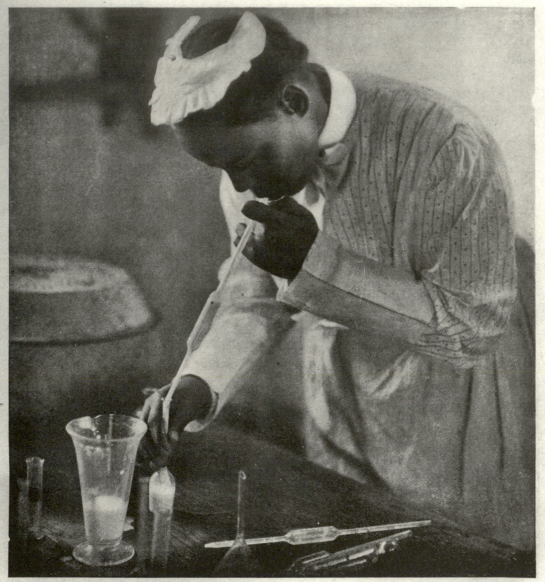

A STUDENT TESTING MILK IN THE DAIRY AT TUSKEGEE
Learning the principles of hygiene and the use of pure food

There are ten other institutions in different parts of the South, founded and taught by Tuskegee graduates. None of them has less than sixty students and some have several hundred. There are altogether not less than 4,000 young colored men and women being educated in them, and more than 200 graduates of the Tuskegee Institute are engaged as teachers in other industrial schools. Isaac Fisher, for example, a poor young man who came to Tuskegee and worked his way through, is principal of the Normal College of Pine Bluff, Ark. Miss Annie Courts has charge of the domestic science department in the public schools at Columbus, Ga., and Mary L. McCrery occupies a similar position in the industrial college for colored people in Oklahoma. India A. Gordon has charge of the dressmaking and millinery department at the East Tennessee Industrial School; J. S. Shanklin is principal of the Port Royal Agricultural School, South Carolina; Lucy Clup-

AN OLD NEGRO COOK
Whose small income is spent in dues to burial societies

ton is matron at Utica Normal Institute; A. B. Lovett is assistant-principal of a public school at Macon, Ga., and many others occupy similar positions.

Upon the recommendation of Secretary Wilson of the Department of Agriculture, three graduates of Tuskegee went to Africa in 1900 to teach cotton-raising to the natives of the German provinces. At the end of the second year, the officers were so well satisfied with their services that they sent for three other students, and in 1903 a hundred bales of cotton were shipped from Togo, Africa, to Berlin.

These are, however, but some of the more conspicuous examples of the work which

TWENTY-FIVE YEARS OF TUSKEGEE   7445

graduates and former students are doing in every part of the South. Humbler men, some of, whom, because they were perhaps less gifted, have had less success, but they have worked silently, patiently, and alone to do their part, however small, in the task of up-building the race. I could name more than one man in our own Macon county, whose patient and persistent effort, doing only a little but doing all that he could, has been an inspiration to me in my work.

In conclusion, I might add that the school

I think it is true that Tuskegee gives employment to a larger number of Negro college graduates than other school in this country or elsewhere. Of the 156 teachers and officers of the school about 40 are college or university graduates. Several come from technical schools, such as the Massachusetts Institute of Technology, the Drexel Institute in Philadelphia, and the Pratt Institute in Brooklyn. Fully one-third of the entire corps of officers and instructors came from Hampton Institute, and another third graduated at Tuskegee.

LEARNING SEWING AT TUSKEGEE

at Tuskegee has been a source of strength and encouragement to the colored people of this country, because it has been from the first a distinctly Negro school founded and conducted, in the main, by members of the Negro race. Its teachers and all of its active officers have been Negroes. It has been a service to the Negro race, also, in so far as it has given an opportunity to so large a number of exceptional Negro men and women to hold positions of such high responsibility and at the same time to be of such genuine service to members of their own race and to the nation.

I think it is true that Mr. P. C. Parkes, superintendent of the school-farm, is managing the largest farm, measured by the number of people employed—though there have probably been farms of larger acreage—ever conducted by a colored man. Mr. Warren Logan our treasurer, probably handles more money every year than is handled by any other colored man in the country, with the exception of Mr. Charles W. Anderson, the colored collector of internal revenue at New York.

It is probable also that our business agent,

7446 TWENTY-FIVE YEARS OF TUSKEGEE

A PROFITLESS STREET DISCUSSION

Lloyd Wheeler, does more business in connection with the purchasing department of the school than any other colored man, with only two or three exceptions. We consume on an average two and a quarter barrels of flour a day, to say nothing of cornmeal. We use on an average two beeves a day, and it requires twenty-five bushels of sweet potatoes a mea for the students and teachers who dine at the school.

D. S. Smith, a graduate of the Massachusetts Institute of Technology, is undoubtedly conducting at Tuskegee the largest electrical plant operated by any colored man in this country. I think Emmett J. Scott, my executive secretary, probably handles the largest correspondence and has charge of the largest office-force, with one or two exceptions, of all colored men in the country. It is probably also true that Roscoe C. Bruce, the head of the academic department, is in charge of the largest school of academic studies to be found among our people in the world. The very fact that it can be said of these men that they occupy positions so exceptional shows to what extent every man who accomplishes anything unusual is a pioneer of his race.

It is because the school at Tuskegee has been to so large an extent built up and directed by members of the Negro race, that it and its achievements, it seems to me, may be fairly taken as an example of what the Negro race is capable of under reasonably favorable circumstances. We are too often inclined to pass judgment upon the Negro upon the basis of what the race as a whole or

PLOWING WITH AN OX
The kind of agriculture that keeps even the industrious Negro poor

TWENTY-FIVE YEARS OF TUSKEGEE

CAPT. GEO. A. AUSTIN

One of the Military Instructors at Tuskegee Institute

MR. WARREN J. LOGAN

Treasurer of Tuskegee Institute

A TUSKEGEE STUDENT FROM AFRICA

Who will return to teach his people

REV. J. M. JONES

A teacher in Phelps Hall Bible Training School

FOUR MEN OF TUSKEGEE

ANYTHING RATHER THAN WALK

on the average has accomplished since emancipation. To a certain extent that is just, and I do not believe the Negro people have reason to be ashamed of their record. But we should not forget that the condition in which the great mass of the race has lived before and since emancipation has not been such as to bring out all, or even the best, there is in any

A TYPICAL ACCIDENT
Thoughtlessness and improvidence meeting the inevitable misfortune

TWENTY-FIVE YEARS OF TUSKEGEE   7449

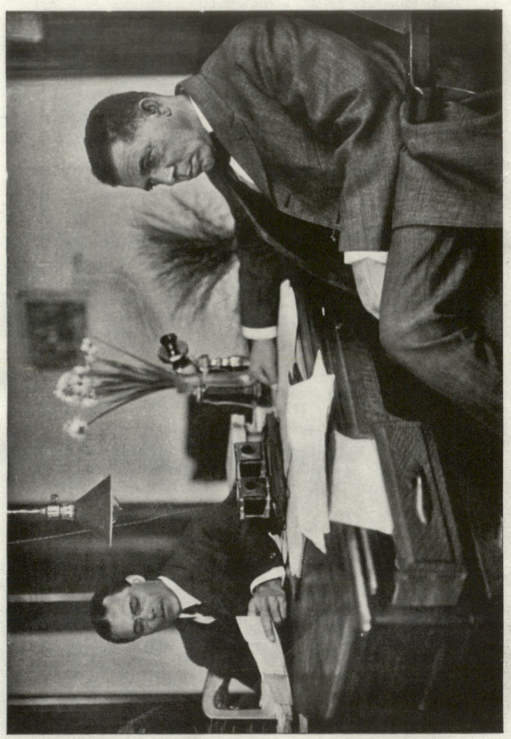

DR. BOOKER T. WASHINGTON

The Founder and Principal of Tuskegee Institute with his Secretary, Mr. Emmett J. Scott

THE BAND AT TUSKEGEE

of the Negro people. The school at Tuskegee is an example of what the Negro can do under favorable circumstances, and even these circumstances are not especially favorable when compared with opportunities that members of the other race have in other parts of the country.

Whatever its success has been, Tuskegee is, I believe, an evidence of the possibilities of the race as a whole; and, so far as it has succeeded, it is a pledge that the Negro will not, in the long run, betray the hopes of those who have devoted their time, their strength, and their money to his uplifting.

Capt. Geo. A. Austin   Elbert Williams, Bandmaster   Maj. J. B. Ramsey   Captain Brown

THE MEN WHO TEACH TUSKEGEE STUDENTS DISCIPLINE AND EFFICIENCY

Souvenir National Medical Association

August 27, 28, 29 ~ 1912

Tuskegee, Ala.

Booker T. Washington, Principal

John A. Andrew Memorial Hospital

Tuskegee Normal Industrial Institute

Dr. John A. Kenney, Medical Director

4

Work

No phrase captures Booker T. Washington's thoughts on work more than "the dignity of labor." Like his other familiar phrases, from "cast down your buckets" to "head, heart, and hand," this one was carefully appropriated. These borrowed words are the mark of a pragmatic Christian reformer, a man whose cautious nature directed him toward building upward from the bottom on rhetoric audiences knew as tried and true. The message he sent with the phrase *dignity of labor* was twofold. First, he was primarily concerned with racial uplift and self-help. His message told Whites that the Black community could provide hard workers equal or superior to the new mass of immigrants that were arriving at the beginning of the twentieth century. Equally important was what the phrase did not say. His relative silence on strikebreaking and lack of demand for immediate inclusion in organized labor comforted Whites and segments of the Black bourgeoisie.

Unraveling the phrase dignity of labor, we see how carefully Washington's ideas on education, racial uplift, and social advancement were woven together. The dignity of labor appears in early Tuskegee catalogs as the third piece of his educational plan, following "mental training" and "vocations." Depending on the context, Washington used dignity of labor to emphasize moral or character education, community service and racial uplift, the intellect in work, economic advancement, or, increasingly, to link work with beauty and grace as a sign of social equality. Even his later critics select the dignity of labor as the key phrase to characterize the Tuskegee plan.[1] Yet after 1900, with resistance mounting from Black intellectuals, Washington began to develop ideas around work directed at the middle class. He formed the National Negro Business League, began writing increasingly about Black entrepreneurship, and eventually, shifted some attention toward the professions.

Washington's concept of work, signified in the dignity of labor, fit within two interconnected, idealized views of labor. The first was a widespread belief among elites that manual labor was good for the mind and soul. These believers encouraged real men to leave their desks and pick up an ax or hammer. Among these calloused-hand intellectuals were the followers of the Social Gospel Movement and several of Washington's friends, including Harvard president Charles W. Eliot. Eliot represents a certain elite group of thinkers, including Washington, who believed that the new cultivated man combined the lofty with the physical.[2] However, Washington racialized this idea, offering a second meaning of labor distinct from Eliot's.

Although Washington must have first heard the words dignity of labor from his Hampton mentor Samuel Chapman Armstrong, he soon transformed its meanings. The older Armstrong had used the phrase with an emphasis on control and order.[3] But Washington, like many of his contemporaries, was steeped in the new Arts and Crafts movement. From the 1895 Atlanta Exposition on, he repeatedly told audiences some variation of the following: "No race can prosper until it learns there is as much dignity in tilling a field as in writing a poem";[4] and "The negro throughout the South is beginning to see the dignity and beauty of labor."[5] Among Washington's writings, the 1896 "The Awakening of the Negro" demonstrates how the dignity of labor embodies the Tuskegee plan. He firmly believed that his labor-based industrial system of education would lead to prosperity, a virtuous life, and the end of "friction between the races." Industrially trained laborers, learning modern systems of teaching skills, would find in their work the dignity of self-help, racial uplift through assisting their communities, and all of the Christian character virtues necessary to provide the "moral backbone" for the climb to "civilization." "With newer methods of labor, which teach promptness and system, and emphasize the beautiful,—the moral value of the well-painted house, and the fence with every paling and nail in its place,—we are bringing to bear upon the South an influence that is making it a new country in industry, education, and religion."[6] Cultured Victorian men like Washington saw aesthetics at the peak of this ascent to civilization.

The notion of labor as beautiful and dignified may be found both literally on the walls of Tuskegee and in several of Washington's writings. The display of high-art print reproductions at the school, explored in chapter 6, included romantic images of workers by noted European artists, such as Raphael, Millet, and Jules Breton. Classroom walls were adorned with prints of works of art such as Jules Breton's *The Song of the Lark*, Raphael's *Sistine Madonna*, and *The Apollo Belvedere*. Similarly, when Washington wrote about education and work for elite White publications, he often enlisted the expertise of noted artists to portray his concept of labor and beauty. For example, when Washington wrote a lengthy article about Tuskegee for *The World's Work* titled "The

Successful Training of the Negro," he hired one of America's leading photographers, Frances Benjamin Johnston, to visualize his ideas.[7]

For Washington, of course, the dignity of labor also pointed the way to racial uplift. It endures because, since its use early in the nineteenth century, its transformative nature allowed for as many connotations as one could conjure. While it typically carried a message of respect for workers with a quasi-religious tone, it quickly took on two meanings—either used derisively by those who saw a form of suppression or worn as a badge of honor for those aligning it with self-determination. On the one hand, thinkers such as Friedrich Nietzsche, Oscar Wilde, and Jack London saw the term as a lie perpetuated by those in power to maintain a compliant workforce.[8] On the other hand, missionary associations, organized labor, and leaders of the Arts and Crafts movement used the phrase with pride.[9] Shifting in between, always eager to please both capital and labor, was the protean Booker T. Washington, repeating this phrase like a magical epigram.

It became a favored term of industrial and progressive education, but here too its meanings varied. C. M. Woodward and the manual training movement used the phrase to describe a new kind of skilled worker-engineer who would run the mighty engines of the new age.[10] Other educators called for industrial drawing as a way of "dignifying labor" by raising the status of manual work in the eyes of those who did not work with their hands.[11] John Dewey argued that simply providing new sentiments about the dignity of labor was not enough. It was time to challenge the old division between manual and intellectual skills.[12]

Black educators grafted the dignity of labor onto the equally complex phrase "racial uplift." Racial uplift could mean many things, but most often, it emphasized salvation, morality, and community service. For those engaged in racial uplift, the terms *work* and *dignity of labor* often suggested similar meaning.[13] The dignity of labor appears in both Black liberal and industrial education catalogs, from the African Methodist Episcopal schools to Tuskegee. As late as 1909, Clark College president William Crogman launched an agricultural program to "dignify farm labor and raise the standard of living among our people."[14] Similarly, W. E. B. Du Bois made "a belief in the dignity of labor" the seventh and final platform item for the Niagara Movement, writing: "The seventh statement emphasizes the fact that labor is not only profitable but honorable. There is dignity in working not for yourself alone but for the world about you."[15]

Sometime after 1900, as pressure mounted from Black intellectuals, Washington recognized the need to use his influence to promote white-collar jobs and higher education in the professions. After forming the National Negro Business League in 1900, Washington wrote several essays on the need to develop a Black middle class, particularly a network of Black businessmen. (Women played little role in his plan for a white-collar army of bankers, storekeepers, and insurance salesman.) Typical of these writings is his submission to the magazine *Charities*, in which he encouraged Black businessmen to return to the South and to escape the evils of northern cities, to increase their wealth through emerging opportunities, and to serve the race. In doing so, according to Washington, the businessman uplifts the Black community and "gives[s] a dignity to his work and a significance to his whole life."[16] Knowing Washington's disdain for northern cities, it is not surprising that, when he chose to profile a "typical Negro community" in his most complete work on the Black middle class, the 1907 *The Negro in Business*, he looked south.[17]

Washington paints an optimistic picture of a thriving Black community in Pensacola, Florida.[18] In 1908, he went so far as to tell readers of the Chicago-based *Home Herald* that, after considering the work of Black banks in the South, "there is no higher test of intellectual and moral fiber of a people than its capacity to conduct a business like a bank."[19] During this same period, Washington began to write about Black professionals and to see change from the top down. For example, in "The Negro Doctor in the South," which appeared in *The Independent* in 1907, Washington states, "there are few stronger forces at work, in the elevation of the race, than those represented by negro doctors."[20] Soon after, the National Medical Association, the nation's oldest organization of African American health professionals, was added to the list of meetings hosted at Tuskegee (a list that hitherto had included mostly farmers' groups). Ironically, the medical group first gathered in 1895 during the Cotton States Exposition in Atlanta while Washington was delivering his famous speech.

Late in life, when Washington wrote an account of his second European tour titled *The Man Farthest Down*, he once again embraced the college-trained farmer. Washington's use of the dignity of labor here embodies his vacillation between the notion as emanating from the top or percolating from the bottom. He offered his audience both. In this publication, the reader learns of Washington's complete admiration for Denmark and its people. It is a country where, as Washington describes it, the typical farmer speaks three languages, the children are happy in school, and the masses live in harmony with the land. One finds on their shelves not only technical and literary magazines but also, in one case, a copy of the English art journal *Studio*.[21] The Danish fully understood, in his estimation, how to start at the bottom. Here was the living model for the southern Black worker, which he had been developing in his mind since his days as a student at Hampton Institute: a self-sufficient landowner who possessed both the scientific knowledge to raise crops efficiently and the aesthetic wisdom to find beauty in the simple, bucolic life. This picture summarized the Janus-headed nature of his educational philosophy. Washington ended the book by identifying with the common man: "The man who is down, looking up, may catch a glimpse now and then of heaven, but the man who is so situated that he can only look down is pretty likely to see another and quite different place."[22] This book, like most of his writings, was directly aimed at the men looking down, knowing that they had the power and resources to effect change.

Contents

Published
Every Saturday

October 7, 1905
Volume 15, No. 1

CHARITIES

CHARITY TO-DAY MAY BE JUSTICE TO-MORROW

The Negro in the Cities of the North

1—The Italian in America, May, 1904
2—The Slav in America, December, 1904

New York
The Charity Organization Society
105 East 22d Street

Entered at the Post Office, New York, N. Y., as second-class matter

Ten Cents a Copy $2 a Year be subject to their order until I have fulfilled this contract, forfeiting all claims to said personal effects after sixty days from this date should I fail to comply with agreement.

One month's service is the usual period inserted in the bargain. The agreement and baggage check are sent to the correspondent. In return transportation—usually steerage on boats—is provided. The boat stewardesses say the majority of the girls going North have agency tickets. Here comes the profit. The steerage fare from Norfolk to New York is but $5.50, but the agent's charge is often double. From Savannah or Charleston there is likewise a heavy overcharge.

I have tried to show how this migration has naturally arisen out of existing conditions. As yet foreign immigration has not appreciably affected the Southern situation. This is true, although we hear from time to time of attempts being made to get Italians into the South and likewise hear of the successes of numbers of small colonies of Italians. We must bear in mind, however, that there are thousands of acres of untilled land in the South and that in many districts, as for instance in the delta regions of the Mississippi, many new farms are being opened with a corresponding increase in the demand for labor. In the districts under consideration in this article, the Italian as yet plays absolutely no part in causing the exodus of native blacks. This may, however, come at any time, for Italians are being sought for plantation work. There is need for the Negro in the South, but so long as unskilled labor elsewhere yields such large returns together with city opportunities, the migration will continue. Meanwhile, it must be borne in mind by the reader that the South is passing through a great industrial revolution which involves in many ways the life of the Negro. As yet the black has not become in any sense a factory hand in the cotton mills, but wherever large masses of relatively unskilled labor are employed, as in the mines or in the iron mills about Birmingham, a new source of livelihood has been opened for thousands; and these thousands have largely come from the rural districts. This industrial transformation means that the old dominant type of the Southern planter with the patriarchal system of plantation life and the deep sense of personal responsibility for the welfare of the blacks is in one sense a thing of the past. The South as well as the North is beginning to demand efficiency, and the Negro is more and more left to himself to work out his salvation. No wonder, then, with the poverty of natural resource and scanty means of training at his command that the young man dreams of larger opportunities in the North.

It is only necessary in closing to suggest that many ex-convicts and otherwise undesirable individuals find it advantageous to leave home. Many of these seek the North and to them the older Negro city dwellers ascribe a considerable part of the crime which has attracted attention in recent years.

Why Should Negro Business Men Go South?

Booker T. Washington
Tuskegee Institute

In a recent address to the members of the National Negro Business League, at their sixth annual meeting in New York, I said: "In commending opportunities for progress in business and commerce we should not disregard the fact that of the ten million members of our race, the great masses are in the South, and there, in my opinion, they will remain. While there are evils of which no one should lose sight—in creating and securing labor, in conducting business enterprises, and in securing homes—there is no other part of the United States that begins to offer a field more inviting than the South. We should see to it that we do not lose in the South that which we now possess. We should not grasp at a shadow, and lose the substance. If we neglect to occupy the field that is now before us in the South, it will become there as it is in the North—we will be excluded by those who are strangers to our tongue and customs."

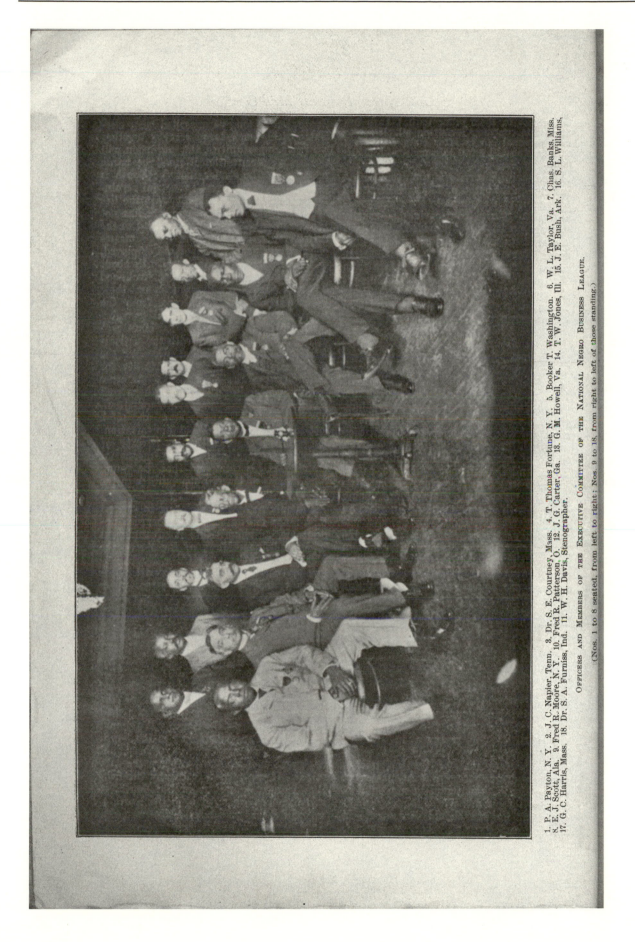

1. P. A. Payton, N. Y. 2. J. C. Napier, Tenn. 3. Dr. S. E. Courtney, Mass. 4. T. Thomas Fortune, N. Y. 5. Booker T. Washington. 6. W. L. Taylor, Va. 7. Chas. Banks, Miss. 8. E. J. Scott, Ala. 9. Fred R. Moore, N. Y. 10. Fred R. Patterson, O. 12. J. G. Carter, Ga. 13. G. M. Howell, Va. 14. T. W. Jones, Ill. 15. J. E. Bush, Ark. 16. S. L. Williams. 17. G. C. Harris, Mass. 18. Dr. S. A. Furniss, Ind. 11. W. H. Davis, Stenographer.

OFFICERS AND MEMBERS OF THE EXECUTIVE COMMITTEE OF THE NATIONAL NEGRO BUSINESS LEAGUE.

(Nos. 1 to 8 seated, from right to left; Nos. 9 to 18, from left to right; from right to left, of those standing.)

Why Should Negro Business Men Go South ?　　19

In seeking to answer briefly the question that has been proposed to me, "Why should the Negro business man go South?" I believe I cannot do better than enlarge somewhat and make more specific the statement I have just quoted.

Emphasis should be put on the fact that the masses of the Negro people are now, and are likely to be for all time, in the South, for the most part on the farms and in the small towns, rather than the large cities.

They were born there, bred there, and even were it possible to remove them in any great numbers, I believe they are better fitted to live there than elsewhere, either on this continent or in Africa.

I saw the statement recently that until the beginning of the nineteenth century, no city has ever increased in size by the natural growth of its native population. Where great cities sprang up, they grew and maintained their population by constant accessions from the country districts. In other words, the population produced in the country went to the city only to die. It was not bad sanitary conditions alone that brought this about. The same causes which operated to destroy the population of the cities a hundred years ago, are still operating to-day, though to a less degree, no doubt, in the crowded city districts which most of the colored people usually live in, in the North.

I do not believe the masses of colored people are yet fitted to survive and prosper in the great northern cities to which so many of them are crowding. The temptations are too great, and the competition with the foreign population, with which they there come in contact, is too fierce.

I am convinced that for a long time to come the great mass of the prosperous, successful colored people will be found on the farms and in the small towns of the South.

But where the great masses of the Negro population are, there are the best opportunities for Negro business men. Experience has shown, I believe, even in the North, that the largest opportunities for the Negro in business are in providing for those needs of other members of his race, which the white business man, either through neglect, or lack of knowledge, has failed, or been unable to provide. The Negro knows the members of his own race. He knows the Negro people of his neighborhood, in their church, and in their family life, and is able to discriminate in his dealings with them. This superiority in the matter of credits is in itself a business advantage, of which competition cannot easily deprive the Negro, and one which, with the extension of the modern methods of business, is likely to become of increasing importance.

Every condition which favors the Negro in the South, the cheapness of land, of the cost of living, opportunities for work, and his natural adaptation to the soil, favor also the Negro in business in the South. Indeed the great need of the masses of the Negro people for direction in the matter of buying and selling, saving and investing, makes opportunities for the Negro who possesses training in business affairs.

But there are other reasons which must appeal more and more to one who considers the matter thoughtfully. Money earned by the Negro in the way of business in the South is ordinarily worth more than money earned in the same way in the North. It is worth more, not merely because it goes further, but because the business man, in earning it, can be of more service to his race. The Negro banker who, in the course of his business, finds it necessary to encourage thrift and industry among his people, the Negro tradesman, who, for his own protection, must constantly discriminate between the honest and industrious members of his race, is at the same time performing a service to his people and the community as a whole, which should and does give a dignity to his work and a significance to his whole life.

The Negro who, in the course of his own business, is doing something which at the same time makes the world better, will in the long run stand higher in the community among his neighbors of both races, than he who, making more, and spending more, spends it, as he is tempted to do, for the superficial things which make life in the great northern cities so attractive to large numbers of the people of my race.

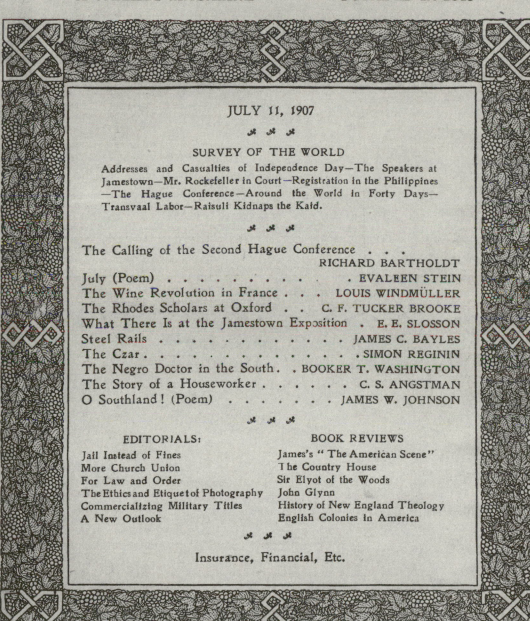

Ten Cents a Copy   Two Dollars a Year

The Independent

A WEEKLY MAGAZINE   FOUNDED IN 1848

JULY 11, 1907

❧ ❧ ❧

SURVEY OF THE WORLD

Addresses and Casualties of Independence Day—The Speakers at Jamestown—Mr. Rockefeller in Court—Registration in the Philippines—The Hague Conference—Around the World in Forty Days—Transvaal Labor—Raisuli Kidnaps the Kaid.

❧ ❧ ❧

❧ ❧ ❧

❧ ❧ ❧

Insurance, Financial, Etc.

130 Fulton Street, New York

him a successor to the throne, because He regarded Nicholas as unworthy of the Russian people. The people who are now the "Black Hundreds" took up this agitation of Father John of Kronstadt. The people were seized with a spirit of discontent which threatened to develop into a rebellion on religious grounds. If the son had not been born Nicholas II would have been forced to abdicate in favor of his brother, Mikhail. Yanishev, the Czar's confessor, then persuaded the Czar to renounce the spiritualists and devote himself entirely to prayer. And to strengthen this religious fanaticism in the Czar, it was resolved to discover some new saint. Such a saint was soon discovered by the Holy Synod in the person of the old recluse Seraphim, who was buried in the forest of Sarov. The Czar and the Czarina went to pray at Seraphim's grave, and soon after the Czarina gave birth to a son. Is it strange after this that the Czar is guided in all serious matters by some mysterious elements and leads the nation astray?

During the recent war with Japan the Czar kept sending trainloads of ikons, instead of cannon and guns to the battlefield. The well-known strategist and military writer, General Dragomirov, said at one of the military conferences at the time: "The Czar is sending us ikons for the Japanese, while the Japanese are sending us bullets. He sends us some more ikons and they send us some more bullets. We will thus fight with prayers, and they with cannon, and, of course, we will come out victorious."

Such is the attitude of the more or less intelligent bureaucrats toward the Czar; but the majority of the court clique deride Nicholas, and frequently ignore him altogether.

What is the attitude of the revolutionaries toward the Czar? The Russian Emperor has demonstrated better than any of the revolutionary groups, or all of them taken together, how ruinous to Russia the autocracy has been, and thus the revolutionary party has found in the person of Nicholas II a valuable ally, and it is hardly in their interests to lose him.

New York City.

The Negro Doctor in the South

BY BOOKER T. WASHINGTON, LL.D.

Principal of Tuskegee Institute, Alabama

WHEN I went to Alabama in 1881, there was not a negro doctor, dentist or pharmacist in the State; three years later Doctor C. N. Dorsett located in Montgomery, Ala., and received a hearty reception from the white physicians and colored citizens generally. At the present time there are more than one hundred negro doctors, dentists and pharmacists in the State. In the district of Birmingham alone, there are over twenty-five. It might be well to mention here, that the first woman of any race, who was permitted to practice medicine in the State of Alabama, was a negro woman, Dr. Sadie Dillard, a daughter of Bishop Benjamin Tanner.

A few days ago the State Negro Medical, Dental and Pharmaceutical Association held its annual session in Birmingham, Ala. There were present seventy-one men and women connected with the medical profession. Aside from those who reside in the State there were present medical men of national reputation such as Dr. Geo. C. Hall, of Chicago; Dr. A. M. Curtis, of Washington, D. C., and Doctors Boyd, Stewart and Roman, of Nashville, Tenn.

The progress that I have mentioned as having taken place in the State of Alabama is a fair sample of what is going on thruout the South. One does not hear much of the negro doctor, but there are few stronger forces at work, in the elevation of the race, than those represented by the negro doctors. The negro physician is well treated by the white physician. In many instances the white doctor is willing to lend the negro doctor books, instruments and, with few exceptions, is glad to go into the consultation room with him. He receives practically the same consideration at the drug stores that is accorded the white physician. In almost every section of the South, where I have gone, I have observed that the negro doctor is not only treated with high respect by the colored people, but

community in which he lives, and owning valuable property. In Montgomery, Ala., for instance, the negro doctors own and operate four drug stores; in Birmingham and Mobile they own and control equally as many drug stores.

One of the largest and most successful wholesale drug stores in the city of Anniston, Ala., is owned by Dr. Charles I. Thomas, and there is nothing in its ap-

THE ALABAMA MEDICAL, DENTAL AND PHARMACEUTICAL ASSOCIATION, BIRMINGHAM, ALABAMA.

equally so by the white people. There are comparatively few cases where the negro doctor has not held his own from a moral point of view. The number who have gone down on account of drink or other bad habits is very small.

The influence of the negro doctor, in the elevation of the race, has extended further than the mere practice of medicine. In many cases it will be found that he is a successful business man in the

pearance, outside or inside, that indicates it is not in the hands of a white man. Nearly every town or city of any size in Alabama has its negro drug store, and its patrons are not confined to the negro race, altho the practice of the negro doctor is confined almost exclusively to the members of his own race.

The influence of the negro doctor has gone still further: In nearly every large city in the State there are hospitals or infirmaries, where good surgical and medical attention is provided and nurses are trained. In some instances the institution is owned and controlled by the public, in other instances they are owned by individual doctors.

The majority of the negro doctors, dentists and pharmacists in the South have been educated at Howard University, Washington, D. C.; Meharry Medical College, at Nashville, Tenn., or at the Leonard Medical College, at Raleigh, N. C. At the Leonard Medical College, from the beginning, a majority of the professors have been Southern white men residing in Raleigh.

Last April I had the pleasure of delivering the commencement address to the graduating class of the Meharry Medical College when ninety-six received diplomas in medicine, dentistry and pharmacy. A majority of these, of course, will practice in the South.

The evolution of the negro doctor has been a gradual but constant one, and his influence for good will be felt in an increasingly strong manner thruout the South each year.

TUSKEGEE, ALA.

The Story of a Houseworker

BY C. S. ANGSTMAN

MY maid was very taciturn, but evidently quite a superior girl, so I was interested to find out why she was doing housework, and led her on talk of herself at two or three different times, and this is what she told me:

"You see, we girls had a stepmother, and she soon had children of her own, for whom perhaps it was natural that she should want all that there was, but, anyway, we were always short of clothes and the many things which girls are always needing. We continued to go to school, however, till my father died, after which the family was soon separated. At this time I was thru the second year of high school and sixteen years old. Having now to take care of ourselves my sister and I turned naturally to housework, because we had been well trained in that at home and because we could always get it without much trouble, tho after a number of years I have come to see that it is almost as hard for a girl to get a satisfactory place in which to work as it is for a lady to get a satisfactory helper.

"After working in our home city for a while, we went to the large city of ———. Soon after our arrival, I secured a place in a knitting factory, lured on by the stories of evenings and Sundays to one's self and big wages, told by the girls at our boarding-place, who thought housework quite beneath them. Work in the factory was paid by the piece, so the faster we worked the more we earned. Being naturally quick motioned, by much hurrying I soon made $12 a week. But, oh, the noise of the machines! They seemed to be going all night long, and I was always hurrying, hurrying with everything, even in my dreams. It seemed that as I outdistanced many girls in the number of socks which I could finish in a day, and so made more money than they did, that a perfect fever took possession of me to accomplish always more.

"The room in which two hundred of us girls worked the machines was low, long and narrow and dark, lighted from small windows at the front and back only. These windows were not opened all winter long, and as there was no system of ventilation you can imagine what the atmosphere was. We hardly realized that there was a sun or even daylight. All winter long we went to work in the dark and went home in the dark. Seeing occasionally a little more brightness thru the dingy windows than at other times, we could only guess that the sun might be out.

"After a year of this life, I gave out

Chapel, Tuskegee Inst., Ala.

5
Philanthropy

Booker T. Washington and philanthropy can be examined in at least three basic ways. The first, which dominates the scholarship on this topic, considers Washington as the passive recipient of northern industrialists' money. This approach narrowly defines philanthropy as the distribution of money from those in power, most often the province of the White elite.[1] A second way of analyzing the theme of Washington and philanthropy involves a different perspective, one that sees philanthropy much more broadly. Here philanthropy expands to include multiple forms of support, not only monetary, such as giving time and goods. In this way, the Black community's complex methods of agency and uplift are recognized as powerful methods of philanthropy in the literal sense of the phrase: "love to mankind."[2] From this vantage point, Washington often appears as an activist within the Black community: one who raised funds, secured loans and jobs, and used his name to assist Black individuals and causes. Finally, a third perception of Washington and philanthropy changes the focus. Instead of perceiving Washington as a lackey of northern industrialists, one may ask how and why Washington made himself such an attractive recipient of power and money. Rather than confronting Whites as Du Bois did, Washington pushed for change by demonstrating Black intellectual and cultural equality with Whites.[3]

Washington's role as gatekeeper for northern White industrialist philanthropy constitutes the main narrative in Washington scholarship. Its construction begins with Du Bois and runs through the writings of Louis Harlan and James Anderson. From their point of view, Washington was selected by northern industrialists because he naively traded in social and political rights, along with demands for higher education and for basic economic security. As a reward, Washington was given a token authority in a number of philanthropic organizations to help divert funds toward industrial rather than higher education efforts for African Americans. Clearly, Washington used his power to support the programs he favored over those he did not. Furthermore, there is no doubt that Washington used his power to destroy the careers of those who did not support his industrial plan.

Washington's critics may choose from a number of writings to point out his obsequious relationship with the industrial philanthropists. For example, a 1902 article for *The World To-Day* is as much a celebration of his benefactors as it is a description of the Tuskegee plan. Recipients of Washington's praise include a who's who of Progressive Age philanthropy, as he thanks such men as Robert Ogden, Andrew Carnegie, Collis P. Huntington, George Foster Peabody, and John D. Rockefeller to name a few. Moreover, this article includes two themes that infuriated his later critics. The first was his willingness to tell potentially demeaning dialect stories in White journals.[4] The second was his willingness to accentuate the positive aspects of White power and ignore its blatant embrace of Jim Crow racism. For example, here he notes how "easily accessible" Tuskegee is by traveling on the Southern Railroad, ignoring the segregation of its passengers.[5]

Whereas Washington rarely missed a chance to thank a benefactor publicly, he also rarely missed a chance to privately attack his detractors. Washington was careful not to leave a record of these attacks by outmaneuvering his enemies in the shadows. No story of Washington's wrath is sadder than that of William E. Benson (18?–1915), a Howard University graduate who served as an administrator at the nearby Kowaliga Academic and Industrial Institute. Benson, whose family was friends with Washington, secured Washington as a Kowaliga trustee and an advisor. Washington endorsed Benson and his school in national publications and introduced Benson to influential friends. However, Benson mistakenly went directly to one of Washington's philanthropist friends, Emily Howland, without first consulting Washington. In the example included in this chapter, Washington fired off a letter to Howland labeling Benson "whimsical, spasmodic and rather superficial."[6] Washington evidently worked against Benson for several more years.[7] Du Bois would later use the case of Benson's demise to demonstrate Washington's tyrannical control over resources handed out by the industrial philanthropists.[8]

In addition to being seen as a gatekeeper for industrial philanthropy, Washington supported many causes and people. Emmett J. Scott, Washington's personal secretary, described it best when he outlined Tuskegee's support of local farmer conferences: "Here is a program that calls for real philanthropy—a philanthropy not only of money, but of service as well."[9] In contrast to how he treated Benson, Washington lavishly supported farmers and local schools, writing articles on behalf of friends and penning forewords to books, securing jobs for Blacks at every level of society, and lending his name for numerous causes. He was careful to let White readers know how much Blacks contributed financially toward self-help.[10] Whereas many of Washington's efforts are well documented, his quiet assistance for struggling artists is not.[11] Included in this chapter are two examples. The first, an 1897 introduction to a volume of poetry by African American poet Mary Weston Fordham, demonstrates Washington's support for someone about whom little else is known.[12] Finally, Washington launched the careers of several Black photographers, several of whom became nationally known, such as C. M. Battey and A. P. Bedou. Washington's connections made it possible for these photographers to photograph White and Black elite as well as to publish their work in many venues. Even late in his career, Washington continued to reach out to emerging Black talent. In 1906, an unknown Washington, D.C., photographer, G. Addison Turner, wrote to Washington, introducing himself as a member of the Negro Business League, looking for a chance to build his career by photographing Washington.[13] Always willing to help a fellow member of the league, the Tuskegee leader sat for the unknown photographer.

A third way of viewing Washington and philanthropy shows Washington's ability to make himself an attractive recipient of industrialists' money. Here, the Tuskegee principals's early years as a house servant for wealthy New Englanders came in handy. A quick study, Washington saw both their paternalistic racism and their Christian charity. He understood how these men (and a few women) were believers in the Darwinian social ladder, in which *taste* was to be at the highest rung. For these Victorians, who looked to thinkers like John Ruskin for inspiration, taste represented joining work, morality, and aesthetics.

Washington molded his own image into that of the Victorian man of highest tastes. He made sure the design and typography of his articles and books sent north for publishing and for potential northern benefactors equaled the Arts and Crafts splendor of the best work from Boston and New York. For example, his first book, *Daily Resolves*, a sumptuously decorated collection, was designed in an Arts and Crafts movement illuminated manuscript revival style (which is discussed in depth in chapter 6).[14]

Washington also used flattery to gain support of industrial philanthropists. At times, the flattery was quite blatant. For example, the frontispiece for this chapter shows the Tuskegee campus literally inscribed with the names of important donors.[15] However, Washington was usually more subtle. He adopted the high-art style of his benefactors in his articles and books to show that he shared their values concerning work, morality, and aesthetics. That artistic style, known as Pictorialism, dominated lofty northern journals. Washington's images of industrious labor in the agrarian South provided precisely the romantic image of progress that good-hearted, enlightened White philanthropists sought. Washington reflected a flattering image of their paternalistic dreams. He also sent the message that Blacks would remain at peace in the Sunny South. Prominent White photographers, such as Frances Benjamin Johnston, Gertrude Kasebier, Clifton Johnson, and Julian Dimock, were hired to create soft-focused views of Washington and his worker paradise.

Perhaps no illustrated article by Washington better captures his desire to evoke a tranquil, bygone country paradise than the 1901 piece "Chicken, Pigs, and People."[16] In this visual essay, Washington performs in the role of pastoral shepherd. He feeds the animals and smells the dogwoods. It is here, in nature and not in books, Washington states that the true and the good are discovered: "To me there is nothing more delightful and restful than to spend a portion of each Sabbath afternoon in the woods with my family, near some little stream where we can gather wild flowers and listen to the singing of the mocking-birds and the ripple of the water. This, after a good sermon in the morning, seems to take us very near to nature's God."[17] Of course, this is a fiction—enacted by a gentleman farmer in a suit—not Christian virtue. In reality, Jim Crow ruled Macon County, Alabama, and the "gentleman farmer" spent more time on the road promoting his programs and raising money than he did gathering flowers.

Contents

VOL. 68, NO. 5   *June 1, 1901*   PRICE TEN CENTS

THE
OUTLOOK
TWELFTH ANNUAL
RECREATION
NUMBER

CHICKENS, PIGS AND PEOPLE

By

Booker T. Washington

ILLUSTRATED WITH

PHOTOGRAPHS BY

CLIFTON JOHNSON

I HAVE always been intensely fond of outdoor life. Perhaps the explanation for this lies partly in the fact that I was born nearly out-of-doors. I have also, from my earliest childhood, been very fond of animals and fowls. When I was but a child, and a slave, I had close and interesting acquaintances with animals.

During my childhood days, as a slave, I did not see very much of my mother, since she was obliged to leave her children very early in the morning to begin her day's work. The early departure of my mother often made the matter of my securing breakfast uncertain. This led to my first intimate acquaintance with animals.

In those days it was the custom upon the plantation to boil the Indian corn that was fed to the cows and pigs. At times, when I had failed to get any other breakfast, I used to go to the places where the cows and pigs were fed, and make my breakfast off this boiled corn, or else go to the place where it was the custom to boil the corn, and get my share there before it was taken to the animals.

If I was not there at the exact moment of feeding, I could still find enough corn scattered around the fence or the trough to satisfy me. Some people may think that this was a pretty bad way in which to get one's food, but, leaving out the name and the associations, there was nothing very bad about it. Any one who has eaten hard boiled corn knows that it has a delicious taste. I never pass a pot of boiled corn now without yielding to the temptation to eat a few grains.

Another thing that helped in developing my fondness for animals was my contact with the best breeds of fowls and animals when I was a student at the Hampton Institute. Notwithstanding the fact that my work there was not directly connected with the stock, the mere fact that I saw the best kinds of animals and fowls day after day increased my love for them, and made me resolve that when I went out into the world I would have some as nearly like them as possible.

I think that I owe a great deal of my present strength and ability to work to my love of outdoor life. It is true that the amount of time that I can spend in the open air is now very limited. Taken on an average, it is perhaps not more than an hour a day, but I make the most of that hour. In addition to this I get much pleasure out of the anticipation and the planning for that hour.

I do not believe that any one who has not worked in a garden can begin to un-

MAKING FRIENDS WITH THE COLT

derstand how much pleasure and strength of body and mind and soul can be derived from one's garden, no matter how small it may be; the smaller it is, the better, I think, in some respects. If the garden be very small, a man can have the gratifying experience of finding out how much can be produced on a small plot carefully laid out, thoroughly fertilized, and well cultivated. And then, when the garden is small, but the vegetables and plants large, there springs up a feeling of kinship between the man and the plant, as he tends and watches the growth of each individual plant from day to day. Each day there is some new development. The rain, the dew, the sunshine, each causes some new growth.

The letter or the address that one began writing the day before never budges or moves forward one iota until you return and take up the work where it was left off; not so with the plant. Some change has taken place during the night; there is the appearance of bud or blossom or fruit. This sense of newness, of expectancy, brings to me a freshness, an inspiration for each day, that it is difficult to describe.

It is not only a pleasure to grow good vegetables for one's own table, but I get

much satisfaction from sending some of the best specimens to some neighbor whose garden is backward, or to some one who has not learned the art of raising the best or the earliest varieties, and who is therefore surprised to receive some new potatoes two weeks in advance of any one else.

When I am at my home at Tuskegee, I usually find a way, by rising early in the morning, to spend at least half an hour in my garden, or with my fowls, pigs, or cows. As far as I can get the time, I like to find the new eggs each morning myself, and when at home am selfish enough to permit no one else to do this in my place. As with the growing plants, there is a sense of freshness and newness and of restfulness in connection with the finding and handling of newly laid eggs that is delightful to me. Both the anticipation and the realization are most pleasing. I begin the day by seeing how many eggs I can find, or how many little chickens there are that are just beginning to peep through the shells.

Speaking of little chickens coming into life, a few days ago one of our students called my attention to something in connection with the chickens owned by the school itself that I had not previously

Chickens, Pigs, and People   293

known. That was that, when some of the first little chickens come out of their shells, they began almost immediately from the outside to help others not so forward to break their way out. It was delightful to me to hear that the chickens raised at the school had, so early in life, caught the Tuskegee spirit of helpfulness for others.

I am deeply interested in the different kinds of fowls, and, aside from the large number grown by the school in its poultry house and yards, I grow at my own home common chickens, Plymouth Rocks, Buff Cochins and Brahmas, Peking ducks, and fan-tailed pigeons.

The pig, I think, is my favorite animal. I do not know how this will strike the taste of my readers, but it is true. In addition to some common-bred pigs, I keep a few Berkshires and some Poland Chinas ; and it is a real pleasure to me to watch their development and increase from month to month. Practically all the pork used in my family is of my own raising.

Speaking of pigs, and of the Tuskegee spirit, I heard a story of one of our graduates not long ago that gave me great satisfaction.

A man had occasion to go to the village of Benton, Ala., in which Mr. A. J. Wood, one of our graduates, had settled ten years

IN SEARCH OF THE FOREST FLOWERS

The Outlook

before, and gone into business as a general merchant. In this time he has built up a good trade and has obtained for himself a reputation as one of the best and most reliable business men in the place. While the visitor was there, he happened to step to the open back door of the store, and stood looking out into a little yard behind the building. The merchant, joining him there, began to call, "Ho, Suke! Ho, Suke!" and finally, in response to this calling, there came crawling out from beneath the store, with much grunting, because he was altogether too big to get comfortably from under the building, an enormous black hog.

"You see that hog," the man said. "That's my hog. I raise one like that every year as an object-lesson to the colored farmers around here who come to the store to trade. About all I feed him is the waste from the store. When the farmers come in here, I show them my hog, and tell them that if they would shut their pigs up in a pen of rails, and have the children pick up acorns in the woods to feed them on, they might have just such hogs as I do, instead of the razorbacks they have now running around wild in the woods.

"Perhaps I can't teach a school here," the man added, "but if I can't do that, I can at least teach the men around here how to raise hogs as I learned to raise them at Tuskegee."

In securing the best breeds of fowls and animals I have the added satisfaction at Tuskegee of seeing a better grade of stock being gradually introduced among the farmers who live near the school.

My favorite cow is the Jersey. The Jersey, when properly taken care of, not only repays one in her yield of milk and butter, but she soon becomes a great pet. I get much satisfaction in leading these cows around, and in holding them by a rope in the yard while they eat a tempting portion of green grass or oats.

After I have gathered my eggs, and have at least said "good-morning" to my pigs, cows, and horse, the next morning duty—no, I will not say duty, but delight—is to gather the vegetables for the family dinner. There are no peas, no turnips, no radishes, no beets or salads, that taste so good as those which one has raised and gathered with his own hands in his own garden.

In comparison with these all the high-sounding and long-named dishes found in the most expensive restaurants seem tame and flavorless. One feels, when eating his own fresh vegetables, that he is getting near to the heart of nature; that is, not a second-hand, stale imitation of something, but the genuine thing. How delightful the change, after one has spent weeks eating in restaurants or hotels, and has had a bill of fare pushed before his eyes three times a day, or has heard the familiar sound for a month from a waiter's lips: "Steak, pork chops, fried eggs, and potatoes!"

As I go from bed to bed in the garden, gathering my lettuce, peas, spinach, radishes, beets, onions, and the relishes with which to garnish the dishes, and note the growth of each plant since the previous day, I feel a nearness and kinship to the plants which makes them seem to me like members of my own family. When engaged in this work, how short the half-hour is, how quickly each minute goes, bringing nearer the time when I must go to my office! When I do go there, though, it is with a vigor and freshness and with a steadiness of nerve that prepares me thoroughly for what perhaps is to be a difficult and trying day—a preparation that I could not have had but for the half-hour spent in my garden.

All through the day, too, I am enabled to do more work and better work because of the delightful anticipation of being permitted to have another half-hour, or perhaps more than that, in my garden after the office work is done. I get so much pleasure out of this that I frequently find myself beseeching Mrs. Washington to delay the dinner hour that I may take advantage of the last bit of daylight for my outdoor work.

The time spent in my garden in the evening is usually devoted to laying out new beds, planting new vegetables, in hoeing the plants, or in pruning my peach-trees.

While I am fond of shrubbery and flowers, I must confess that they do not possess enough of the industrial or economic element to particularly appeal to me, and all that part of the gardening I leave to Mrs. Washington.

My own experience in outdoor life leads me to hope that the time will soon come

A FRIENDLY VISIT TO THE CHICKENS

296 The Outlook

when there will be a revolution in our methods of educating children, especially the children in the schools of the smaller towns and rural districts. I think that it is almost a sin to take a number of children whose homes are on farms, and whose parents earn their living by farming, and cage them up, as if they were so many wild beasts, for six or seven hours during the day, in a close room where the air is often impure.

I have known teachers to go so far as to frost the windows in a school-room, or have them made high up in the wall, or keep the curtains to the windows down, so that the children could not even see nature. For six hours the life of these children is an artificial one. As a rule, the apparatus which they use is artificial, and they are taught in an artificial manner about artificial things. To even whisper about the song of a mocking-bird or the chirp of a squirrel in a near-by tree, or to point to a stalk of corn or a wild flower, or to speak about a Holstein cow and her calf, or a little colt and its mother grazing in an adjoining field, is a sin for which they must be speedily and often severely punished. I have seen teachers keep children caged up on a beautiful,

bright day in June, when all nature was at her best, making them learn—or try to learn—a lesson about hills, or mountains, or lakes, or islands, by means of an artificial map or globe, when the land surrounding the school-house would be full of representations of these things. I have seen a teacher work for an hour with children, trying to impress upon them the meaning of the words lake, island, peninsula, when a brook not a quarter of a mile away would have afforded the little ones an opportunity to pull off their shoes and stockings and wade through the water, and find, not one artificial island or lake, on an artificial globe, but dozens of real islands, peninsulas, and bays. Besides the delight of wading through the water, out in the pure bracing air, in this way they would learn more about these natural divisions of the earth in five minutes than they could learn in an hour by the book method. A reading lesson taught out on the green grass under a spreading oak-tree is a lesson that one has to use little effort to get a boy to pay good attention to, to say nothing of the sense of delight and relief that comes to the teacher.

I have seen teachers make students

A YOKE OF INSTITUTE OXEN

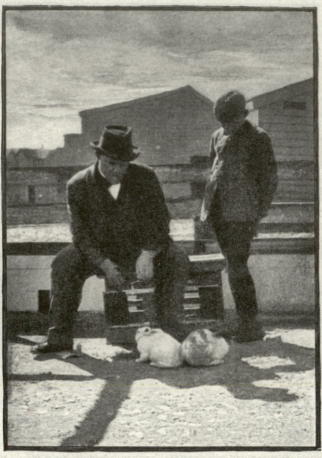

THE RABBITS—GARDEN PETS OF MR. WASHINGTON

puzzle for hours over the problem of the working of the pulley, when not a block from the school-house there would be workmen with pulleys in actual operation, hoisting bricks with which to construct the walls of a new building.

I believe that the time is not far distant when every school in the rural districts and in the small towns is going to be surrounded by a garden, and that it will be one of the main objects aimed at by the course of study to teach the child something about real country life, and about the occupations that his parents are engaged in. As it is, a very large proportion of the subjects taught in the schools have to do more or less directly with city life. Since the greater part of the child's education bears upon city life, as soon as he gets old enough, he natu-rally goes to the city for occupation and for residence.

I am glad to say that at the Tuskegee Institute we now have in process of erec-tion a new school-house in and about which, so far as we can do so, the little children of the town and vicinity will be taught, in addition to books, the real things which they will be called upon to use in their homes. Since Tuskegee is surrounded by people who earn their living by agriculture, there will be about this school-house three acres of ground on which the children are to be taught to cultivate flowers, shrubbery, vegetables, grains, cotton, and other crops. In addi-tion they are to be taught cooking, laun-dering, sewing, sweeping, and dusting, how to set a table, and how to make a bed—the things by which they are to live.

297

OF ALL THE DOMESTIC ANIMALS THE PIGS ARE MOST INTERESTING

I have referred to this building as a "school-house," but we are not going to call it that, because the name is too formal. We are going to call it "The Children's House."

Also, in the training of the negro ministers for our people, especially those who are to work among the people who live in the smaller towns and country districts, where, in the Gulf States, eighty-five per cent. of our people reside, I wish that something of the real conditions these ministers are to meet might be kept in mind.

In this, as in too many other things, the negro minister is trained to meet conditions that exist in New York or in Chicago—in a word, it is too often taken for granted that there is no difference between the work to be done by negro ministers among our people after only thirty-five years of freedom, and that to be done among the white people who have had the advantages of centuries of freedom and development.

The negro ministers, except those who go to the large cities, go among an agricultural people, as a rule—people who, of course, lead an outdoor life. They are poor, without homes or ownership in farms, without proper knowledge of agriculture, in most cases people who are able to pay their minister but a small and uncertain salary—such a small salary that no one can live on it honestly and pay his bills promptly.

During the three or four years that the minister has spent in the theological classroom, scarcely a single subject that concerns the every-day life of his future people has been discussed. He is taught more about the soil of the valley of the Nile, or of the valley of the river Jordan, than about the soil of the State in which the people of his church are to live and to work.

What I urge is that the negro minister should be taught something about the outdoor life of the people whom he is to

298

Chickens, Pigs, and People   299

lead. More than that, it would help matters immensely if in some more practical and direct manner this minister could be taught to get the larger portion of his own living from the soil—be taught to love outdoor work, and to make his garden, his farm, and his farm-house object-lessons for his people.

The negro minister who earns his living in a large part on the farm is independent, and can reprove and rebuke the people when they do wrong. It is not so with the one who is wholly dependent upon his congregation for his bread. What is equally important, an interest in

agricultural production and a love for work tend to keep a minister from that idleness which, in the case of some men not so employed, proves a cause for their yielding to temptation.

To me there is nothing more delightful and restful than to spend a portion of each Sabbath afternoon in the woods with my family, near some little stream where we can gather wild flowers and listen to the singing of the mocking-birds and the ripple of the water. This, after a good sermon in the morning, seems to take us very near to nature's God, and prepares me not only for my evening "talk" in the

AMONG THE DOGWOOD BLOSSOMS

300 The Outlook

chapel to our students and teachers, but also for the week's work.

At least once a week I make it a practice to spend an hour or more among the people of Tuskegee and vicinity—among the merchants and farmers, white and black. In these talks with the real people I can get at the actual needs and conditions of the people for whom our institution is at work.

When talking to a farmer, I always feel that I am talking with a real man and not an artificial one—one who can keep me in close touch with the world as it actually exists. When talking with a simple, honest cultivator of the soil, I am sure of getting first-hand, original information. I have secured more illustrations that I have found useful in public addresses in a half-hour's talk with some white or colored farmer than from hours of reading books.

If I were a minister, I think I should make it a point to spend a day in each week in close, unconventional touch with the masses of the people. A vacation spent in visiting farmers, it seems to me, would often prepare one as thoroughly for his winter's work as a vacation spent in visiting the cities of Europe.

Apart

By Mabel Earle

Had it been mine to choose, I should have prayed,
"Let me go forth, my Lord, and meet the brunt
Of strife against Thy foemen, fierce arrayed,
Fighting or falling at the battle's front.
Comfort me not with ease," I should have said,
"Or peaceful days, lest sword and spear grow blunt;
Give me to share the fight my brothers share;
Their wounds, their want, their triumph, their despair."

God chose instead, and set mine eager feet
Close within walls I cannot pass at will;
The noise of shouting where His armies meet
Drifts to me faint from yonder far-off hill;
My days are silent; pastures green and sweet
Beside me spread, and healing waters still.
Alas, my brothers! was I faint of heart
Or weak of hand, so to be set apart?

Yet in the silence here the self-same foe
Creeps in upon me still through sun and shade.
He fronts me sudden for the overthrow,
He follows on my steps with poisoned blade.
The weary watch by day and night I know,
The wounds, the thirst, the looking forth for aid.
So did my God, denying, grant my prayer;
So, set apart, my brothers' lot I bear.

THE BARNS AT TUSKEGEE.

The Tuskegee
Normal and Industrial Institute.

A Practical Institution—The Work It Is Doing.

BY

BOOKER T. WASHINGTON.

IN the year 1881 the Legislature of Alabama decided to establish a normal school for colored pupils in the town of Tuskegee, in Macon county, and appropriated the sum of $2,000 annually for the support of this school. The members of the Board of Commissioners in whose hands the Legislature had placed the control of this institution, two white men and one colored man, residents of the town of Tuskegee, wrote to the late General S. C. Armstrong, who was then at the head of the Hampton Institute, in Virginia, to know if he could recommend a teacher for the newly established Alabama school. General Armstrong was so good as to recommend me for the place, and after some correspondence I was engaged. I had graduated from the Hampton Institute about four years before that, and after taking a course of advanced study at Wayland College, in Washington, D. C., and teaching

for two or three years in my old home in Malden, West Virginia, I had returned to Hampton, at General Armstrong's request and was engaged in teaching the Indian students there. As soon as I could arrange to leave my work at Hampton I came to Alabama.

When I arrived at Tuskegee I found that although the Legislature had appropriated money to pay the teacher, it had done nothing in the way of providing a building for the school, furniture, books or apparatus of any kind. These the teacher and the people must secure for themselves. The colored people of the community were greatly pleased at the prospect of having a school and were willing to help in every way that they could, but so far as money was concerned they had but little to give. I finally secured the privilege of using an old abandoned Negro church and one out-building— neither of which was really a shelter from

1722   TUSKEGEE INSTITUTE.

the elements—and into these
rude and inconvenient quarters I gathered, on the Fourth
of July, 1881, thirty men and
women as pupils. One of
these was a man fifty years
of age, the pastor of one of
the colored churches in Tuskegee, who was glad to have
this opportunity to supplement his scanty earlier education.

That was the beginning of
what is now an institution
owning and occupying more

PHELPS HALL, THE BIBLE TRAINING SCHOOL BUILDING.

than fifty buildings—many of them three
and four story brick structures—and all but
the first three built almost wholly by the students themselves as a part of their industrial
education. The school possesses 2,700
acres of land—800 acres of which are cultivated by the young men students each year
as a part of their training—several hundred
head of live stock, machinery, wagons and
tools, and property altogether valued at
$400,000, on all of which there is no mort-
gage or claim whatsoever. In addition to
this the institution has an endowment fund
of $300,000, and twenty-five thousand acres
of mineral land given it by the Federal government, the proceeds of which when sold
will be added to the endowment fund. The
thirty students have increased to fourteen
hundred each year, and there are in the
neighborhood of one hundred teachers and
instructors, all colored men or women, since
there is no one connected with the institution except some of the members of the
Board of Trustees and one or two persons
not resident at the school who is not of the
race which the institution is designed to educate.

HUNTINGTON HALL, A GIRLS' DORMITORY.

The little school in the old church grew
rapidly. The students were men and
women who were old enough to appreciate
the advantages which had come so late in
life to the most of them. They were determined to have an education. It very
quickly became necessary to provide another
teacher and increased accommodations for
the school. Miss Olivia Davidson was sent
from Hampton to help me, and the newly
organized classes were held in the old out-
building near the church. Both these buildings were so worn with age that when it
rained it was often necessary for a pupil to
hold an umbrella over the teacher that the
lessons could go on. Poor as these buildings were, however, they were better than
the most of those in which the country colored schools were started. Many of those
first schools began their work in brush ar-
bors or under trees.

I had not taught this school many weeks
when I became convinced that it would be
impossible for me to obtain the results I
wished unless I could be able to exert a
closer and more constant influence on the
lives of the pupils than was possible when
I came in contact with them merely during
the hours of the school day. The pupils,
almost without exception, came from one-
room cabin homes in which they could
have had no training in habits of personal
cleanliness or in right living. They needed
to be taught the use and advantages of the
bath, the tooth brush, the night shirt, as
much as they needed to be taught morality,
religion and how to read and write and
cipher.

In addition to this, almost all of the students were so poor that small as were their
expenses while attending the school they
could not afford to remain long enough to
get much real benefit unless some way could

TUSKEGEE INSTITUTE. 1723

CHAPEL AND GIRLS' INDUSTRIAL BUILDING.

be provided by which they could pay a part or all of their expenses while they were there. Most of them, too, needed to be taught to work, about as much as they needed to be taught books. Many of them had come from small, rented plantations which had been cultivated in a slip-shod way. They knew little of the modern ways of work as I had learned them at Hampton. What they needed, in fact, using the word in its broadest sense, was to learn how to live.

While I was studying over the future of the school more and more anxiously every day, a plantation of one hundred acres, situated about one mile out of the town, was offered for sale for $500. I found that I could buy this piece of land by paying only a small part of the money down, and I resolved at once to found a Hampton in Alabama. A friend loaned me the money necessary to make the first payment. I bought the place and moved the school on to it.

The plantation house on the place had been destroyed by fire, leaving only three small buildings and a henhouse. The school began its work in these three little old out-buildings, but new scholars came so rapidly that I was soon obliged to have the hen-house cleaned out and utilized as a class room. The removal of the school into these quarters, cramped and inconvenient as they were, made many improvements possible. A considerable number of the students could now live at the school, and I could have them with me all of the time. I taught the young men in the class room a portion of the day, and then took them out of doors to work with me on the land. We cleared up the fields and planted crops. The young women did the housework, the cooking and the laundry work. They had training in sewing and mending, and later,

as soon as we could afford it, a sewing machine was bought and they began to have more systematic instruction in sewing and dressmaking. Some one gave us a horse to work on the land, and by degrees tools and supplies were given. The people of the town of Tuskegee and the surrounding country, both white and black, showed their interest by their gifts. When we wanted to open up a clay pit on the place and begin to make bricks, a white man at Tuskegee gave us a whole outfit of brickmaking tools. During all the years that the school has been in operation the relations with the white people in the community have been kindly and helpful.

The school kept out-growing its accommodations. We built—largely by our own labor—a three-story wooden building which we named Porter Hall. The basement of this building, damp and dark as it was, we used as a dining room. There was one large room which we used as a chapel and general assembly room; the rest of the building furnished class rooms and sleeping rooms. Gradually the most of these rooms have been outgrown and replaced with better ones. Our dining room—attached to Alabama Hall—affords room for practically all of the students to sit down at one time. The chapel, outgrown again and again, is now a beautiful and commodious brick structure capable of seating 2,400 persons. Some of the executive offices still remain in Porter Hall, although much cramped, but during the past year the money has been given by a friend of the school to build a large and convenient Administration Building, and the students are already at work upon it. Very recently, too, Mrs. C. P. Huntington has signified her wish to give the money to erect an Academic Building at Tuskegee in memory of her husband, the late C. P. Huntington, the president of the Southern Pacific Railroad, to be known as the C. P. Huntington Memorial Building. Mr. Huntington was one of the best friends the school has had. Besides innumerable smaller gifts of money and machinery, he gave $50,000 to the endowment fund not long before his death, and Mrs. Huntington gave the money to build Huntington Hall, our finest dormitory for girls. The sum

1724   TUSKEGEE INSTITUTE.

which she has now put in the hands of the school is sufficient to build—of brick—the largest and finest building which the school has yet had provided. When this building is erected, Porter Hall, which has done us such good service for twenty years, will probably be removed.

When we began to make plans for our second building I determined that, unlike Porter Hall, it should be of brick, being much more durable. We opened up much more widely the clay pit in which we had been at work, made our own bricks and built Alabama Hall, now one of our dormitories for girls. Since then all of our large buildings but one have been of brick, made by ourselves. Into one building—the chapel—we put one million, two hundred thousand bricks. In addition to what we have used ourselves we have made many hundred thousand bricks to be sold for use in the surrounding country. Not long ago one of our graduates who had gone into business as a grocer in Tuskegee town, and had built up a good trade there, decided to build a brick block. He placed an order with us for one hundred thousand bricks, and accompanied the order with a check to pay for the whole bill.

This man, I may add, is among the most successful merchants in the town, and no one there would question his credit.

The young men who work in the brick yard learn brickmaking as a trade. Others who lay the bricks in the walls learn practical brick-masonry. At the same time they are not only paying their expenses at the school—except for the tuition—but they are laying up a credit to be drawn on later. Students who work all day, as these do and as all do who work in any of the departments, attend night school for two hours each evening. As a general thing an industrious student can lay up enough above his expenses in two years so that he can spend the next two years in the day school.

Every student, however, no matter how well able his or her parents may be to pay their child's expenses, must work at some trade or industry six days in every month. We have innumerable students, men and women both, who come here with hardly a cent over what it has taken them to pay their traveling expenses here, and who stay five or more years working their way all of the time and with no money except what they can earn during vacations. Some do not have even money enough to pay their traveling expenses. Many students walk long distances to get here. Two boys walked from their home in North Carolina, five hundred and fifty miles.

At first the students were not anxious for industrial education. The traditions of slavery led many to look upon manual labor as

THE BRICKYARD AT TUSKEGEE.

a badge of servitude to be avoided. They were apt to think that getting an education meant acquiring a smattering of Latin and Greek, and that its chief object was to enable one to live a life of ease.

An old Negro coming in from hoeing in the fields one very hot day was heard to exclaim: "De sun am so hot, an' de cotton am so grassy, dat dis darkey b'lieves he am called to preach."

Too many of the early teachers as well as preachers were "called" for similar reasons. Conditions in this respect, though, are rapidly growing better in the South.

During the days of slavery there was an old colored man who wanted to learn to play on the guitar, and who went to a young

TUSKEGEE INSTITUTE.   1725

white man who was a good musician, with the request that he give him lessons. The young man, because he did not think that the slave, at his age, could learn enough about the guitar to make it worth while for him to try, endeavored to discourage him indirectly by telling him: "Very well, Sam, I will give you lessons, since you wish me to, but I shall have to charge you two dollars for the first lesson, one dollar for the next, fifty cents for the third lesson, and twenty-five cents for the last lesson."

"Dat's all right, boss," said the Negro. "I 'gages you on dem terms. But boss, I wants to ax you one thing. I wants yo' to be sure an' give me dat 'ere las' lesson first."

This man Sam was a type of the race in the earlier days of freedom. The men and women of that time simply wanted to get the last lesson first. The mass of the Negro race is coming to see now that there must be a firm foundation laid in industry, in the ownership of property and in right habits of living. The students of to-day seek industrial education. In almost all of the trades there are more applicants than we can accommodate. In the early days of the school the students were glad to work, it is true, but it was as a means to an end. Now, in addition to this, they realize the dignity and beauty of work for work's own sake.

A few days ago the annual industrial exercises for the present year were held—those which correspond to the usual Commencement exercises in a purely academic school. Our commodious chapel was crowded for the occasion. The governor of the State, Hon. W. D. Jelks, was present, and spoke most encouraging words. With the governor were some of the most successful business men of the South, the State Superintendent of Education, and several of the most notable educators in the State. The prominent citizens of Tuskegee and the neighboring community to the number of several hundred were present. Mr. Robert C. Ogden, of New York, and a party of distinguished educators and philanthropists who had been attending the Southern Educational Conference at Athens, Georgia, were present, and with all these hundreds of parents and friends of the students.

What did these people see? They saw, first, the roomy platform in the chapel covered with the products of the industry of the Institute and the instruments with which those products are obtained. They saw a complete, double carriage, made, wood-

work, iron-work and trimming, in the shops of the school by students. They saw castings from the foundry, and dresses and bonnets from the dressmaking and millinery shops. They saw an incubator in operation, and coops of a dozen or more varieties of standard-bred fowls. They saw an ingenious steam engine running, the work of one of the students in the machine shop, in which he has embodied novel and valuable inventions of his own. They saw shoes, and boots, and harness, and suits of clothes, and

THE HOSPITAL BUILDING.

butter and cream, and vegetables, and fruit trees. And among all these things they saw move about young men in overalls and young women in calico dresses and work aprons who demonstrated by actual work that they knew how to use the tools and make the articles to be seen upon the platform.

A graduate of the agricultural department brought upon the stage a large and unique reproduction of a model farm, with the various crops growing, and explained how each should be treated to get the best results, and what these results ought to be. A young woman discussed the best methods of raising poultry, illustrating her talk with eggs, live fowls and an incubator in operation. Another young woman cooked. A wheelwright showed how a pony phaeton should be built, and another explained the invention and operation of the engine to which I have referred, which, as he had connected it for the occasion with the boiler room of the machine shop, was in motion. A young woman illustrated by actual work the most approved methods of scientific and wholesome laundry work. Two young men

1726   TUSKEGEE INSTITUTE.

nurses from the school's hospital and nurse-training department showed by means of screens, a bed, rubber sheets, bath utensils, thermometer, medicines and foods, and—not least important—a student who posed as a patient, how they would treat a fever case.

The courses of training in the various industries last from one to four years. Students who complete a course satisfactorily are given a certificate of proficiency. Seventy such certificates were given at this industrial commencement. The academic commencement comes a little later in the season, at the close of the regular school year. The graduates from the academic department receive diplomas.

A CLASS IN COOKING, TUSKEGEE INSTITUTE.

I ought not to dismiss this industrial commencement of which I am speaking without a reference to the music which was interspersed between the various numbers, because the training of all the students in music is one of the features which the school emphasizes. All the students have instruction in vocal music. In addition to this a choir of one hundred and twenty-five voices, an orchestra, and a band have special instruction, and ample opportunity is afforded for such as wish to take a special course in piano instruction. Along with thorough training in the best classical and modern music, however, the school has always insisted upon the students retaining and singing those beautiful, old-time Negro melodies which are so essentially a part of the

history of the race. At all of our church services, chapel exercises and public gatherings these melodies are sung, and at this commencement gathering to which I have referred the music ranged from the "Inflammatus," which I may perhaps be allowed to say was sung in such a manner as to elicit unstinted praise from the audience, to some of the unique and inspiring of the Negro songs.

Because I have spoken so strongly in favor of industrial training I would not have it understood that I undervalue academic education. I would have every pupil get all the mental training that his pocketbook and time will allow. The race needs professional men and women, but the rank and file must have industrial training before the people of the race can come to possess that general prosperity which alone supplies a foundation for the proper support of the professional class. Our aim at the Tuskegee Normal and Industrial Institute is to so balance industrial and academic, and moral and religious training as to best fit each individual who is a student here to go out into the world and do the most efficient work of which he or she is capable.

I do not think that I can explain in any better way how Tuskegee does its work than by giving a description of the grounds and buildings as one coming here now sees them. As I have said, the school was started, twenty-one years ago, with three small, old buildings and one hundred acres of practically unimproved land. We now have more than fifty buildings, several of them three and four story brick structures, and twenty-seven hundred acres of land, eight hundred of which are cultivated by the young men each year. The men who do this work on the land not only pay their way by doing it, but, under the direction of thoroughly trained men, are learning the best methods of modern farming, stock raising, dairying, gardening and fruit culture. Most of them expect to make farming their life work. Among them are to be found not only the sons of farmers, but men who own farms themselves and who have left home deliberately and come

TUSKEGEE INSTITUTE. 1727

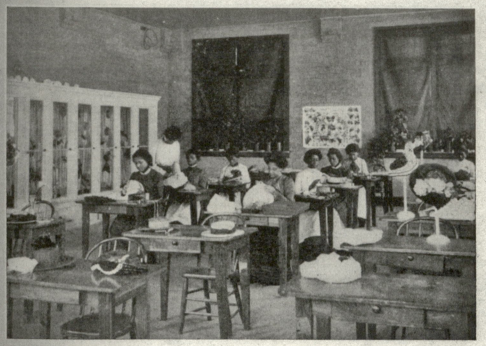

TEACHER AND CLASS IN MILLINERY, TUSKEGEE INSTITUTE.

here to learn how to carry on their farms more successfully.

Tuskegee is the county seat of Macon county. It is situated in the southeastern part of the state, forty miles from Montgomery and one hundred and forty from Atlanta. It is only five miles from a direct line of rail from New York to New Orleans, and is connected with this by a local railroad. It is easily accessible from the North by the trains of the Southern Railroad and the Western Railway of Alabama. The Institute is located about one mile from the town. One entering the school grounds at the gate nearest the town sees first two brick buildings originally used as shops, but now, since the Trades Building was erected, converted into dormitories for boys. One of these—Cassedy Hall—the generosity of Mr. George Foster Peabody made possible to refit so thoroughly that it is now one of the best dormitories for boys that we have. Near these buildings are the saw mill, carpenter shop and machine shop and foundry, in all of which classes of young men are doing practical, thorough work. In the machine shop, for instance, the course of training requires three years, and the stu-

dents obtain a great deal of practical work which apprentices in a shop would not get. They are required to take their turns in running the various engines upon the place. One of these is a seventy-five horsepower engine given by the late Mr. C. P. Huntington. They have also built a number of engines which are employed in various places about the school. The plumbing and steam heating division is connected with the machine shop. Under the direction of the teacher in this department the young men have put in all the plumbing and steam-heating apparatus required by the many buildings upon the grounds. The foreman in the foundry is a young man who took a four years' course in the machine shop here, and then went into a large foundry in Chattanooga for further instruction. All these shops, I ought to say here, will eventually be removed to the other end of the grounds, as soon as it is possible to complete the Trades Building by adding suitable shop rooms to receive these classes. The ground on which they now stand will be utilized at some future time as the site for another boys' dormitory, to accommodate the constantly increasing number of

1728   TUSKEGEE INSTITUTE.

students who apply for admission, and only a part of whom it is possible now to receive.

The next two buildings are Olivia Davidson Hall and Science Hall, respectively, four story and three story brick buildings, used for class rooms and dormitories for boys. Beyond them is Porter Hall, the old wooden building which I have said is soon to be replaced by two new and more commodious brick structures. Behind this is a group of little, old, wooden buildings, hardly more than shanties, among which are the ones in which the life of the school began, still utilized—so crowded are we—as class rooms. Still farther out in this part of the grounds is now being built the four-story brick building which Mr. John D. Rockefeller has given us for a boys' dormitory. This is to be called Rockefeller Hall, and will be one of our best buildings. The new academic building—the Collis P. Huntington Memorial Building—will occupy the site of Porter Hall and extend farther down the main avenue of the grounds. This reference to these large and much needed donations to the school reminds me to emphasize here one fact upon which I wish the general public might be thoroughly well informed. Because Tuskegee has been so favored of late with generous gifts from men and women whose means allow them to give large sums for specific purposes, I hope that people will not make the mistake of thinking—as in fact I have had reason to think some have thought—that the small gifts, which carry with them just as much of interest and encouragement and helpfulness, are no longer wanted or needed by the institution. It is the aggregate of these small gifts from individuals, from Sunday Schools, from churches and from various other organizations that, in years past, has very largely made the work of the school—indeed, its very life—possible; and it is to them that it must look for a large proportion of its support in the future. Not only are the demands upon the institution constantly increasing from the larger and larger number of young men and women who wish to come here, but the very increase in the number of large new buildings brings increased expenses in the care and operation of them so that the students can get from them the greatest good which they can afford. I most earnestly hope that the friends who have helped us in the past by their gifts—which if they may seem small to the givers, in many cases represent self-denials

which make them comparatively large—will continue to help us, and that new friends of this kind may be added. I assure these people that their help is not only wished, but is absolutely essential to the success of the institution, not only in the financial assistance, but in the encouragement which comes from their interest.

Across the street from Porter Hall stands Phelps Hall, the home of the Bible Training School. This building was given by two ladies in New York as a memorial to their mother. The Bible School is essentially non-sectarian and not theological. Its students number about seventy-five men and women each year, who include among their number representatives of about all the many sects and divisions of sects to be found in the South. In connection with their work in the Bible School they pursue some of the trades in the industrial department of the school. The need of the little country Negro churches in the South is not yet so much preachers who are trained in theological doctrines as men of wholesome moral and industrial life who will teach the people of their churches not only religion but also practical daily life. Such men the Bible School aims to train, and it has been successful to an encouraging degree. The country churches cannot afford to pay a man enough to support him, nor do they require that a preacher give all his time to pastoral work. The Bible School teaches him to have some trade or industry by which to supplement the salary which his people pay him, and by the practice of which he can teach them the dignity and value of labor. Among the graduates of the school who are preaching are farmers, a tailor, a painter, several brick masons, and men following other trades. I have in mind one very encouraging example—a man who is preaching to two colored churches not far from Tuskegee and who has bought, paid for, and manages in thoroughly good shape, a farm of over two hundred acres of land. This man's moral life is not only a model for his people, but his home and his farm are models for theirs; and the improvement in the people among whom he lives shows that all these models are being followed.

Adjoining Phelps Hall is the site for the new Administration Building, upon which work has already been begun. One of the photographs which I use as an illustration for this article shows an arithmetic class with their teacher studying measurements in the excavations for this foundation. I speak of this here because I wish to call attention to the effort which we make to have our academic classes teach in a practical working way the things which the students will need to know in their daily life. A great deal of our class work is done out of doors, about the barns and farms, and in the fields. Something over a year ago a friend of the school gave the money to build a commodious and well equipped training school building. For many years the Institute has maintained a practice school—containing kindergarten, primary and elementary grades—for the training of the normal students as teachers. There are about three hundred pupils in this school, the children of the members of the faculty and from families in the neighborhood. The new building of which I have spoken furnished the first adequate accommodation which this school has ever had, and when the new building was erected—upon a hill near the other buildings of the Institute—three acres of land were set off around it to be laid out into gardens in which the children will have practical work each day in learning to raise the vegetables and crops which can be cultivated to advantage in this climate. We do not call this building a schoolhouse, because we think that term too formal to be associated with the training of young children. We call it, instead, "The Children's House."

Beyond the site for the Administration Building is the Carnegie Library, our newest completed building, and one which we prize highly. About a year and a half ago Mr. Carnegie gave us $20,000 with which to build a library. This building, one hundred and ten by fifty feet, two stories high, is the result. The building is Colonial in general style—particularly appropriate to the South—with a lofty portico supported by Ionic columns. It was designed by Mr. R. R. Taylor, who is at the head of the industrial department of the school, and who has designed all of our later large buildings. The work of construction, from the digging of the foundation and the making of the bricks to the making of the furniture and the installation of the electric lighting fixtures was done almost wholly by the students as a part of their industrial education. This building was dedicated when the Ogden party was here, the addresses being made by Dr. Albert Shaw, the editor of the Review of Reviews, and by State Super-

CLASS IN ARITHMETIC STUDYING MEASUREMENTS.

intendent of Education, John W. Abercrombie. Our library numbers about ten thousand volumes. Now that we have ample accommodations it is hoped that this may be increased, for there is no part of the school's equipment which the students use more eagerly and to more profit.

From in front of the Library an avenue leads to the girls' dormitories. The largest and oldest of these is Alabama Hall, a four-story brick building in which are also the dining rooms and kitchens for the students and teachers. Beyond this is Huntington Hall, the beautiful dormitory for girls for which the school is indebted to Mrs. Huntington, and a large, modern cottage house known as "The Senior Home." This building was given by two friends of the school in Brooklyn as a memorial to their daughter. It is furnished throughout as a good modern home should be, and is used each year as the home for the young women of that year's senior class. In living here and taking care of the "Home" these young women have practical training in good housekeeping.

The next large building beyond the Library is the Slater-Armstrong Memorial Agricultural Building, in which are the agricultural museum, the agricultural chemistry laboratory, and a number of class rooms. The original appropriation of the State was increased some years ago to $3,000 annually, and in addition to this amount the State now appropriates $1,500 annually to support an agricultural experiment station here, which is conducted in connection with the work of the agricultural department. The Negro farmers of Macon county also hold monthly institute meetings at this building, and from it one of the officers of

1730   TUSKEGEE INSTITUTE.

the Institute issues at frequent intervals leaf-
lets of nature study for schools, and practical hints and suggestions for farmers. All
the produce raised on the place is consumed
by the students and teachers of the school.
Two years ago forty acres were set out in
peach trees, of varieties which had shown
themselves to be well adapted to this climate.
These trees have done remarkably well since
then, and the orchard promises to become
a valuable part of the school's plant. The
horticultural work of the school is in
charge of a young man who came here a
few years ago absolutely ignorant of any
information as to farming or any work
connected with the cultivation of the land.
He developed so much interest, however,
and showed so much ability, that when he
came to graduate he was hired to remain
as one of the instructors. During the long
summer vacation the school operates a steam
canning plant of its own. This furnishes
work for a number of students who wish to
remain here through the vacation, and also
teaches them a profitable industry. As
many as 2,500 gallons of blackberries are
put up each year, bought from the people
in the surrounding country, and along with
these many hundred gallons of fruit raised
upon the place. One gallon tin cans are
used, mostly made by the students in the
school's tin shop.

Just below the Agricultural Building are
the Trades Buildings. The building in
which the men are taught is the largest on
the grounds. In addition to the trades and
industries which I have mentioned in the
course of this article they are taught blacksmithing, painting, architectural and mechanical drawing, harness making and sad-
dlery, shoemaking, tailoring, and printing.
The young women are taught laundry work,
cooking, dressmaking and millinery, mattress making, basket making, dairying, poultry raising, market gardening and the care
of bees. All girls, no matter what course
they are taking, have to take practice in
cooking and sewing. Special attention is
given to model housekeeping. A suite of
rooms is fitted up as kitchen, dining-room,
sitting-room, bedroom, bath-room and
closet, and classes of girls have drill under
a capable woman in working in these rooms.

Beyond the Trades Buildings is the
Chapel, built of brick, and capable of seating, as I have said, 2,400 persons. The
bricks for this building were made by the

students, the plan for it was drawn by our
architect, and the students did practically all
the work upon it. One of the students designed the pews, and they were made in
the school's woodworking shops. This is
the building in which the late President
McKinley spoke when he visited Tuskegee.

Surmounting the crest of a well-drained
ridge of land beyond the Chapel are the
barns. The first of these is the poultry
barn, a large and convenient building with
commodious yards adjoining it. Beyond
this is the dairy, a good brick building, containing separators, churns, and all the necessary utensils for making first-class butter
and cheese. The school has about one hundred and fifty cows. The dairy furnishes
all the milk, cream, butter and buttermilk
which the students and teachers consume.
The work is done by young men and women
under the direction of an expert dairyman,
a graduate of one of the best scientific
schools in the country. In the dairy there
is a good lecture room, in which the classes
gather for oral instruction from the teacher.
Beyond the dairy are the large and thoroughly well-fitted up stock barns, one for
the cattle and the other for the mules and
horses. The horse barn is the gift of Mr.
Morris K. Jesup, of New York. In addition to the mules and horses used only for
draft, the school has some excellent breeding
animals and is constantly increasing its
stock in this way.

Somewhat remote from the other buildings and situated in a beautiful oak grove
is the school's hospital, maintained both for
the care of such sick as there may happen to
be among the students, and for the training
of nurses. This hospital is the gift of a lady
in New England, given about a year and a
half ago. It takes the place of some smaller
and much less convenient buildings, and has
made it possible for us to increase the size
of the class taking nurse-training. Twenty-
four students, men and women, can now be
accommodated in this class. The course requires three years to complete. It is a popular course with the students and the school
has at no time been able to begin to furnish
as many trained nurses as it has been asked
for, at good wages.

At some little distance from the school
in another direction is the brickyard, one of
the first industries to be started here, and
through all these years one of the most profitable in every way. I have already spoken

TUSKEGEE INSTITUTE.   1731

of the great number of bricks which the yard has turned out. The buildings upon the school grounds show the evolution of this industry. The older buildings are constructed of hand-made brick, rough and uneven. Several years ago we were able to install a brickmaking machine, and the buildings put up since then show much smoother walls. This year we have just put in a second and still more improved machine, and its result is already to be seen in the greater smoothness and beauty of the bricks which the yard is beginning to turn out.

No account of the work of Tuskegee Institute would be complete that did not contain some reference to the Tuskegee Negro Conference. About ten years ago I was led to wish that the school might be able to do something to benefit the older people—the fathers and mothers of the students. This older generation is made up largely of people who cannot be taught from books because the majority of them cannot read or write. They must be reached by means of object lessons. And yet there is evident in these people such a remarkable degree of common sense that I felt sure if a way could be pointed out to them they would do much to better their condition.

With this thought in mind I sent out invitations to about seventy-five farmers and their wives, and professional men who lived in the neighborhood of Tuskegee, to come

to the school at an appointed day to spend the time in "talking over" things. To my surprise four hundred men and women appeared in response to my invitation, and the meeting was felt to be so helpful that another was planned for the next year. From that time on the Tuskegee Negro Conference has grown in numbers and importance. Local conferences have been organized in many parts of the state and in adjoining states which hold meetings at regular times and report to this central body. Frequently nearly every Southern state will be represented at our meetings. The sessions of the Conference are always held the last week in February. Sometimes as many as a thousand farmers and their wives will be present.

The men and women themselves are the speakers here. We discuss very practical matters—things which vitally concern them —such as the need of getting to own land, how to get out of debt and keep out, the necessity of getting better homes and schools, the advantage of living a wholesome moral life. A set of declarations is adopted each year, and then being neatly printed in the Tuskegee printing office a copy of them is given to every person present to take home for guidance during the coming year. Those who cannot read for themselves are admonished to get some of their neighbors who can read to do this service for them.

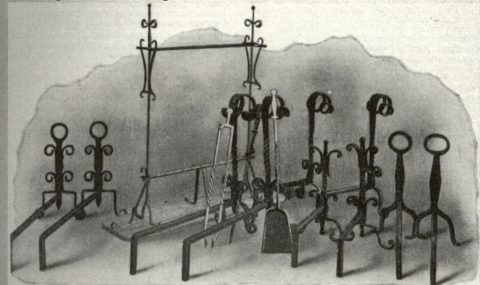

EXAMPLES OF THE WORK OF STUDENTS IN THE BLACKSMITH DIVISION OF TUSKEGEE MISSION.

Principal Washington.

Mrs. B. T. Washington.

Principal Washington's Home, Tuskegee Institute, Ala.

6

Aesthetics

Aesthetics is in the mind of the beholder. Most accounts of aesthetics reflect on perception, experience, and point of view when considering the meaning of art, beauty, and taste. Expressions of these aspects of aesthetics range from the scholarly, theoretical, and philosophical to the common, everyday descriptions of art, beauty, and taste. Culturally determined values about everything from morality, gender, race, representation, and power are contained within aesthetic judgments, whether conveyed by a philosopher or by the woman on the street. Furthermore, delineating who is worthy of making aesthetic judgments reveals a great deal about a culture.

Booker T. Washington and aesthetics? During his lifetime, this was not a surprising juxtaposition of terms. He spoke and wrote about art, beauty, and taste—in other words, aesthetics. Furthermore, he was a patron and a supporter of the arts, a performance artist on the public-speaking stage, and a leader who saw the power of art for advancing his various programs. Soon after his death, the erasure of his role in the arts began. Howard University professor James Porter's 1943 landmark book, *Modern Negro Art*, created the narrative that long exiled Washington from his role in the arts: "These facts are well recorded, including the diminution of the national interest in Negro cultural advancement as a result of Booker T. Washington's industrial education program."[1] It would take fifty years before the restoration of Washington's place in African American art slowly began.[2]

Washington's statements on art, architecture, music, and literature embody the tensions of early Modernist aesthetics. On the one hand, his writings reflect the mainstream aesthetics of the day that emphasized form and universal truths. Like many Americans of the period, Washington freely selected aspects of John Ruskin and the Arts and Crafts movement (in particular, linking the useful, the beautiful, and the good), John Dewey's ideas on linking art and audience, a general disdain for the emerging European abstraction "art for art's sake," and a distinction drawn between high culture and mass culture. On the other hand, Washington was Black. For mainstream America, Black art was at best craft or folk art, not art. Washington found particular beauty in African American music, African art, and Black people. On African art, Washington wrote: "I have frequently been impressed with the beauty of some of the designs that native craftsmen have worked out upon their spears and in their homespun cotton cloth. The leather tanned by some of these native tanners is often surprisingly beautiful in colour, design and finish. Some of the specimens of the native handicrafts have been placed on exhibition in the museum at Tuskegee, and in one or two cases we have been able to reproduce in our classes in basketry the shapes and designs of some of the native articles."[3]

The "two-ness" that emerges in his writings are as conflicted as the age. During the age of Washington, business was conducted in steel skyscrapers, worship was conducted in spaces illuminated by Tiffany glass, and sumptuously designed journals guided readers to exotic places, to the latest fashions, and into the lives of the powerful. The age also openly, and with little resistance, reproduced countless vicious racist representations of African Americans. As Lisa Farrington stated, it was a time that not only produced the jolly Mammy but also produced "a larger group of stereotypes that included the Black Brute, the Happy Darkie, the sundry Sambos and pickaninnies. The rise of depictions of black whores, servants, villains, idlers, idiots, and clowns was accompanied by virulent racism, which found both legal and illegal expression in Post-Reconstruction and Jim Crow America."[4] Black writers of the age, including Washington and W. E. B. Du Bois, struggled with measuring up to White taste, celebrating Black art, and challenging racist representations.

Washington used mainstream art to demonstrate racial equality by displaying his good taste and, by association, the intellectual capacity of Blacks for understanding and embracing all that high culture meant. Included in this chapter, for example, is one of Washington's many letters to publication editors. This one, to *The Colored America Magazine*, urged African Americans to find ways to celebrate the life and work of the poet John Greenleaf Whittier.[5] At the same time, he advanced the careers of Black artists, photographers, architects, musicians, and writers who forged a new identity in the face of the widespread acceptance of racial stereotypes that abounded during the Age of Booker T. Washington. Speaking directly to such representations, Washington wrote in 1909:

> It seems to me now, as I recall my first definite impressions of my race in Africa, that the books I read when I was a boy always put the pictures of Africa and African life in an unnecessarily cruel contrast with the pictures of the civilized and

highly cultured Europeans and Americans. One picture I recall vividly was in the first geography I studied. It was a picture of George Washington placed side by side with a naked African, having a ring in his nose and a dagger in his hand. Here, as elsewhere, in order to put the lofty position to which the white race has attained in sharper contrast with the lowly condition of a more primitive people, the best among the white people was contrasted with the worse among the black.[6]

Washington's thoughts on aesthetics reveal him using both art as propaganda to reach his benefactors and as a means to counter the distortions of Blacks in the media by providing signs of intellectual and moral progress.

In spring 1900, Booker T. Washington watched members of the Tuskegee staff and faculty perform *Othello* in the interior of his new Victorian mansion, The Oaks.[7] Surrounded by such cultural finery, Washington may have barely felt the sting of rejection from the young Du Bois, who had turned down a job at Tuskegee in favor of what he believed to be greener cultural pastures. Said Du Bois: "The only opening that would attract me now would be one that brought me nearer the centres of culture & learning and thus gave me larger literary activity."[8] Tuskegee, a remote Washington dreamland-in-the-making in rural Alabama, did not meet his standards of refined culture. Only a few months later, the artistic photographic displays of both Washington and Du Bois would be placed together at the World's Fair in Paris. This meeting marked the beginning of a fifteen-year aesthetic competition. Yet these fierce adversaries, who agreed on very little, strongly supported the development of Black arts for similar reasons. Who could have imagined that the intellectual common ground shared by these two would be aesthetics? Along the way, they both believed in the ability of art to persuade, wrestled with ways in which to incorporate African art into their Victorian taste, crafted complex mixed-media publications, had their writings printed together, and even hired some of the same artists. In the final year of Washington's life, they shared in their public anger at the release of the racist film *A Birth of a Nation*. Soon after, the recognition by scholars of Washington's support for the arts and his evolving understanding of culture and race faded, while Du Bois's advocacy of the arts became foundational in the literature.

Before urban, vibrant, and northern Harlem erupted as a Black arts mecca in the 1920s, work by African American artists could be found at the turn of the twentieth century on the southern campuses of historically Black colleges and universities. During this earlier period, Black artists strove for inclusion and acceptance by demonstrating their ability to perform and create within White Victorian standards of taste. The talented Adrienne Herndon directed Shakespeare at Atlanta University. The Fisk Jubilee Singers were founded as a fund-raising effort for the university. John Henry Adams Jr. (W. E. B. Du Bois's first illustrator) created a classically based studio art program at Morris Brown College. William Benson envisioned a photography school at Kowaliga Institute in Alabama. Robert R. Taylor's elegant architecture rose on the remote, pastoral, romantic grounds of Tuskegee. In the case of Tuskegee, the identification with blackness was subtle and fit within Washington's notion of quiet resistance. Even though Taylor's buildings are in European revival forms, they are, like the character of Othello, the work of a Black hero.

With very little formal education compared with Du Bois, Washington, the former slave, achieved his cultural sophistication as a keen listener to the people who knew about such things. Perhaps his earliest, and most important, cultural influences were the women in his life. The first was the Vermont-born Viola Ruffner, the White Victorian woman who took the ten- or eleven-year-old boy Booker into her Malden, West Virginia, home as a house servant for her family. There, he received a thorough education in proper New England tastes. Washington's second and third wives, Olivia and Margaret, refined those skills with their intelligence and social sophistication. His lessons in culture continued through his work with his ghostwriter Max Bennett Thrasher, Paul Laurence Dunbar, Charles Chesnutt, Thomas Calloway, the family of Rev. Benjamin Tanner, his powerful New England philanthropist friends, and those men and women he hired, such as Robert R. Taylor, William Pittman, George Washington Carver, C. M. Battey, A. P. Bedou, and Frances Benjamin Johnston.

Whereas many of these intellectuals believed art to be a venue for social critique, Washington was more pragmatic about it. He knew that cultural sophistication could attract donors and demonstrate the equality of the races. Washington's first work of art was himself, a living object lesson crafted to show how his ideals would lead to material and social success. For all of his talk about industrial education and rising up from the bottom, Washington performed on the American social stage as a member of the cultural elite. By 1900, this international celebrity, known for his simple, yet dignified taste, had traveled to Europe, written many books and articles, helped design buildings, and worked with many leading Black poets, painters, sculptors, and composers. This cultural capital allowed him to show members of Progressive White America that he was schooled in the graces of the "higher civilization"—that he was their equal in intelligence and cultural refinement and thus worthy of their largesse. George Washington Carver, the Leonardo da Vinci of Tuskegee, wrote to Washington in 1903 describing how White "lovers of art" in town were asking for Carver's art criticism. Carver felt that Washington would be excited to hear this news since "this is in direct line and a substantiation of what you have always maintained with reference to the races."[9]

Using art as a measure of equality led Washington to comment frequently on the need for Black artists to present only the highest-quality work, or risk ridicule. He understood that many Whites were quick to diminish any Black artistic efforts as primitive. In 1907, Washington wrote to Thomas J. Calloway, his old friend and assistant who was now in charge of organizing the display of Black art at the 1907 Jamestown Exposition:

> One thing I am very anxious about, and that is that you stick to the policy of seeing that the exhibit at Jamestown represents real and fundamental progress of the race rather than mere lightness and artificiality. The progress of a people is indicated mainly by what they get from the soil, by their progress in wood, in iron, in

domestic economy, etc. It would be a great blunder if you have at Jamestown cheap imitations of art. There are one or two colored people who can do something worth while in art, but outside of Tanner and one or two others, we make ourselves ridiculous when we attempt to exhibit paintings, statuary, etc. It is always wiser, in my opinion, for us to stick to the things we can do well or excel some other fellow in rather than try to imitate in a poor way some other man or race . . . Of course this is a good deal of advice for a man who is taking no part in the exhibition to give, but I feel deeply on the subject.[10]

The foundation of this aesthetic position was first mapped out in his 1895 Atlanta speech in which he described his familiar themes of the "dignity of labor," or the beauty in utility, and how, eventually, but not "just now," Blacks would be in a position "to spend a dollar in an opera house."[11] The consistent theme one finds in Washington's early writings and in the art he supported is a concern with taste. In his view, the simple and the practical could rise to the level of taste. Like his rise up from slavery, he believed change for Black Americans needed to come from the bottom up. Civil rights would follow economic empowerment. Cultural achievements by Blacks, he felt, could change White people's minds about Black inferiority. This meant that a sliding scale of art existed for each class as it found its natural and rightful expression. Most Blacks had not reached, in his estimation, a level of economic and cultural attainment commensurate with such middle- or upper-class attainments as having a piano, learning French, reciting poetry, or dressing in fancy clothes. As he wrote in 1902, "the southern White people had the idea that every Negro educated would become a minister, or teacher, or dude: that an educated Negro meant as a rule a high hat, a big walking-cane, kid gloves and patent leather shoes."[12] Instead, he espoused a restrained high taste that showed modesty in the Arts and Crafts tradition of simplicity steeped in the handcrafted aesthetics of John Ruskin. In drawing on Ruskin, Washington was in the mainstream of educational thinkers. Ruskin's thought, in particular, on art filled American education journals of the period. Moreover, African American thinkers, both inside and outside the Washington camp, frequently quoted Ruskin (completely free of his later political and social economic ideas).

Washington's Arts and Crafts sensibility is most evident in the layout of his writings and in his interest in displaying high art around the campus.[13] The books and articles created by Washington brought Ruskin to the Black Belt. Washington's first book, *Daily Resolves* (1896), became the first in a series of sumptuously produced books aimed at fund-raising.[14] Most Washington articles were illustrated with soft-focused Pictorialist images, the photographic expression of the Arts and Crafts movement. When looking at views of Tuskegee in these articles, one sees how Washington championed the dignified, Christian, self-determined worker who thinks with his head rather than using Rodin-like muscles. In context, Washington's workers are not the classical half-dressed young men of Constantin Meunier or Max Liebermann's world but pastoral gentlemen. Although Booker T. Washington never published theoretical works on aesthetics like Du Bois, he nonetheless understood many of art's powers and frequently wrote on the topic. Some of Washington's references to art are hard to catch, appearing perhaps as merely a passing reference to a painting or a mention of a visit to Roycroft, Elbert Hubbard's Arts and Crafts utopia in Upstate New York.[15] Washington's philosophy of art changed over his lifetime. The aesthetics of his early years is one in which art is primarily offered as a sign of progress and served as a way for Blacks to demonstrate intellectual equality by emulating White Victorian taste. However, Washington's views changed over time. He slowly embraced the need to develop an independent Black aesthetic that would not be merely an imitation of White art.

During the early phase, Washington's thoughts on aesthetics are found scattered across his writings, most often in the form of tableaux: illustrative stories. Perhaps the first powerful tableau meant to show the effect of images is in a story he created for White readers in a 1900 article in *The Century Magazine* (included at the end of this chapter). Like the pictures in his articles and the high art on the walls, this tableau demonstrated how the right taste could serve to both uplift Black people and win the battle for the hearts and minds of Whites:

> An object-lesson in civilization is more potent in compelling people to act right than a law compelling them to do so. Some years ago a colored woman who had graduated at Tuskegee began her life-work in a Southern community where the force of white public sentiment was opposed to the starting of what was termed a "nigger school." At first, this girl was tempted to abuse her white sister, but she remembered that perhaps the white woman had been taught from her earliest childhood, through reading and conversation, that education was not good for the Negro, that it would result only in trouble to the community, and that no amount of abuse could change this prejudice. After a while, this colored teacher was married to an educated colored man, and they built a little cottage, which, in connection to her husband's farm, was a model. One morning one of the white women who had been most intense in her feelings was passing the cottage, and her attention was attracted to the colored woman who was at work in her beautiful flower garden. A conversation took place concerning flowers. At another time this same white woman was so attracted to this flower-garden that she came inside the yard, and from the yard she went into the sitting-room and examined the books and papers.[16]

By 1903, Washington, writing in *The Negro Problem*, had reduced these thoughts into his aesthetics syllogism: "Without industrial education there can be no wealth; without wealth there can be no leisure; without leisure no opportunity for thoughtful reflection and the cultivation of the higher arts. I would set no limits to the attainments of the Negro in arts, in letters, or statesmanship."[17] A few years later in 1906, Emmett J. Scott, Washington's secretary, essentially described Tuskegee within the Ruskinian aesthetic equation of work, beauty, and morality:

> I do not believe that any person is educated until he has learned to want to live in a clean room made attractive with pictures and books . . . In a word, I wish to say again that education is meant to give us that culture, that refinement, that taste, which will make us deal truthfully and sympathetically with our fellow men, and will make us see what is beautiful, elevating, and inspiring in what God has created.[18]

Taste was developed from the bottom up. It was slowly earned through work with the hands, served as a mark of civilizing forces, and directed a man or woman toward noble thought. Like Du Bois, Ruskin, and Dewey, Washington eschewed the new modernist idea of "art for art's sake," endorsing art that was useful. The art Washington supported was never mere ornament, or what Dewey would call bijoux, for as such it would lack direct connection to people's needs. When Washington decided to build arts programs on campus, he focused on the functional arts of photography and architecture. Both photography and architecture were the perfect media for Washington since they required technical training and utilitarianism but could nevertheless aspire to be fine art.[19] With respect to photography, no American of his generation worked with as many leading Black and White photographers as Booker T. Washington. Yet the only writings by Washington on photography are found in the hundreds of private correspondences with dozens of photographers.[20]

At the same time, Washington frequently wrote about architecture, particularly houses. Architecture reigned supreme as a sign of success. For the Tuskegee leader and many of his generation, a home came to signify independence, success, equality with Whites, economic security, and culture and, by extension, intellectual capability that equaled Whites'. The home also served, in the divided world of Jim Crow, the very practical need of the other meeting place (alongside the church and the Mason Hall). Washington's first article on the subject, published for a Black audience (and included in this chapter), describes how White Americans are cut off from seeing the private world of Black spaces: "To see the better side of the home life of the Negro is not an easy thing for a stranger to do." The Tuskegee leader tried to counter popular culture caricatures of Blacks with a description of Black homes as cultured spaces filled with books and pictures of "taste."[21] A few years later in *The Century Magazine*, Washington wrote an extravagantly illustrated article on the same topic, this time aimed primarily at a White northern audience. Black homes, he told *The Century* readership, represented the moral, intellectual, and cultural achievement of Black Americans.[22]

Although Washington used the White press to exhibit the cultural refinement achieved by Blacks, within the Black community, he worked hard to support individual artists. He served as an inspiration to many artists by writing articles and endorsements supporting their work, using his network of connections to help market their work, and, of course, patronizing them. Washington worked to support established artists and to assist others in launching their careers. He wrote articles on Tanner and encouraged Blacks to buy photographs of the paintings if they could not afford an original.[23] Washington helped start the career of Isaac Hathaway, a sculptor who worked with him and would go on to start one of the first ceramics departments at a historically Black college or university. With respect to literature, as early as 1897, Washington wrote the introduction to a book of poems by Mary Weston Fordham, a Black author.[24] A few years later, Washington would commission Paul Laurence Dunbar to write the school song.[25] He hired the Harvard-educated and activist poet Leslie Pinckney Hill for the English Department. In music, he wrote the introduction to a new book on composer Samuel Coleridge-Taylor, helped to launch the career of the composer and musician N. Clark Smith, as well as write stories about Black entertainers such as Bert Williams.[26] When the young photographer C. M. Battey was trying to establish a business, Washington furnished him with prominent Black and White sitters for portraits, found agents to distribute his works, and wrote endorsements to accompany his photographs.[27]

It was not just C. M. Battey who counted on Washington for help in securing White patronage. Other artists turned to the Tuskegee leader as well.[28] For A. P. Bedou, becoming Washington's personal photographer was the ticket to recognition. Even the painter Henry O. Tanner pushed Washington to connect him with Andrew Carnegie after another White philanthropist, Olivia Stokes, bought one of his paintings.[29]

That aesthetic achievement in the White domain would prove Black equality had clearly shifted by the time of the 1906 Atlanta Race Riot, the Brownsville affair, and the birth of the Niagara Movement. In 1905, Washington had written a strong endorsement of African music and its connections to this country's spirituals in his introduction to the work of Coleridge-Taylor. The fifty-year-old Washington began to voice publicly his more private thoughts on racial inequalities, making outspoken calls for Black history as well as a Black art. Washington wrote in 1906, "so long as the Negro was taught that everything that was good was White and everything that was bad was Black . . . it was natural and inevitable that he should desire to become in everything—in style, manners, thought, and in the color of his skin—White."[30] He admitted the following:

> The feelings that divided my mind and confused my purposes when I was a young man, have also divided the members of my race. The continual adverse criticism has led some of us to disavow our racial identity, to seek rest and try our successes as members of another race than that to which we were born. It has led others of us to seek to get away as far as possible from association with our own race, and to keep as far away from Africa, from its history and its traditions, as it was possible for us to do.[31]

Washington now began to find parallels between southern, African American blacksmiths and the village blacksmiths of Africa.[32] Late in life, Washington fully supported the study of one's own culture. In the 1911 *My Larger Education*, he wrote

> Cultural education has usually been associated in my mind with the learning of some foreign language, with learning the history and traditions of some other peo-

ple. I found in Denmark a kind of education which . . . sought to inspire an interest and enthusiasm in the art, the traditions, the language, and the history of Denmark . . . I saw that a cultural education could be and should be a kind of education that helps us to awaken, enlighten, and inspire interest, enthusiasm, and faith in one's self, in one's race and in mankind.[33]

It is a remarkable statement of transformation by a man known for not celebrating Black culture. Washington had come a long way from his initial stance on emulating White culture. Long gone from his comments was any mention of the uselessness of French lessons or the sight of a piano in a country shack.[34] In one of his last articles, published shortly after his death in the elite weekly journal *Musical Courier*, Washington lifted African American music to a universal level, describing how White composers found inspiration in Black music.[35]

Contents

THE COLORED AMERICAN MAGAZINE

· 15 CENTS A NUMBER   SEPTEMBER, 1902 $1.50 A YEAR.

AN ILLUSTRATED MONTHLY DEVOTED TO LITERATURE, SCIENCE, MUSIC, ART, RELIGION, FACTS, FICTION AND TRADITIONS OF THE NEGRO RACE.

WHEATLEY.

DOUGLASS.

Mrs. MARSHALL WALTER TAYLOR.
(Mrs. Major Taylor.)
Hartford, Conn.   See page 344.

PUBLISHED BY
THE COLORED CO-OPERATIVE
PUBLISHING COMPANY
5 PARK SQUARE, BOSTON, MASS.

copies can be obtained from him at any time.

———

Miss Lottie Johnson, the subject of this sketch, was born in Richmond, Va. Her public career began when she was seven years of age under Cornelius Minns, Esq. After finishing the prescribed courses of study in the Grammar school, she was sent to the famous Warren Street School in Philadelphia, where she graduated with high honors.

About this time Mrs. Johnson became deeply impressed with the idea that her daughter should have a trade, so she arranged for Miss Johnson to go to Brooklyn, N. Y., where she entered the Dress-making and Millinery Departments of the Young Women's Christian Association. Being naturally gifted with the needle Miss Johnson made rapid progress in the art of dress-making, and graduated from the department in June, 1901, standing 100% in the final examination. Miss Johnson continued her studies in millinery and graduated from that department as professor in June, 1902. During the whole course of study at the Young Women's Christian Association Miss Johnson was held in the highest esteem by her teachers and classmates, she being the only colored girl in the millinery class. She has already received several calls to teach from various schools, the last and most favorable call being from Richmond, Va., which she has partly decided to accept. She is a firm believer in the highest possibilities of the young women of the race, and thinks that the various industrial vocations should be strictly adhered to as well as other professions. All through her studies her mother was her bosom companion, from whom she received much inspiration and encouragement. She is of a sweet and loving disposition, and by natural and loving disposition and by nature and training, a born teacher.

———

NEGRO HOMES.

BOOKER T. WASHINGTON.

I do not believe it is possible for any one to judge very thoroughly of the life of any individual or race unless he gets into the homes. How I recall that in my own case I have completely misjudged the real worth of individuals because I was led to pass my opinion upon them because their dress was coarse or their language broken or their face uninviting. It has only been when I have seen the evidences of culture, convenience, thoughtfulness and gentleness displayed inside the homes of such people that I have been made to see the mistake of judging people outside of their homes. So, with regard to the Negro, if one wants to get an idea of the progress that the race has made within a few years, he should not pass judgment until he has had an opportunity to get into the homes of the race. To see the better side of the home life of the Negro is not an easy thing for a stranger or for a member of another race to do. During the last three years I have spent considerable time in traveling through the South. During this time I have seen my people in the fields, in the shops, in schools, in colleges, in churches, in prisons, and in their homes, but in no place have I noted such evidence of progress as in their homes. Behind the development of nearly every home there was a history, in many cases both romantic and pathetic, a history of struggle or self-sacrifice, of failure, and then final success. Let me tell in brief the story of one of these homes I found in Mississippi. I found myself one night not long ago a guest in a home in Mississippi of a member of my race. There were in it seven rooms. The parlor, the kitchen, the dining room and bath and bed rooms were as clean, sweet, comfortable, conveniently arranged and attractive as one would expect to find in Massachusetts. On the table of the sitting-room were to be found the daily paper, a weekly paper and several magazines; many of the books on the shelves of the library were standard books. The pictures on the walls were not of the cheap, "dawdy", flashy character, but had been selected with taste and care. I saw little about the house except the color of the occupants to remind me that I was in the house of a Negro. There was from kitchen to parlor a delicacy, sweetness and refinement that made one feel that life was worth living. Another thing that pleased me as much as what I saw was the pride with which each member of the family referred to his own race, and

cated, the more he finds comfort and satisfaction in the company of educated members of his own people.

There are other evidences of the activity of the race in home-getting. In Alabama, for example, there are at the present time three incorporated towns or cities where practically all the in-

Miss LOTTIE JOHNSTON, BROOKLYN, N. Y.
See page 378.

the faith all exhibited in the success of the race. I neither heard nor saw anything that led me to believe that any member of the family was ashamed of his people or wanted to discard the race to which Providence had assigned him for another race. Many people, I think, have the feeling that the average Negro is continually seeking to get away from his own people, forgetting that every sensible Negro has as much pride in his own as is true of other races. As the Negro becomes edu-

habitants are Negroes, and where all the town officials are of the same race. Their names are Hobson City, Douglass City and Booker City. In the case of one of these towns within a few weeks one hundred lots were sold to members of the race, and out of this number I was informed on good authority that there was only one purchaser who could not read and understand the papers bearing upon the purchase of the property.—Christian Work.

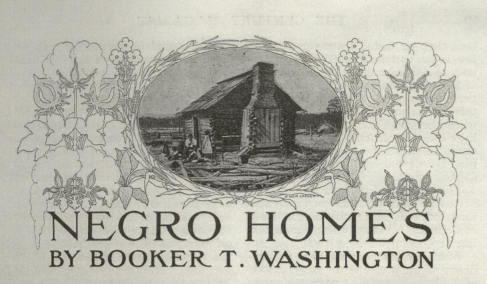

NEGRO HOMES
BY BOOKER T. WASHINGTON

THE first Negro home that I remember was a log-cabin about fourteen by sixteen feet square. It had a small, narrow door, which hung on rusty, worn-out hinges. The windows were mere openings in the wall, protected by a rickety shutter, which sometimes was closed in winter, but which usually hung dejectedly on uncertain hinges against the walls of the house.

Such a thing as a glass window was unknown to this house. There was no floor, or, rather, there was a floor, but it was nothing more than the naked earth. There was only one room, which served as kitchen, parlor, and bedroom for a family of five, which consisted of my mother, my elder brother, my sister, myself, and the cat. In this cabin we all ate and slept, my mother being the cook on the place. My own bed was a heap of rags on the floor in the corner of the room next to the fireplace. It was not until after the emancipation that I enjoyed for the first time in my life the luxury of sleeping in a bed. It was at times, I suppose, somewhat crowded in those narrow quarters, though I do not now remember having suffered on that account, especially as the cabin was always pretty thoroughly ventilated, particularly in winter, through the wide openings between the logs in the walls.

I mention these facts here because the little slaves' cabin in which I lived as a child, and which is associated with all my earliest memories, is typical of the places in which the great mass of the Negro people lived a little more than forty years ago; and there are thousands of Negro men and women living to-day in comfortable and well-kept homes who will recognize what I have written as a good description of the homes in which they were born and reared.

Probably there is no single object that so accurately represents and typifies the mental and moral condition of the larger proportion of the members of my race fifty years ago as this same little slave cabin. For the same reason it may be said that the best evidence of the progress which the race has made since emancipation is the character and quality of the homes which they are building for themselves to-day.

In spite of difficulties and discouragements, this progress has been considerable. Starting at the close of the war with almost nothing in the way of property, and with no traditions and with little training to fit them for freedom, Negro farmers alone had acquired by 1890 nearly as much land as is contained in the European states of Holland and Belgium combined. Meanwhile there has been a marked improvement in the character of the Negro farmer's home. The old, one-roomed log-cabins are slowly but steadily disappearing. Year by year the number of neat and comfortable farmers' cottages has increased. From my home in Tuskegee I can drive in some directions for a distance of five or six miles and not see a single one-roomed cabin, though I can see thousands of acres of land that are owned by our people. A few miles northwest of Tuskegee Institute, in a district that used to be known as the "Big Hungry," the Southern Improvement Association has settled something like over fifty Negro families, for whom they have built neat and attractive little cottages. During the first six years nearly all of these settlers have paid for their houses and land from the earnings of their farms.

The success of this experiment has helped to improve conditions throughout the county. Similar results have obtained at Calhoun, Alabama, where a somewhat like experiment has been tried.

What I have said in regard to the condition of the people in the neighborhood of Tuskegee is equally true of Gloucester County, Virginia, where the influence of Hampton has been much felt. My friend Major R. R. Moton of the Hampton Institute writes:

In traveling over some fifty miles of Gloucester County last May, visiting schools and farms of the colored people, I did not see a single one-room house occupied by colored people. Not only that, but the houses of the colored people, I might add, were for the most part either painted or whitewashed, as were the fences and outbuildings. While, on the other hand, in a travel of about eight miles in York County, which is separated from Gloucester County by the York River only, I counted as many as a dozen dilapidated one-room dwellings of colored people. The reason of this is due largely to the influence of the fifty or more graduates and former students who have settled in Gloucester County, while York County has not been touched by the former students and graduates of Hampton Institute.

At Mound Bayou, Mississippi, in the center of the Mississippi-Yazoo delta, where the Negroes outnumber the whites sometimes as high as ten to one, a Negro colony, founded by Negroes, has come into possession of thirty thousand acres of land, and has built a Negro town in which, during the twenty years of its existence, no white man has ever lived. Another and large Negro town has grown up at Boley, Indian Territory, within the last five years, where all business, schools, and town-government are in the hands of Negroes, most of them from the farms and country towns of northern Texas, Arkansas, and Mississippi.

With regard to the progress made by Negroes in the cities we have less complete and definite information. But the number of those who possess homes, particularly in the Southern cities, is, I am convinced, much larger than most people, even those who are best informed, are aware. And this progress has been made for the most part in recent years, for after emancipation the freedmen did not at once understand the importance of acquiring property and building homes. They have had to learn that, as they have had to learn, in the first forty years of freedom, so many other simple and elementary principles of civilization.

I remember that the Reverend W. R. Pettiford, President of the Alabama Penny Savings Bank at Birmingham, Alabama, told us in one of his reports at the National Negro Business League that when he began his campaign among the miners and laborers of that region, before he could induce them to save money he had first to convince some of them of the necessity of giving up the loose connections in which they had been accustomed to live in slavery, and to establish permanent family relations for the benefit of their children. Many of these people who had been living together for years were ashamed to go through the legal form of marriage: it was a sort of acknowledgment that they had been in the wrong. It was only after their responsibility to their children was explained to them that they could be induced to do so. Others were led to take the step through the influence of the church, or were drawn to it by the growing strictness in such matters of the community in which they lived.

So an increasing number of Negro homes has gone along with an increasing sense of the importance of the safeguards which the home throws about the family, and of the household virtues which it encourages and makes possible.

In every Southern city there is a Negro quarter. It is often merely a clutter of wrecked hovels, situated in the most dismal and unhealthy part of the city. A few years ago there might be two or three of these quarters, but there was very little choice between them. They all had the same dingy, dirty, and God-forsaken appearance. These are the places that are still usually pointed out as the Negro homes. But in recent years there have grown up, usually in the neighborhood of a school, small Negro settlements of an entirely different character. Most of the houses in these settlements are still modest cottages, but they are clean and neat. There are curtains in the windows, flowers in the gardens, the doorways are swept, there is a little vine growing over the porch, and altogether they have a wholesome air of comfort and thrift.

If you should enter these homes, you would find pictures on the walls, a few books on the table, and an atmosphere of self-respect and decency which is conspicuously absent in the other quarters to which I have referred. These are the homes of a thrifty laboring class, usually of the second generation of freedmen. You would find, if you should inquire, that the owners had all had some education. Many of them have gone through colleges or an industrial school, or at least are sending their children there; and if you should inquire at the places where they are employed, you would learn that they were steady, thrifty workmen, who had won the entire respect of their employers. Many of them were perhaps born and reared in the dingy hovels to which I have referred. Many of them had come originally from farms, and, after leaving school, have settled permanently in the city.

In these same communities, however, you will frequently find other homes, larger and more comfortable, many of them handsome modern buildings, with all the evidences of taste and culture that you might expect to find in any other home of the same size and appearance. If you should inquire here, you would learn that the people living in these homes were successful merchants, lawyers, doctors, and teachers. There is nothing picturesque about these dwellings, and nothing to distinguish them from any other houses of the same class near-by; they are not usually recognized as Negro homes.

Now, the fact is, that white men know almost nothing about the better class of Negro homes. They know the criminals and the loafers, because they have dealt with them in the courts, or because they have to collect the rents from the places in which they congregate and live. They

know to a certain extent the laboring classes whom they employ, and they know something, too, of the Negro business men with whom they have dealings; but they know almost nothing about the doctors, lawyers, teachers, and preachers, who are usually the leaders of the Negro people, the men whose opinions, teaching, and influence are, to a very large extent, directing and shaping the healthful, hopeful constructive forces in these communities.

In the course of my travels about the country I have had the opportunity to visit the homes of many of the people of this influential class. I have talked with them, by their firesides, of their own personal struggles. I have had opportunity to learn of their difficulties, temptations, aspirations, and mistakes, as well as to counsel and advise with them in some of the common undertakings in which we were engaged.

If it were possible, I should like to describe in detail some of the homes that I have visited, and to tell some of the histories that I have heard, because most that has been written about the Negro race in recent years has been written by those who have looked upon them from the outside, so to speak, and have seen them merely through the dull, gray light of social statistics. It is my experience that a house is like a face: it is not difficult to perceive and feel the subtle influences that find expression there, but it is hard to describe them. But I can make here only a few random notes upon my own impressions; I must leave to a poet like the late Paul Laurence Dunbar, and to a novelist like Charles W. Chestnutt, the task of telling the new thoughts that are now stirring in plantation cabins, or the ambitions and struggles of the men and women who have gone out from them to win success in the bigger world outside.

One of the most beautiful and interesting homes with which I am acquainted is that of W. H. Lewis, Special Assistant to the United States District Attorney at Boston. Mr. Lewis lives in Cambridge. His home is on Upton Road, one of the many pleasant avenues of that beautiful university city. The house itself was designed especially for Mr. Lewis, who has chosen to put the entrance rather near the street, in order to give more room and privacy for the fine lawn at the back. On the rear porch, looking out across the lawn, the family sometimes have their meals in summer. The interior is designed with all the ingenuity and taste that have made modern houses models of comfort and convenience, and is at once large enough to be airy, and snug enough to be warm. Mr. Lewis is extremely fond of old furniture, and he has many trophies to show for his prowls among the antiquaries. I might mention also that in the library and study, which is the place which he regards as particularly his own, Mr. Lewis has a good collection of the books which concern the history of his race, and other races, and the walls are hung with the portraits of the men, both black and white, who have distinguished themselves by service to the Negro race. Mr. Lewis was born in Virginia thirty-nine years ago. Both his father and mother had been slaves, and he got his early education in the Virginia Normal and Collegiate Institute, a school for colored youth. As a boy he peddled matches along the wharves at Portsmouth, Virginia, and in one way or another he made his way until he was able to enter Amherst College. While he was in Amherst he was captain of the foot-ball team. He won the Hardy Prize Debate and the Hardy Prize Oration, and at his graduation, in 1892, was chosen class orator. He was graduated from the Harvard Law School in 1895. During all this time he made his own way, working at various occupations which chance offered. He worked for a time, during this period, as a waiter in Young's Hotel, Boston. After his graduation he began the practice of law. He was three times chosen representative from Cambridge to the legislature, and was finally appointed, in 1903, to the position of United States District Attorney. Such, in brief, is the history of one of the more successful of those who are sometimes referred to in the South as the "new issue."

The limits of this article will not permit me to describe at the same length the homes of Dr. Samuel G. Elbert of Wilmington, Delaware; of Professor William S. Scarborough of Wilberforce, Ohio; nor that of A. D. Langston of St. Louis, Missouri, all of whom are, like Mr. Lewis, men of scholarly attainments, whose homes reflect the best influence of modern American life.

Dr. Elbert, who was graduated from the Harvard Medical School in 1891, and after several years' experience, first as interne, and then as assistant resident physician, at the Freedman's Hospital in Washington, completed his medical education by a three years' graduate course at the Medical School at the University of Pennsylvania, is still a zealous student, and has collected a private library of some 5000 volumes. Professor W. S. Scarborough, who is the head of the department of Greek at the Wilberforce University, is author of a Greek textbook and a member of a number of learned societies to whose proceedings he is a valuable contributor. Mr. A. D. Langston, who is the son of the Hon. John Mercer Langston, the only colored man ever chosen from the State of Virginia as United States representative, is, as his father was before him, a graduate of Oberlin College. He has been for the larger part of his life a teacher, and is at present the head of the Dumas School at St. Louis, Missouri, where he is doing valuable work for the education of his race.

A Negro home very different from any of these is that of Paul Chretien, who owns a large plantation of 360 acres two miles from St. Martinsville, in St. Martin's Parish, Louisiana. Mr. Chretien's father was a Creole Negro who made a fortune before the war raising cattle on the low and swampy prairies of southwestern Louisiana. When he died, he left each of his children, three boys and two girls, 360 acres of land, and to Paul he gave the quaint and beautiful country place in which he lived. It was a vast, roomy structure of brick and wood, with a wide gallery across the front, and a porch set into the building at the back. The house stands in the midst of a large garden in which flowers and fruits blossom and bear in tropical profusion. Side by side with such fruits as Northern people are familiar with, grow oranges and figs, which lend an air of luxuriance to eyes accustomed to soberer Northern landscapes.

Among the other Negro homes that I have visited, which have preserved either in their exterior or interior something of

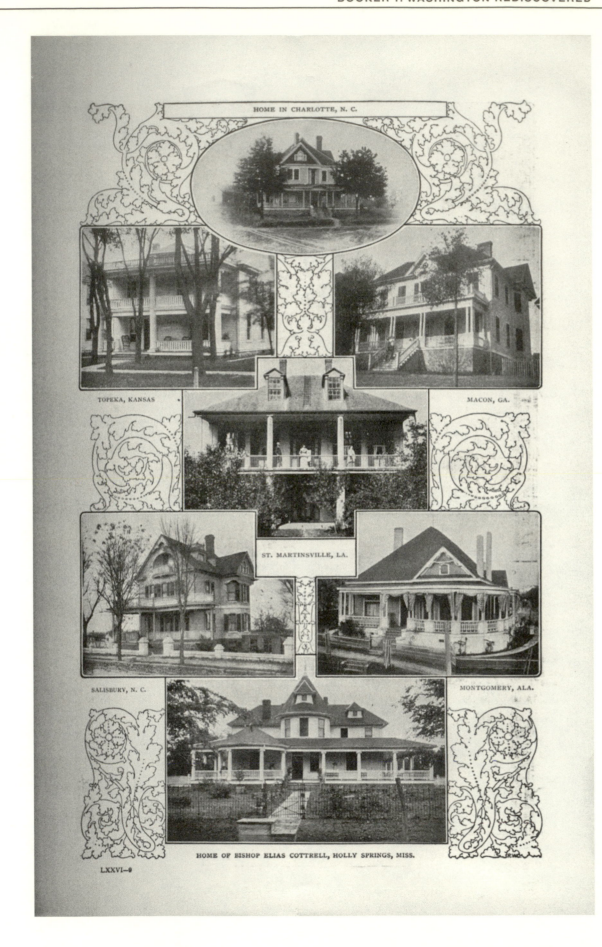

HOME IN CHARLOTTE, N. C.

TOPEKA, KANSAS

MACON, GA.

ST. MARTINSVILLE, LA.

SALISBURY, N. C.

MONTGOMERY, ALA.

HOME OF BISHOP ELIAS COTTRELL, HOLLY SPRINGS, MISS.

LXXVI—9

WILMINGTON, DEL.

WILMINGTON, DEL.

WILMINGTON, DEL.

CAMBRIDGE, MASS.

ST. LOUIS, MO.

CAMBRIDGE, MASS.

WILBERFORCE, OHIO

TUSKEGEE, ALA.

NEGRO HOMES   77

the quality of the old Southern mansion, I might mention those of Bishop Elias Cottrell at Holly Springs, Mississippi; A. J. Wilborn of Tuskegee, Alabama; John Sunday of Pensacola, Florida; G. E. Davis of Charlotte, North Carolina; and that of Nicholas Chiles of Topeka, Kansas.

Bishop Cottrell, who will be remembered among the Negroes of Mississippi for the useful and courageous work he has done and is doing for Negro education in that State, has served the Colored Methodist Church of Mississippi in one capacity or another since 1875, and has been a bishop since 1894. A. J. Wilborn, a graduate of the Tuskegee Institute, is a merchant in Tuskegee, where he was born a year before the breaking out of the war. He was one of the first students of the Tuskegee Normal and Industrial Institute. At the present time he owns one of the best business blocks in the town, and does a large and profitable business, particularly among the farmers in the surrounding country.

Professor G. E. Davis has been for twenty-one years a teacher in Biddle University at Charlotte, North Carolina. I quote the following passage from a letter from Mr. Davis because it illustrates one of the curious family traditions—where there were family traditions—that have been handed down to the new generation from the days of slavery.

My mother's father was born free. His father, a native Scotchman, was a man of means, and left my maternal grandfather considerable wealth, entirely in gold coins, in strong iron chests. My maternal grandfather's wife, and consequently his children, were slaves, with a kind master. The father and husband hired the entire time of his wife and all his children, ten in number, and gave his sons the trade which he followed — mason and plasterer — and the girls the refining influence of a Christian home.

I might add that the struggle for freedom which his ancestors began, Mr. Davis has faithfully and honorably continued, adding to the hard-won freedom his father gained that other freedom that comes of economic independence, knowledge, and discipline.

John Sunday was a wheelwright before the war; then he became a soldier, and was afterward a member of the Florida legislature. Since then he has been in business. He tells me that in 1906 his total taxes amounted to $1079.45. He has eight sons and two daughters, all of whom he educated at his own expense. Three of them went to Fisk University, and two of his sons are physicians.

Nicholas Chiles conducts a newspaper in Topeka, Kansas. He made his money, however, in real estate. Turned adrift, like many Negro boys after the war, to shift for himself, after years of aimless wanderings and adventure he attracted attention some years ago by buying a house in the same block with the Governor's mansion, and making of it a beautiful home.

An interesting fact with regard to the home of W. H. Goler of Salisbury, North Carolina, is that he built it almost wholly with his own hands. Mr. Goler learned the trade of mason at Halifax, Nova Scotia, where he was born. He recalls that he worked at a later period on the old Adelphi Theater Building in Boston,—afterward the store of Jordan & Marsh,—and that when the men employed there refused to work with a Negro, he organized a gang of Negro bricklayers to take the place of the men who struck on that account. It was from the money he earned as a bricklayer in Boston that he was able to pay his way through Lincoln University, Pennsylvania, which he entered in 1873 at the mature age of twenty-seven. He completed his collegiate course there in 1878, and three years later was graduated from the theological department. After two years as pastor of a church at Greensboro, North Carolina, he became a teacher at Livingston College, where, in addition to his other work, he superintended the industries of the college and, with the help of the students, made the brick and laid the walls of most of the college buildings. He is now president of that college.

J. H. Phillips was born on the "Carter Place," a few miles from Tuskegee. He studied at Hampton Institute, and went from there to the Phillips Academy, Andover, Massachusetts. He has a beautiful home in Montgomery, which, he informs me, is insured for $7500.

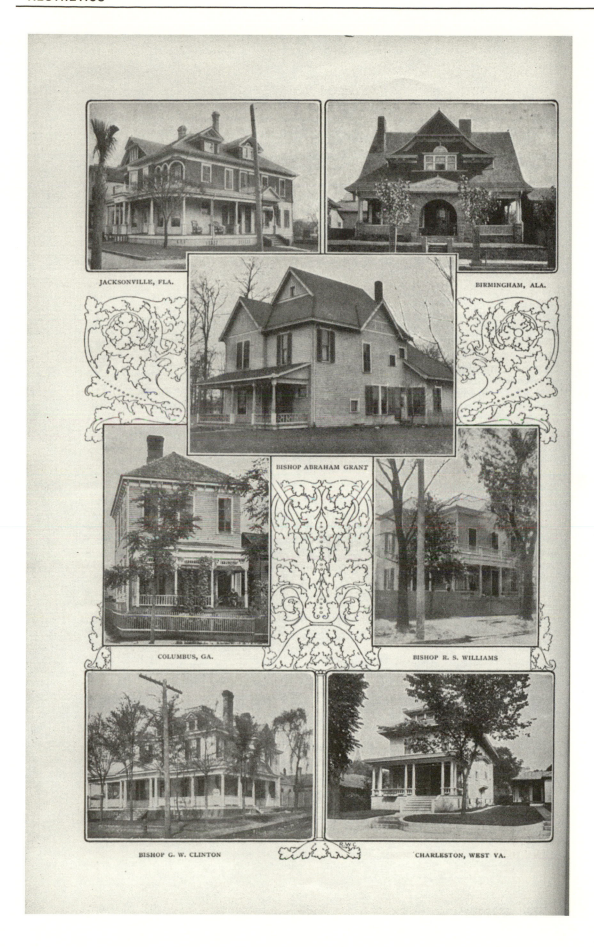

JACKSONVILLE, FLA.

BIRMINGHAM, ALA.

BISHOP ABRAHAM GRANT

COLUMBUS, GA.

BISHOP R. S. WILLIAMS

BISHOP G. W. CLINTON

CHARLESTON, WEST VA.

NEGRO HOMES   79

Mr. Phillips once said to me:

In building and furnishing our home, we may have been a little extravagant; but the homes in which we were born and reared were neither ceiled nor plastered, the walls were without pictures, our beds without springs, and the kitchen was without a stove. On the floor there was no matting, or carpet, except a burlap sack I used to stand upon on cold mornings. We are trying to make up, my wife and I, for all we missed in our childhood.

I have room to say but little of the wonderful career of Bishop Abraham Grant, who was born in an ox-cart while his mother was being carried home from the slave-market; was himself sold for $6000, Confederate currency, during the war; and has since traveled over a large part of the world—through Europe, Africa, and the West Indies—largely in the interests of his church. Bishop Grant's present residence is in Kansas City, Kansas, although his home, as he says, is in Indianapolis.

I can only mention the names of Bishop R. S. Williams of the Colored Methodist Church, whose home is in Augusta, Georgia; and Bishop G. W. Clinton of the Zion African Methodist, who lives at Charlotte, North Carolina; C. W. Hadnott, a contractor and builder of Birmingham, Alabama; and Andrew M. Monroe, who has been for many years collector for the Merchants' National Bank at Savannah, Georgia,—men whose homes, if less pretentious than some others I have named, still have about them, in a more than usual degree, the cheerful, wholesome atmosphere of a home.

One of the most imposing Negro residences of which I know is that of Dr. Seth Hills of Jacksonville, Florida. Dr. Hills is still a young man, and has been singularly favored by fortune and unusually successful in his profession. His father, a very practical man, who was at the same time preacher and carpenter, set him at an early age to learning the cigar trade. It was with this trade that he supported himself for the most part during the years he studied at Walden University, and afterward at the Long Island Medical College of Brooklyn, New York. While there he was fortunate enough to make friends who helped him to complete his education there and abroad.

His home is one of the many handsome Negro residences of Jacksonville.

There are other Negro physicians whose homes attracted me; among them are Dr. C. S. Swan of Columbus, Georgia, and Dr. Richard Carey of Macon, Georgia. Dr. Carey was graduated from Howard University, studied afterward in New York, and in Vienna, Austria. Since his return from Europe he has confined his practice almost wholly to diseases of the eye, ear, nose, and throat. I might mention also the names of J. M. Hazelwood, S. W. Starks of Charleston, West Virginia, whose residences are as handsome and complete as any that I know, and Dr. Ulysses Grant Mason of Birmingham, Alabama, who, after completing his course at Meharry Medical College, Nashville, went abroad in order to take a special course in surgery at the Royal Hospital of Edinburgh. In 1895 Dr. Mason was elected to the position of assistant city physician, a post not held before that time by a colored man.

There are other Negro homes that are quite as deserving of notice as any that I have mentioned. I have written of those that have come in my way, and they have served the purpose of this article, which has been to throw some new light on the deep and silent influences that are working for the upbuilding of the Negro people in this country.

The average person who does not live in the South has the impression that the Southern white people do not like to see Negroes live in good homes. Of course there are narrow-minded white people living in the South, as well as in the North and elsewhere; but as I have gone through the South, and constantly come into contact with the members of my race, I am surprised at the large numbers who have been helped and encouraged to buy beautiful homes by the best element of white people in their communities. I think I am safe in saying that the sight of a well-kept, attractive home belonging to a Negro does not call for as much adverse comment in the South as it does in Northern States.

The fact is that human nature is pretty much the same the world over, and economy, industry, and good character always bring their rewards, whether the person concerned lives in the North or in the South.

The Survey, June 19, 1915

Photo by Bedou

LOOSENING UP LOUISIANA

The story of a missionary junket carrying the gospel of co-operation, educational and economic, to black folk and white

By

William Anthony Aery

HAMPTON INSTITUTE

BOOKER T. WASHINGTON IN ACTION

Fifty thousand Negroes and hundreds of whites attended the outdoor meetings arranged through Hampton and Tuskegee Institutes.

7

Race

Washington learned about race from being born a poor, southern, fatherless mulatto boy and raised on a small plantation in rural Virginia. In many ways, he typifies Black Americans of his generation, a Black Everyman of the Post-Reconstruction era. He was but one of millions of Blacks living in the agrarian south without property, formal education, and many possessions, as well as a member of a complex family structure existing under the control of White people. This control by the dominant race, often expressed through intimidation and violence, necessitated developing a separate Black sphere. A complex Black world of churches, schools, clubs, and political networks operated largely unseen by the powerful. From behind this veiled Black world, the young Booker watched and absorbed the values of the transplanted White Victorian culture he served in southern homes.

Booker T. Washington's early writings on race express the hopefulness of the first phase of the New Negro.[1] He answered the so-called Negro Problem with optimistic race pride, declaring a new era of advancement in culture, education, business ownership, home ownership, and investment in the Black community. Only a few months before delivering his famous Cotton States Exposition speech in September 1895, the progressive Congregationalist weekly paper *The Advance* heralded Washington as being sent by "Providence." They placed his image on the cover and applauded (like most White Progressives) his choice of self-reliance as the best path to solving the "Negro Problem."[2] The article he presented in *The Advance* contains ideas that are, in context, simultaneously passive and activist. On the one hand, the New Negro ideology was built on the premise of success as measured by White standards of what constituted civilization. Like many Americans from the second half of the nineteenth century, Booker T. Washington grew up accepting the social Darwinist model of race as a pyramid.[3] He did not question the accepted proposition that Whites peered down from the apex of civilization to view the world's other races as struggling to make the climb. To his critics, his great failing, as seen in the article, was to let White power entirely off the hook and place the burden for change on the backs of African Americans. On the other hand, to proclaim publicly oneself as a New Negro during this period increasingly meant taking a risk.[4] To own land, to demonstrate cultural sophistication, and to show intelligence could cost you everything.

Washington's critics failed to see that he saw industrial education as a means to an end. His plan called for Blacks to gain economic clout and offer goods the White man needed. Political and social change would follow. "Let us go with this industrial education for a few years, interlacing our business interests till a Black man can get a mortgage on a White man's home which he can foreclose at will—will that White man want to drive that Negro away from the polls when he sees him going up to vote? It is along this line that the problem must be solved."[5] Washington could not have gained power, received so much from philanthropists, or been offered so much space to publish in popular journals if he did not share or, at the very least, espouse, the Christian, social Darwinist ideas of White Progressives. He believed, as they did, in a formulation of race that was profoundly simple. In the heavenly eyes of God, there is only the human race. In the earthly eyes of humankind, the White race represented progress and enlightenment. All the other races should be proud, while recognizing the need to measure themselves against a White scale of achievement. As a result, Washington parted from Black nationalists such as Edward Blyden. The Tuskegee leader strongly rejected any back-to-Africa schemes, seeing Africa as suffering from ignorance resulting from a lack of Christian values and Western educational models.

Only months after his Atlanta Cotton States speech in Atlanta propelled him to national attention, Washington traveled to Harvard as the university's first African American recipient of an honorary degree. The speech he delivered embodied his belief in how the blending of social Darwinism with Christian idealism would serve as not only the blueprint for Black success but also, ultimately, the higher goal of a divinely guided racial harmony. Washington opened his Harvard speech with characteristic deference, telling the audience how he was but a humble soul, a representative of the many "crawling up" from the lower rungs of the "Black Belt of the South," who had traveled to receive honors near "the mansions on yon Beacon street." This juxtaposition of low and high culture, a rhetorical device Washington frequently used, serves as a metaphor for the heavenly and the earthly journey to the respective promised lands. In words recalling how one must render unto Caesar what is Caesar's, and to the Lord what is the Lord's, Washington stated, "If my life in the past has meant anything in the lifting up of my people and the bringing about of better relations between your race and mine, I assure you that it will mean doubly more. In the economy of God, there is but one standard by which an individual can succeed—there is but one for a race. This county demands that every race measure itself by the American standard."[6]

The race optimism displayed on the stages of Atlanta and Harvard would slowly turn toward disillusionment by the turn of the century as Washington learned how, despite his best efforts, skin color permanently fixed Blacks in separate spaces. During his first twenty years as Tuskegee's principal, a position that began in 1881, Washington never complained that he frequently traveled around Jim Crow America in separate rail cars, stayed in separate hotels, worshiped in separate churches, ate in separate restaurants, attended the burial of the dead in separate cemeteries, and spoke to segregated audiences.

Washington was riding high on his international fame when he was invited (as the only Black speaker) to make an address at the 1898 Peace Jubilee in Chicago, one of the victory celebrations taking place soon after the end of the Spanish-American War. After his speech in the elegant Auditorium Building, Washington attended a sumptuous banquet created for the many dignitaries. He never commented on how he was intentionally seated at one of the lesser tables, far from President William McKinley, the other keynote speakers, and all White southerners. One month later, when Atlanta hosted its own Peace Jubilee parade, no Black presence existed. Not even Washington, whose famous 1895 speech brought thunderous applause from New South Whites, was asked to attend. Then, in 1901, at the invitation of the new president, Theodore Roosevelt, Washington shared a meal in the White House. Southerners were outraged at such a violation of the social codes—of this darkening of the White House by a Black man who entered the sacred White space.

These setbacks coincided with Washington's newfound interest in a new type of race pride as he began to sound more like W. E. B. Du Bois. These later writings actively voiced support for Black empowerment and come close to what Tommy Shelby has described as pragmatic nationalism.[7] This is the late Washington that the young Marcus Garvey admired. During this late period, Washington increasingly redirected his travels and writings to the Black community, suggesting various intermediate steps toward Black progress until integration and the promises of America became a reality. No longer did Washington overtly construct blackness in opposition to whiteness; instead, he crafted three distinct kinds of race pride writings: (1) celebrations of individual Black achievements; (2) a broad, contextual look at Black history; (3) and the need for separate Black spheres of empowerment.

Washington's first writings on the heroic accomplishments by Black individuals were quite cautious, deferring to Whites in the hopes of winning their favor. Among these writings are his first two autobiographies, *The Story of My Life and Work* (1900) and *Up from Slavery* (1901), as well as a few short articles. For example, Washington's 1903 article "Heroes in Black Skins" provides stories of Black character almost entirely as it pertained to pleasing and assisting Whites.[8] However, soon Washington began to shift the focus toward celebrating Black achievement with a larger historical framework and used his own prestige to assist Black individuals and causes. An early work in this direction was his preface to a collection of works by the composer Samuel Coleridge-Taylor (1904), in which Washington places a Black artist within the framework of the African diaspora.[9] This work was followed by *Tuskegee and Its People* (1905) in which Washington moved aside to allow Black men and women to speak for themselves. The following year he published, with the help of S. Laing and Fannie Barrier Williams, a biography of Frederick Douglass. Washington became involved in the fund-raising effort to save Douglass's home and wrote in the Black publication *Alexander's Magazine*, "We should make Cedar Hill to the Negro people what Mt. Vernon is to the White race." In 1907, he produced, along with T. Thomas Fortune, *The Negro in Business*, a book largely celebrating the achievements of the National Negro Business League. Among his writings celebrating Black success stories are "Achievements of Negroes" (*Independent*, 1909), "Bert Williams" (*American Magazine*, 1910), "Charles Banks" (*American Magazine*, 1911), and the introduction to Matthew Henson's *A Negro Explorer at the North Pole* (1911).

At about the same time that his writings on individual Black achievement began to change, Washington started to write about Black history. The catalysts for Washington's move toward Black pride many be found in his growing loss of faith in White support and the rise of criticism from Black intellectuals. His place of power in the White world was severely diminished after 1906, when his influence on President Theodore Roosevelt waned. At the same time, the criticisms of intellectuals, such as Du Bois and Monroe Trotter, eroded his power in the Black world. Washington responded by embarking on tours of southern Black towns and increasingly writing about the historical struggles and successes of Black people.

Near the end of his life, Booker T. Washington began to see the struggle of Black people in a larger historical and global context. Washington's largest work on Black history is his two-volume *The Story of the Negro* (1909). In this book, one sees the growing influence of sociologist Robert E. Park with the Negro struggles increasingly defined in global times. Washington no longer refers to "the Negro problem," as he had early in this life—now there is a "so called Negro problem."[10] The book opens in a Du Boisian tone with a marked interest in contributionism and the double consciousness of Black Americans.[11] It is not only his anger at the exclusion of Blacks from history that is striking but also his desire to tell Black history as a global struggle. Writing this book gave him the confidence to draft a lengthy critique of the 1910 book *The Negro in the New World* written by the well-traveled, highly prolific Sir Harry Johnston.[12] The essay is striking on a number accounts, including Washington's interest in visual depictions of Blacks, in his awareness of issues facing Blacks in the diaspora, and in how much of his knowledge of these issues came from listening to the African and Afro-Caribbean students who had attended Tuskegee. Who could have imagined that the man on the stage in Atlanta in 1895 would tell an audience at Western University, nearly twenty years later: "It is indeed true that many of our own race go to institutions where they study all races, history of the Jews, history of the Greeks, history of the Germans, but they never study the history of our own race."[13]

Washington's third type of writing on race focused on the need for nurturing and supporting separate Black spaces or spheres. As he aged, he increasingly visited and supported all-Black towns from coast to coast. He was remembered, in this regard, by the number of schools and even a few towns named after him (e.g., Bookertee, Oklahoma). Adamantly opposed to any back-to-Africa plans, Washington continued to believe that there was ultimately one race under God. However, in the interim, before the divine plan was realized on earth, the pragmatic Washington supported separate Black towns and campuses as places of safety, economic development, intellectual growth, and cultural expression. Moreover, these separate spaces would serve as model communities, demonstrating Black potential to the White race.

Booker T. Washington's writings on Black communities began with his own ventures. He wrote not only about his own campus but also about the projects he directly assisted, such as the Greenwood community adjacent to Tuskegee and an experimental farming colony on Hilton Head Island.[14] At the same time, he began publishing many articles in support of Black towns. These include essays on Wilberforce, Ohio (1907, *The World's Work*), and Boley, Oklahoma (1908, *The Outlook*). However, his most passionate support was directed at Mound Bayou, Mississippi. In the illustrated 1907 article, "A Town Owned by Negroes," Washington told readers of the elite White journal *The World's Work* of the great promise for America embodied in this Black colony in the rural delta.[15] Here, at Mound Bayou, White America could see how economic rather than political solutions were winning the day, how Blacks were capable of self-government, and how morality and sobriety ruled over chaos and lawlessness. Readers were then shown in photographs how success had led to ownership of tasteful Victorian homes. However, the dream of Mound Bayou, like Washington's belief in the role of Black towns overall, failed to be realized. Not long after his death, towns such as Bookertee disappeared and so did the vision of economic self-determination. The separate Black space faded into a ghost town subsumed by White supremacy and economic and political disenfranchisement.

Booker T. Washington's views on race changed over time and, in many cases, became more complicated. We should apply Vladimir Nabokov's caution to the writing of history: "In art as in science there is no delight without the detail . . . All 'general ideas' (so easily acquired, so profitably resold) must necessarily remain but worn passports allowing their bearers shortcuts from one area of ignorance to another." Simplifying Washington into general ideas (based on only the most familiar writings) not only misses the variety and texture of his thought but also runs the risk of incorrectly abstracting him into a single position.

Contents

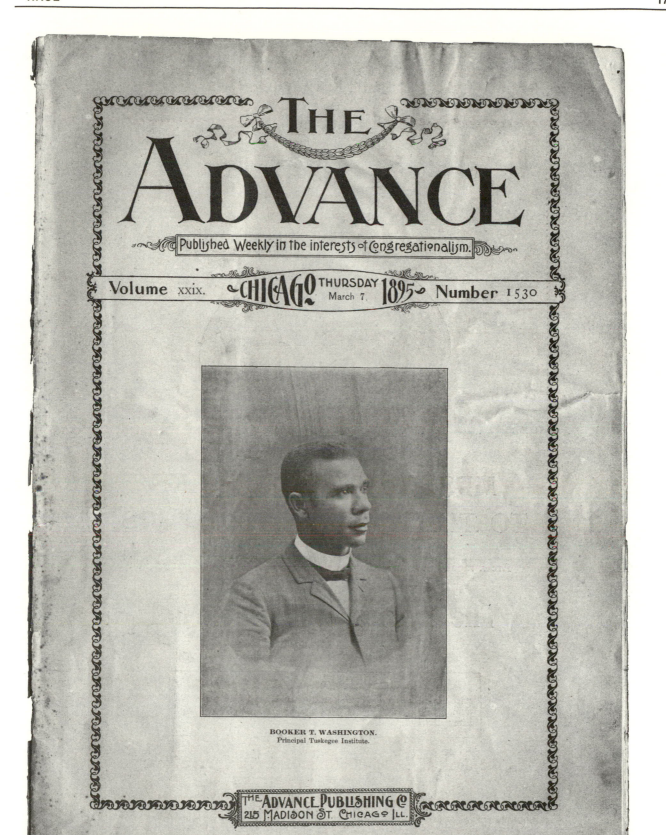

THE ADVANCE

Published Weekly in the interests of Congregationalism.

Volume XXIX.　CHICAGO THURSDAY March 7 1895　Number 1530

BOOKER T. WASHINGTON.
Principal Tuskegee Institute.

THE ADVANCE PUBLISHING CO
215 MADISON ST. CHICAGO ILL.

GOD'S BIRTHS.

BY GRACE J. WILLIAMS.
Cleveland, O.

Beyond the reach of storm or shock,
 In ocean's vast and silent deep,
The mollusk clings to solid rock
 By ages worn:
A grain of sand within its shell—
 A transformation passing man—
We gaze enrapt in wondrous spell:
 The pearl is born.

Bidden upon earth to creep
 By Him who gavest all things life,
We look ; our thoughts, unwelcome, leap;
 "A worm," we cry.
A silence, rest, a chrysalis—
 A transformation passing man—
Behold ! arrayed in shining dress,
 The butterfly.

The human heart sunk deep in vice,
 Unloved, uncared for and unsought,
The gilded forms of sin entice
 To death, its goal.
A pleading voice, a loving touch
 A transformation passing man—
The prayer of faith availeth much,
 A heaven-born soul.

OUR SOLUTION OF THE NEGRO PROBLEM.

BY BOOKER T. WASHINGTON.
Principal Tuskegee Institute.

The Negro in the South is a hungry man. This means that to a large extent his stomach is empty now or he has no provision for a rainy day, that he is homeless and poorly clad. When a man is hungry he cannot get his political rights. He has not the respect and confidence of his neighbors; and all who have tried it know that it is a hard matter to make a good Christian of a hungry man.

The thing most needed to be done, especially for the negroes who live in the country districts (and ninety per cent live in the rural districts of the "Black-Belt"), is to get them into a position where they can be sure of at least food, clothing and shelter. Without these they cannot educate their children, or practice, in any high degree, morality or religion.

What is the remedy? The North and West cannot educate directly all the colored people in the South, but the North and West can, with the Southern States, educate Christian leaders—furnish levers—who will go among the masses of colored people and show them how to help themselves.

At the Tuskegee Institute we have seven hundred and ninety-five picked young men and women from every state in the South being trained in the book, in industries and in religion to the end that each one may go out and become a center of light. One of the main industries taught at Tuskegee is farming. A young man graduates from the normal work and from the agricultural department. He then goes into some of the country districts of the South, takes the three-months public school as a nucleus for his work. Then he calls the older people together in weekly meetings. He shows them how to stop mortgaging their crops, how to buy land, how to build a decent house, how to cultivate their land better, making his own home and farm a model, how to build a schoolhouse by contributions of labor and money. Then each family taxes itself, and the school term is gradually extended from three to six and even eight months through the efforts of the people themselves. In a few years a large proportion of the people own land and have comfortable schoolhouses and are out of debt, and have a school that means something. All these changes are made, not by the gifts from the outside, but by the people, because they had a leader who could wake them up, guide and stimulate them. This is not an imaginary picture, but a representation of real changes that Tuskegee graduates are making every year.

When the colored people once get the material start, their religion ceases to be so much a matter of the emotions, but is a reality. The average Negro too often spends his time shouting and singing about living in the heavenly mansions, and at the same time his family are living in a one-room cabin in this world, forgetting that right living here is the best preparation for the heavenly life.

In proportion as the negro gets something that the white man in the South wants or respects, prejudice will disappear. The printing office at the Tuskegee institute does the printing for the white people in this section; not only the job printing, the white Democratic paper for the county is printed by Negro students. This industry, (and the same is true of the other nineteen) brings the black man and the white man into business contact. A few years ago a black boy graduated from the Wheelwright department of the Tuskegee Institute, and went into a small town and set up a shop. He manufactured wagons, he produced something that made the white man in that community dependent on the black man for something instead of all the dependence being on the other side. These wagons brought the black man and the white man together.

Let us go on with this industrial education for a few years, interlacing our business interests till a black man can get a mortgage on a white man's home which he can forclose at will—will that white man want to drive that Negro away from the polls when he sees him going up to vote? It is along this line that the problem must be worked out.

Immediately after the war we began at the wrong end. We began working to get to Congress when we should have been working to get land. At Tuskegee we teach the students that it is better for them to spend their time and strength in becoming the leading carpenters, contractors, truck gardeners, dairymen, in this town, instead of being too anxious to make stump speeches or go to Congress.

The Negro has great power of self-help. He works, but he does not know how to control and utilize the results of his labor. It is largely to meet this need that the Tuskegee Negro Conferences are held. They give seven or eight hundred representatives of the common masses a chance to get inspiration and lessons, compare views and lay plans to utilize their strength, and the results in an industrial, educational and religious sense are most encouraging.

—In ancient times when a box on the ear given by a master to a slave meant liberty, little would the freedman care how hard the blow. By a stroke from the sword the warrior was knighted by the monarch; small matter was it to the new-made knight if the royal hand was heavy.—*C. H. Spurgeon.*

"BESIDE THE BONNIE BRIER BUSH."*

AN INTERPRETATION.

BY REV. DAVID BEATON.
Lincoln Park Church, Chicago.

The present outflowering of Scottish literary genius is nowhere more keenly appreciated than in America. Since the recall to nature and simple patriotic themes by Burns, followed by the magic wand of Scott in creating the splendid visions of her past glories, Scotland has never been without a distinctively national school of writers. Brilliant enough, too, have they been; and so universal in sympathies as to attract the attention and find human response in the hearts and minds of thoughtful readers in every land.

The new group which is bringing distinction to the dear old land of the heather and the thistle, is marked with the old-time patriotism, simplicity and God-fearing honesty in the character of its subjects; with the old-time pathos, pawky humor and delicate sense of the purity of language in its literary style; but it has some literary and religious features peculiarly its own. This peculiarity lies in the fact that the literary and religious elements of interest and power are not separated, as they have too often unhappily been, but are wedded into a happy unity by meeting in the hearts and minds of men gifted at once with the artistic and poetic faculty and the high ideas of a simple faith.

The group I refer to includes a few names other than those most familiar to the general reader. And it is most significant to the Christian of wide literary sympathies to observe that this pure stream of Scottish poetry and scholarship arose in the manses of the Scottish ministers. I can see to-day the great mass of Ben a' Hie lifting himself above the valleys of Alford and the Garioch. In the humble manse of Tough, in the former, W. Robertson Smith, the great modern Semitic scholar was born; in Insch, another Free Church manse, William G. Elmslie first saw the light. Round those names you may group (and we give them precedence because they have early been called home) that brilliant galaxy of religious writers familiar to all Americans: Marcus Dods, Alexander Balmain Bruce, George Adam Smith, James Denney and William Robertson Nichol. Now the peculiarity of these names in this connection lies here: you cannot tell where religion ends and literature begins. They are professors and ministers and editors and literary men.

The next group are literary men, editors and ministers: Robert Louis Stevenson, J. M. Barrie, S. R. Crockett and John Watson (Ian Maclaren). I shall leave out here all reference to the strictly theological writers, simply saying that they are profoundly affecting the religious thought and life of Great Britain and America through works that bear the stamp of genuine scholarship, clear, broad, manly thinking and unwavering fidelity to the essential principles of a spiritual, evangelical faith. Of the second group, prose poets and authors of the purest, sweetest fiction of to-day, I wish to say a word. It is not of literary criticism; that you can find in abundance in the current

---

Beside the Bonnie Brier Bush. By Ian Maclaren. New York: Dodd, Mead & Co. $1.25.

HEROES IN BLACK SKINS

BY BOOKER T. WASHINGTON

JOHN MATTHEWS

SOME years ago, when visiting a little town in western Ohio, I found a colored man who made an impression upon me which I shall never forget. This man's name was Matthews. When I saw him he was about sixty years of age. In early life he had been a slave in Virginia.

As a slave Matthews had learned the trade of a carpenter, and his master, seeing that his slave could earn more money for him by taking contracts in various parts of the county in which he lived, permitted him to go about to do so. Matthews, however, soon began to reason, and naturally reached the conclusion that if he could earn money for his master, he could earn it for himself.

So, in 1858, or about that time, he proposed to his master that he would pay fifteen hundred dollars for himself, a certain amount to be paid in cash, and the remainder in yearly instalments. Such a bargain as this was not uncommon in Virginia then. The master, having implicit confidence in the slave, permitted him, after this contract was made, to seek work wherever he could secure the most pay. The result was that Matthews secured a contract for the erection of a building in the State of Ohio.

While the colored man was at work in Ohio the Union armies were declared victorious, the Civil War ended, and freedom came to him, as it did to four million other slaves.

When he was declared a free man by

Abraham Lincoln's proclamation, Matthews still owed his former master, according to his ante-bellum contract, three hundred dollars. As Mr. Matthews told the story to me, he said that he was perfectly well aware that by Lincoln's proclamation he was released from all legal obligations, and that in the eyes of nine tenths of the world he was released from all moral obligations to pay his former master a single cent of the unpaid balance. But he said that he wanted to begin his life of freedom with a clean conscience. In order to do this, he walked from his home in Ohio, a distance of three hundred miles, much of the way over the mountains, and placed in his former master's hand every cent of the money that he had promised years before to pay him for his freedom.

Who will be brave enough to say that such a man is not fit to use the ballot, is not fit for citizenship?

SERGEANT WILLIAM H. CARNEY

DURING the Civil War, in the course of the operations before the city of Charleston, South Carolina, it was decided to concentrate all the available forces of the Federal army on Fort Wagner on Morris Island, in order to bombard the fort, and then to charge it.

After an exhausting march, and without the troops having had time for food, the bombardment began. The line of battle was formed with the Fifty-fourth Massachusetts assigned to the post of honor and danger, in front of the attacking column.

Suddenly such a terrific fire was opened on the regiment when ascending the wall of the fort with full ranks that, using the words of Sergeant Carney, "they melted away almost instantly" before the enemy's fire.

During the attack, Colonel Robert G. Shaw, commanding the brigade, was killed. So disastrous was the fire that the brigade was compelled to retire; but Sergeant Carney, who was with the battalion in the lead of the storming column, and who, with the regimental colors, had pressed forward near the colonel leading the men over the ditch, planted the flag upon the parapet, and, lying down in order to get as much shelter as possible, for half an hour, until the second brigade came up, kept the colors up all the time. He received a severe wound in the head. When this brigade retired, he, creeping on his knees, having by this time received a wound in the thigh also, followed them, but still holding up the flag. Thus he held the flag over the wall of Fort Wagner during the conflict of two brigades, and received two wounds.

When he entered the field hospital where his wounded comrades were, they cheered him and the colors. Nearly exhausted from the loss of blood, he exclaimed: "Boys, the old flag never touched the ground!"

"RUFUS"

RECENTLY a colored man who lives not many miles from the Tuskegee Normal and Industrial Institute, in Alabama, found that when he had harvested his cotton and paid all his debts he had about one hundred dollars remaining. This negro is now about sixty-five years of age, and of course spent a large portion of his early life in slavery. So far as book-learning is concerned, he is ignorant. Notwithstanding this, I have met few persons in all my acquaintance with whom I always feel that I can spend half an hour more profitably than with this seemingly uneducated member of my race. In his own community this man is known simply by the name of "Rufus."

On many occasions Rufus has talked with me about the need of education for young people. This subject seems to be continually in his thoughts.

After Rufus had harvested his crop, as I have said, and evidently had thought the matter over carefully, he appeared at my office one afternoon. As he entered I saw at a glance that he had something unusually weighty upon his mind, and I feared that there had been some misfortune in his family. He wore his usual rough garb of a farmer, and there were no frills in evidence about him. On that day he was simply himself—just plain Rufus, as he always is.

After considerable hesitation he came to the matter about which he wished to consult me. He asked if I would be willing to accept a small gift from him, to be used toward the education of one of our boys or girls. I told him that I should be delighted to accept the gift, if he felt that he could part with any of his hardearned dollars. After searching in his rough garments for a little time, he finally produced from some hidden part of his clothes a rag around which a white cotton string was carefully tied. Unfastening the string slowly and with trembling fingers, he produced a ten-dollar bill, which he begged me to accept as his gift toward the education of some black boy or girl.

I have had the privilege of receiving many gifts for the Tuskegee Institute, but rarely one that has touched my heart and surprised me as this one did.

In a few minutes after having made his offering, Rufus left me and went to his home. The next day he sought out the principal of a white school in his own town, and after going through much the same performance as with me, placed a second ten-dollar bill in the hands of this white teacher, and begged him to use it toward the education of a white boy or girl.

ROBERT SMALLS

IN 1835 there was born a slave-child in Beaufort, South Carolina, who was named Robert, and who, later in life, was known as Robert Smalls.

In 1851 the owner of this young man moved to Charleston, and took Robert with him. In Charleston the slave was put to work as a "rigger," and soon became acquainted with all matters pertaining to ships. In 1861 Smalls was put to work at some menial service on a Confederate steamboat named the *Planter*. This steamer was used as a despatch-boat by General

Ripley, the Confederate commander at Charleston.

After Smalls had been upon the *Planter* long enough to become thoroughly acquainted with her, he planned and decided to undertake a bold and dangerous venture. Notwithstanding the fact that he was employed upon a vessel which was in the service of the Confederates, his sympathies were with the Union forces. In some way he had learned that these forces would be greatly strengthened if they could obtain possession of the *Planter*. Difficult as it would be to do this, he determined to try to put the boat into their hands.

After considering the matter carefully, —he was afraid to advise with any one,— Smalls decided upon a very bold plan. In the middle of the night he seized the vessel, took command, compelled all those on board to obey his orders, and then piloted the boat, still in the hands of the Confederates, to where he could turn it over to one of the Federal gunboats then blockading the port of Charleston.

It was estimated that the cargo of the *Planter*, including guns, ammunition, and other material, was worth between sixty and seventy thousand dollars. Of course this feat of Smalls created a sensation at the time. He was given a position of honor and trust on board the *Planter*, and also was rewarded with money. In many ways Smalls proved himself to be of great value to the Union forces. He knew where the Confederate torpedoes were sunk in the harbor, for he had helped to sink many of them; hence he was able to assist the Federal forces to avoid these dangers.

In 1863, while the *Planter* was sailing through Folly Island Creek under command of Captain Nickerson, the Confederate batteries at Secessionville opened such a hot fire on her that the captain deserted his post and took shelter in the coal-bunker. Smalls, seeing this, entered the pilot-house, took command of the boat, and carried her safely out of reach of the enemy's guns. For this bravery General Gillmore promoted Smalls to be captain of the *Planter*, where he served till the end of the struggle between North and South caused his boat to be put out of commission and sold.

After the war Smalls was elected to membership in Congress at least three times, and also served in many places of trust in South Carolina. General Smalls, as he is now known, still lives in Beaufort, South Carolina, where he enjoys the confidence and respect of the people of both races.

THE GENERAL'S LAST DOLLAR

VERY soon after the close of the Civil War some Union generals were given a dinner by a famous Confederate general in Petersburg, Virginia. The guests were waited upon by a colored man, one of the old type of servants, who was passionately devoted to the Confederate general, who had been his owner for many years.

None of the Union officers realized the fact that General G——, their host, had been stripped of all his property by the war. Indeed, there was little in his fine, courtly bearing, or in the dinner, to apprise them of this fact.

The meal was served by Uncle Zeke, the old colored servant, with all the neatness and formality that had characterized such functions in the more prosperous days of the late slave's owner. When the meal was over, for some unexplained reason the Northern guests forgot, or neglected to remember, Uncle Zeke.

Not so with General G——. He took the only piece of money in his possession, a one-dollar bill, and with great politeness handed it to Uncle Zeke, who bowed and thanked him for it in the most approved manner.

But as soon as the guests were gone, and the old colored servant could speak with General G—— alone and unobserved, he came to him and said: "Massa, I was powerful glad to see you make dat front before dem Yanks, an' teach dem a lesson; but, massa, I knows dat is de las' dollar you 's got, an' I can't keep it. I want you to take it an' git Miss Genie a new dress, 'cause she ain't had no new dress dis year."

MOSES TURNER

DURING the closing days of the Civil War a great many of the slaves in Virginia followed the Northern army as it went through the State from time to time, and thus made themselves free before the Eman-

HEROES IN BLACK SKINS   727

cipation Proclamation was issued. It was comparatively easy at this time for almost any slave to find his way from northern Virginia into a free State.

At the opening of the war there was a white family named Turner that was very prominent in that part of Virginia. In this family there were four sons, four daughters, and their mother. In the first battles of the war two of the sons were killed, and, later on, the third son was slain. Not long before the close of the war the fourth son came home on a furlough. He found his mother and sisters in destitute circumstances. They had no sugar and coffee, and the clothes that they had been able to secure were few. The war had reduced the family to a point where it had none of the comforts and few of the necessities of life.

But for the faithful labor of the dozen or more slaves on the place, there would have been great suffering.

Among the slaves there was one man, just past middle age, called Moses, who was looked up to by the others as a leader. To him had been intrusted the management of the farm.

Before the young master left home at the end of his last furlough, he had a long and earnest talk with Moses, in which he told him that he was going to trust not only the management of the farm to him, but was going to place in his care the safety of the young man's mother and sisters and the valuables in the house and about the place. Moses promised that he would not betray the trust.

A few weeks after the return of the young master to the army, a division of the Northern army came through that region. Some days before the arrival of this force, Moses had word of its possible coming through the agency of that rather mysterious means of communication known among the slaves as the "grape-vine telegraph."

Fearing that there might be those among the Yankees who would be bent upon mischief, Moses decided, after consulting with his mistress, to take all the old silver and other valuable household articles to a near-by swamp and bury them. This he did in the night, and no one knew the hiding-place of these articles but himself.

In the early morning, a few days later,

several companies from a Northern regiment passed the house. Some of the men got into conversation with Moses, and it did not take them long to discover that he was an exceptional man. After questioning him and getting some idea of his history, of their own accord they proposed that they release him from slavery and take him with them or send him North. Moses had no family or relatives, and nothing to bind him to the Virginia plantation.

There was no slave in all the South who had more earnestly longed for freedom than he had, and now the moment had come when he could obtain that for which he had so long wished. I have said that he had nothing to bind him to the Virginia plantation and to slavery. Yes, there was one thing: Moses had given his word to his master that he would protect and support the white people on the plantation during his master's absence, and no promise of freedom could make him break his word.

In the afternoon of the same day another group of straggling Northern soldiers came past the house. Before they reached it they had heard interesting stories of the wealth of the owners of Moses, especially their wealth in old silver plate and similar articles. Some of the more villainous of the soldiers resolved to possess themselves of as much of this silver as possible. When they approached the house they were met by Moses, who informed them politely that the male members of the family were away, and that he was in charge. Without any great amount of hesitation the soldiers told him what they wanted. The slave civilly but firmly gave his hearers to understand that although he knew where the valuables of the family were, it was a secret which he would share with no one. The soldiers at first tried to bribe him with money, and then, when that had no effect, with the offer of freedom, but with the same result. Then they tried to frighten him by threats of bodily harm, but he was not moved.

As a last resort, a rope was procured and he was strung up by his thumbs, but to no purpose. This terrible torture was repeated twice, and then half a dozen times. The slave was finally in such a condition of collapse by reason of this torture that he could scarcely stand or speak, but still he had strength of manhood enough to repeat over and over again, "No, no." Finally, seeing that their efforts were in vain, the soldiers departed, with curses upon their lips, but with greater respect in their hearts for the manhood of the negro race.

WILL PHILIP LINING

"How He Saved St. Michael's" is an old, old poem, and the church which the negro slave saved from destruction is said to have been St. Philip's instead of St. Michael's, but the deed was such a brave one that the story of it has lived for a century, and will continue to live.

Something like a hundred years ago a great fire was raging furiously in the city of Charleston, South Carolina. Building after building had been destroyed, and a gale of wind carried sparks far and wide to spread the conflagration. The lofty spire of St. Philip's Episcopal Church caught fire almost two hundred feet above the ground, and in an apparently inaccessible place, and the people in the streets below saw with dismay that one of their city's dearest possessions seemed about to be lost to them. Some stanzas from the old poem tell the rest of the story best:

Who is it leans from the belfry, with face upturned to the sky,
Clings to a column and measures the dizzy spire with his eye?
Will he dare it, the hero undaunted, that terrible sickening height?
Or will the hot blood of his courage freeze in his veins at the sight?

But see! he has stepped to the railing; he climbs with his feet and his hands,
And firm on a narrow projection, with the belfry beneath him, he stands;
Now once, and once only, they cheer him—a single tempestuous breath—
And there falls on the multitude gazing a hush like the stillness of death.

Slow, steadily mounting, unheeding aught save the goal of the fire,
Still higher and higher, an atom, he moves on the face of the spire.
He stops! Will he fall? Lo! for answer, a gleam like a meteor's track,
And, hurled on the stones of the pavement, the red brand lies shattered and black.

Once more the shouts of the people have rent the quivering air;

At the church door, vestry and people wait with their feet on the stair;
And the eager throng behind them press for a touch of his hand—
The unknown saviour, whose daring could compass a deed so grand.

But why does a sudden tremor seize on them while they gaze?
And what means that stifled murmur of wonder and amaze?
He stands in the gate of the temple he had periled his life to save;
And the face of the hero before them is the sable face of a slave.

History tells that the slave was promptly given his freedom as a reward for what he had done, and that in after life this man was known by the name of Will Philip Lining.

"RUBE" LEE

At the Alabama Constitutional Convention held recently in Montgomery, a member made an attack on the negro race as a whole, charging that it was unreliable, untruthful, insolent, indolent, and entirely wanting in the elements of manhood and womanhood.

An old Montgomery negro named Reuben Lee heard the wholesale charges, and, as the recollections of his slave days came back to him, talked feelingly of the past.

In a trembling voice Mr. Lee told several members of the Constitutional Convention incidents of the dark days during the Civil War. "I cannot believe," said he, "that the younger white men, like the speaker, really understand and know my people, else they would not make such statements about them. I wish he could know something of the relations that existed between master and slave. I remember one night, soon after the war began, my old master had some fresh mutton that had been killed that day, and old mistress wanted their daughter, who lived about three miles away, to have some of it.

"Master said it would be a good thing for her to have some of the mutton if there was any one by whom they could send it. 'Why not send Rube?' said the mistress, and the old man agreed that I should go. When they told me what they wanted, I objected, telling them I was too tired from work in the field that day. They told me

I might ride the old horse, and so I took a leg of mutton and rode over to my young mistress's house.

"When I reached the house and the young woman found out who I was, she rushed to the door to meet me, exclaiming: 'Oh, Rube, I am so glad to see you! I have n't slept any for several nights.

head resting on an old washboard, I remained all night under a hickory-tree at the gate of my young mistress's house. Next morning, with tears in her eyes, she thanked me for staying there and protecting her and her two little children, and said that although there was no house or any other living soul within a distance of

From a portrait bust made by Leila Usher in 1902
BOOKER T. WASHINGTON

My husband and brothers have all gone to the war, and I have been so scared, back here by myself with my two little children, that I could not sleep. You must stay all night, so I can get a little sleep.' I told her that her father and mother were expecting me back that night, but she pleaded so earnestly with me to stay that I could not refuse. Wrapping myself up in some quilts which she gave me, and with my

two miles, she felt safe while I was there, and that she had not slept so well for more than a week. So, for many months after that, I watched first at her house, sleeping under the hickory-tree, and then at my old master's. Perhaps if those who attack my race knew of such incidents as these, which were constantly happening then, and which happen even now, they would not seek to incite such intense feelings of race hatred."

LXVI.—88

own plans, and we have every reason to believe that our request will be granted. Herein lies a great opportunity for colored Americans, with single tax proclivities, to join with us in civilizing that part of Liberia now occupied by semi-civilized tribes of natives and there work out a true civilization that we believe will eventually dominate the earth. And what a grand contribution to the cause of humanity Afro-Americans would thus give to the world can only be estimated by a study of "Social Problems" and "Progress and Poverty" by the late Henry George.

Allotment of Lands.

Each adult immigrant to Liberia is alloted 15 acres of land. This allotment will provide homes of 15 acres each for 2,133,333 families, or for about 12,000,000 persons out of the total area of Liberia, to say nothing of the vast population that will grow up in the cities and towns.

The United States alone can well afford 100,000 Afro-Americans of the best class to assist in accomplishing this great work, and by the time these were well established in Liberia there will have been added two or three millions more to population of Negroes in America through natural processes.

A MEMORIAL TO DOUGLASS

Tuskegee Institute, Ala.,
February 1, 1907.

It is now nearly twelve years since Frederick Douglass, to whom the Negro people owe more than to any other man of our race, for the part he took in securing our freedom, died in Washington, D. C. His home at Anacostia, in the suburbs of Washington, still remains, however, and an effort is now being made to preserve this house with its memories and traditions and make it a permanent memorial to Douglass and the Negro people.

An association, known as the Frederick Douglass Historical Association, has been formed to effect this purpose. The people of our race have a rare opportunity to honor the memory of Frederick Douglass and to show their love and reverence for the man, who during the trying times before and after the war, embodied in his own life, more than any other man of our race, the aspirations and the cause of the Negro people. I have been asked by the officers of the Memorial Association to assist in securing the comparatively small sum of money amounting to $5,400 and interest, necessary to clear off the mort-

gage on the property and so secure the property for all time to the association and the Negro people of the United States. We should make Cedar Hill to the Negro people what Mt. Vernon is to the white race.

All of this can be accomplished if every member of the race would contribute at once, a small sum of money and send it to me by Postoffice order, check or otherwise as soon as this communication is read. I am making this appeal by the authority of the officers of the Frederick Douglass Memorial and Historical Association, and with the approval and sympathy of Mr. Douglass' immediate family. Now is the time when Mr. Douglass' birthday is being celebrated and talked of in all parts of the country, for the race to show its love for Douglass, not only in words, but in deeds. I shall hope to receive within the next few days this money, which can be sent in sums of from twenty-five cents up. After the money has been secured to clear off the mortgage, I am sure that steps will be taken to put the place in condition to serve the purpose mentioned.

The following letter, written to me by the officers of the Frederick Douglass Memorial and Historical Association, will make the situation clear:

Washington, D. C., Dec. 17, '06.

Dr. Booker T. Washington.

Dear Mr. Washington:—There is an encumbrance of fifty-four hundred dollars ($5400), bearing 6% interest, payable semi-annually against the Douglass property. This property consists of about fourteen acres of land in the heart of Anacostia, on a hill giving a beautiful view of the Potomac river and city for several miles. It is the opinion of experts that when the Government completes the new bridge and the reclamation of flats, this property will be worth at least $5,000 an acre. Its actual value is now $1,500 an acre. It is exempt from taxes by the act of Congress incorporating the Frederick Douglass Memorial and Historical Association. The Association needs at least the $5,400 to lift the mortgage. In the course of time about nine acres of the property could be cut up into building lots and sold, and with the proceeds of such sale Cedar Hill could be endowed with ample funds to meet the wants of the Douglass Memorial Association in perpetuity.

ARCHIBALD H. GRIMKE, Pres.
WHITFIELD McKINLEY, Sec.
FRANCIS J. GRIMKE, Treas.

The following pledges have already been received:

Booker T. Washington, Tuskegee, Ala.	$150.00
J. Douglass Wetmore, 5 Beckman St., N. Y.	100.00
Daniel Murray, 934 S St., N. W., Washington, D. C.	5.00
Robert Pekham, 2236 Sixth St., N. W., Washington, D. C.	5.00
Prof. Kelley Miller, Howard Uni., Washington, Pd.	5.00
Wm. L. Board, 1911 13th St., N. W., Washington	5.00
Archibald Grimke, 1413 Corcoran St., Washington, Pd.	5.00
A. U. Craig, Anacostia, D. C.	5.00
H. P. Slaughter, 2236 13th St., N. W., Washington	5.00
Prof. L. B. Moore, Howard Uni. Washington, D. C.	5.00
Dr. F. L. Shadd, 901 R St., N. W., Washington, D. C.	5.00
A. S. Gray, 1833 Vermont Ave., N. W., Washington	5.00
Dr. P. B. Brooks, 306 Third St., N. W., Washington, Pd.	5.00
Dr. P. B. Brooks, paid for daughter	5.00
Judge R. H. Terrell, 326 T St., N. W., Washington	5.00
Whitfield McKinley, 936 F St., N. W., Washington	10.00
Albertus Brown, 1725 Tenth St., N. W., Washington	5.00
James W. Johnson, for Rosamond Johnson, N. Y. City	25.00
J. A. Lankford, for Washington Negro Business League	20.00
Fred McCracken, 1413 Corcoran St., Washington, D. C.	5.00
Mrs. Mary Church Terrell, 326 T St., N. W., Washington	5.00
Miss Angelina Grimke (by Archibald Grimke)	5.00
Wilberforce Graduates (by W. A. Joiner) Washington, D. C.	25.00
Dr. W. S. Lofton, 1543 M St., N. W., Washington, D. C.	5.00
John C. Duncy, 2139 L St., N. W. Washington, D. C.	5.00
Mrs. Booker T. Washington, Tuskegee, Alabama	25.00
J. R. Cox, Tuskegee, Alabama.	10.00
Bernard Walton, 322 Spruce St., N. W., Washington, D. C.	5.00
George Waller, 322 Spruce St., N. W., Washington, D. C.	5.00
R. L. Pendleton, 1826 11th St., Washington, D. C.	5.00
Rev. J. A. Moreland, 1932 11th St., N. W., Washington, D. C.	5.00
William L. Pollard, 609 F St., N. W., Washington, D. C.	5.00
J. L. Goines, 1930 14th St., N. W., Washington, D. C.	5.00
Mrs. A. S. Gray, (By Arthur S. Gray) Washington, D. C.	5.00
W. J. Singleton, 2102 Ward P, N. W., Washington, D. C.	5.00
J. A. Cobb, 609 F St., N. W., Washington, D. C.	5.00

I hope that much additional money will be sent at once. All money will be acknowledged with proper credit. I shall be glad to furnish you with such additional information as you may desire.

BOOKER T. WASHINGTON,
Tuskegee Institute, Ala.

To go up stairs

THE NEGRO IN THE
NEW WORLD

BY

Dr. BOOKER T. WASHINGTON

REPRINTED FROM THE

JOURNAL OF THE AFRICAN SOCIETY

1911

NOTICES

The objects of the African Society are thus set forth in Article 1 of the Society's Constitution :—

"The African Society has been founded in commemoration of the work of Miss Mary Kingsley. It is instituted for the purpose of investigating the usages, institutions, customs, religions, antiquities, history, and languages of the native races of Africa; of facilitating the commercial and industrial development of the Continent in the manner best fitted to secure the welfare of its inhabitants; as a central institution in England for the study of African subjects, the diffusion of knowledge relating to such subjects, and to do all such other things as are incidental or conducive to the attainment of the objects for which the Society is founded or any of them."

Copies of the Rules and Constitution, Candidates' Proposal, and Membership Forms are supplied on application at the Society's Office, The Imperial Institute, London, S.W. Candidates for admission into the Society who may be residents abroad, and unable to obtain the papers, may apply to the Secretary, giving their description and address. On receipt of these the Secretary will prepare the necessary documents for submission to the Council.

Every Ordinary Member shall pay on his election £1 1s. as his first annual subscription; or he may become a Life Member by one payment of £15 15s.

Subscriptions are payable in advance, on the 1st of January.

The privileges of a Member include admission (with the right to introduce friends either personally or by card) to the Dinners and all ordinary meetings of the Society, and the use of the Library.

Each Member is also entitled to receive a copy of the Society's Journal.

———————

Membership forms can also be procured from the BANK OF AFRICA, LTD., at 113 Cannon Street, E.C., and at its Branches in South and East Africa, and from the BANK OF BRITISH WEST AFRICA, 14 CASTLE STREET, LIVERPOOL, or 17 LEADENHALL STREET, LONDON, and its Agencies at HAMBURG, TENERIFFE, and GRAND CANARY. Forms can also be obtained from the branches of the latter Bank at BATHURST, SIERRA LEONE, AXIM, SEKONDI, TARKWA, CAPE COAST CASTLE, ACCRA, and LAGOS.

173

THE NEGRO IN THE NEW WORLD

SIR HARRY H. JOHNSTON under the title "The Negro in the New World" has published a very interesting and in some respects a very remarkable book. It is the only book of its kind; that is, it is the only book that gives detailed information concerning the Negro in every part of the Western Hemisphere.

Until this book was published, there was no accurate statement concerning the number of Negroes in the New World. Even we in America are accustomed to think that the Negroes in the Western Hemisphere consist of the ten million in the United States and a few thousand in the West Indies. It is startling, therefore, for us to learn that there are 24,591,000 Negroes and Negroids in the New World. Their distribution according to Sir Harry's estimate is 30,000 in the Dominion of Canada; 10,000,000 in the United States; 12,500 in the Bermudas; 5,756,000 in the West Indies; 117,000 in Central America; 60,000 in Venezuela and Columbia; 225,500 in the Guianas; 8,300,000 in Brazil, and 90,000 in the remainder of South America.

When one has finished reading the book he knows how the Negroes were brought to the various islands of the West Indies, to the several countries of South America and to the United States. He also knows the conditions of the Negro during his enslavement in these various countries, how his emancipation was brought about, what he has done since his emancipation, what are his present relations with the whites and what is his outlook for the future. The author has shown a remarkable insight into the problem of racial adjustment and has been able to point out the weaknesses and the strong points of the Negro and the white people in contact with whom the Negro lives. The frankness with which Sir Harry Johnston has pointed out the weaknesses of the Negro and of the whites will tend to make the book unpopular. His remarkable powers of observation have enabled him to see practically everything in a country from beautiful landscapes to the women's costumes and he has criticised everything from the landscapes to the costumes.

I am sure that everyone who reads this book will have his outlook concerning the Negro problem broadened, and will also have learnt greater toleration with respect to the Negro.

Although I am not an anthropologist and for this reason cannot presume to discuss the first chapter of the book which deals with the anthropology of the Negro, yet it appears to me that in some instances much more representative types could have been given. For example, the picture of the Kru man from the Kru Coast, Liberia, as representing the typical Negro will, I am afraid, be misleading to the average reader, in that the type here shown does not represent that to which the present Negro race is tending, but rather that away from which it is tending. I think that the anthropological section, in fact the whole book, could have been made much more valuable, if there had been more pictures showing the types toward which the Negro is tending.

I am pleased to note that the author takes a hopeful view of Haiti and says that this little nation is not quite so black as she has been painted. Sir Harry has, I think, correctly indicated what Haiti should do in order to become a progressive nation; which is that the blighting military despotism should be done away with or at least greatly minimized, that there should be great efficiency and justness in the administration of the customs and other public functions, that education should be put on a practical basis, and that instead of the students being taught distant and unpractical things, they should have instruction in "agriculture, forestry, zoology, botany, mineralogy, bacteriology—not a single Haitian interests himself in such pursuits. There are the magnificent pine forests of Alpine Haiti being recklessly destroyed year after year by ignorant peasants or hasty concessionaires. The Government of Haiti, from the President down to the lowest ' buraliste ' in Port-au-Prince, does not care an iota.

"Haiti possesses one of the most magnificent floras in the

world and a wonderful display of bird-life. Do you suppose any Haitian knows or cares anything about the trees, flowers, or fruit, beautiful or useful, of his own country; the birds, the fish, the butterflies, the rocks, minerals, rainfall, or wind force? Not one."

If Haiti should carry out the suggestions of Sir Harry Johnston, the Negroes of that country would take their rightful place as the leaders of all the black people of the New World; for, as he says, Haiti has it in her to become a wealthy and respected Negro community. "She has no enemies because the United States is her all-powerful friend."

My own experience with students who have come from the West Indies to attend Tuskegee Institute, and from letters which I have received from many of them after they have gone back to their homes, causes me to agree with the author that a much more universal and practical education should be aimed at. What Sir Harry Johnston says further on this point in the preface of the book is of such importance that I quote it in full: "And just as the British Government has in a very munificent way taken in hand the agriculture of the West Indies, and grouped its teaching round a Central Institute, and thereby contributed greatly to the revival of prosperity, so in like manner some system of universal, British-West-Indian, practical, collegiate education should be brought into being. Otherwise all intelligent Negroes in these islands, and in British Honduras and Guiana, will look to receive their twentieth-century education at the hands of the United States. A great deal more should be done in the future to unify the British administration of these remarkable West Indian Islands, not merely in the interest of the Black and the Yellow, but also of the White."

I have been very much impressed with the fact that the crime rate among the Negroes of the West Indies is so small. In speaking of Jamaica, the author says that the criminality of the Jamaican Negroes is very slight. This is particularly true with reference to crimes of a serious nature. "Indecent assaults by Negroes on Negro women or children are not uncommon, a little more common, possibly, than they are among people of the same social status in England and in some Scotch towns. But it is scarcely too sweeping an assertion to say that there has been no case in Jamaica or any other British West Indian island of rape, or indecent assault or annoyance on the part of a black man or mulatto against a white woman since the Emancipation of the Slaves."

"There is not much serious crime in the Bahamas; such as there is, is more common, proportionately, among the indigenous white population than among the coloured. The Bahaman Negro bears a good reputation in this American Mediterranean. He is honest in big things, exceedingly good-tempered, brave, law-abiding, and hard-working."

There are probably many reasons why the crime rate among the West Indian Negroes is so low; but one of these reasons and a very important one, I think, is that policing and the administration of justice in the petty courts is to a large extent in the hands of the Negroes themselves. This causes them to have a greater respect for law and for the officers who are the representatives of the law. One of the greatest difficulties that we have in dealing with crime among the Negroes in the United States is, that so often the Negro does not think of the law as something made for his protection and designed to promote his welfare, but as something which is primarily to do him an injury. This is largely due to the fact that we as a people are so recently come out of slavery and have not yet been able to dis-associate law from slavery. I think, if there were throughout our Southland a system of Negro policing somewhat after the fashion of the Negro constabulary in the West Indies, that this would go a long way toward increasing the Negroes' respect for the law and tend to decrease our crime rate. In a few places in North Carolina, Alabama and Georgia this has already been tried with a fair degree of success.

With reference to the problem that confronts the Negro in the New World, it appears that the problem in Haiti is for an independent Black people to develop themselves and the great resources of their rich island. The problem in Cuba, where one-third of the population are Negroes, is to prevent an acute form of the race problem from developing. Since Sir Harry's

visit to the island in 1908 a number of things have
happened to indicate that a race problem similar to what
we have in the United States is likely to arise there. It will
be a surprise to many to find the author saying: "Altogether, socially and materially, in Cuba the American Negro
appears at his best, so far as an average can be struck. Nowhere of course is there the intellectual development of the
United States Negro in his higher types: on the other hand,
I did not see any real squalor, stupid barbarity, aggressive
noisiness, or ill manners. The country homes seemed better
and neater than the worst class of Negro habitations in the
Southern States; the town dwellings might not always be
sanitary, but they had about them the dignity of Spain."

Nowhere in South America is there a race problem in the
sense that we have it in the United States. It is very gratifying to know that Brazil with its very large Negro and Indian
population is developing in such a way that all the races are
living together with mutual goodwill toward each other.
Nowhere in the New World is the race problem so acute as in
the United States. There are a number of reasons for this.
Among these are, first, the long and bitter agitation that
preceded the emancipation of the slave; second, the fierce and
prolonged civil war, by which emancipation was achieved;
third, the further intensification of sectional and racial hatred
engendered during what is known as the "Reconstruction
Period," that is the period immediately following the close
of the civil war; fourth, the injudicious use in recent years of
the Negro as a political issue.

Since, however, it is agreed that the Negro is permanently
to remain in the United States, the problem, then, is to bring
about a better understanding between the races and so to
adjust matters that the two races will be able to live side by
side in peace and harmony, both developing, each mutually
assisting the other and both working for the general development of the nation. It is by means of practical education that
the Negro is to be developed and made a useful citizen. This,
of course, applies to the Negro race everywhere and particularly to that part of the race which is yet in Africa.

Being myself an educator, I am of course especially interested in what the author has to say of education in the various countries in the New World which have large Negro populations. In every instance the author thinks that the backwardness of the people is largely due to the lack of adequate educational facilities of the proper sort. He is, I think, very nearly correct in insisting that education is going a long way towards solving the race problem, not only in the New but in the Old World. It would be well if throughout the New World the Negro teachers, pastors and leaders of every sort would everywhere follow Sir Harry Johnston's advice and direct "their attention to the questions that are really vital : to theories and practices of disease-prevention and cure; to the correlation of intestinal worms and sanitary reform; to the inculcation of the chemistry of nature, of practical agriculture, beautiful horticulture, sound building, modern history, modern science, modern languages, modern religion."

Negro education, Sir Harry Johnston sets forth, should be of the kind that can be transmuted into money. "The one undoubted solution of the Negro's difficulties throughout the world is for him to turn his strong arms and sturdy legs, his fine sight, subtle hearing, deft fingers, and rapidly-developed brain to the making of Money, money being indeed but transmuted intellect and work, accumulated energy and courage."

BOOKER T. WASHINGTON.

Tuskegee Institute,
    Alabama, U.S.A.

H78

V11980—Booker T. Washington and Distinguished Guests,
Tuskegee Institute, Alabama.

8

Religion

Readers searching for scholarship on Booker T. Washington's contribution to the Black church will find little or nothing at all. This is not surprising, since he was not a pastor, a writer on theological philosophy, nor an activist church leader. He intentionally stayed clear of these roles, preferring to seek truth in the Bible as an inspirational book for daily living. Among his most important spiritual guides was the well-known White Congregationalist preacher and writer Lyman Abbott, whose journals frequently provided space for Washington's articles.[1] Washington's acceptance of the New England liberal Protestantism of the Progressive Age guided him away from a biblical tradition shared by many Black theologians and abolitionists and toward the Social Gospelers.[2] As a result, the legacy of his religious thoughts is found in today's inspirational thinkers, such as Clifford Taulburt, rather than the intellectual analysis of Cornel West.[3]

Throughout his life, Washington believed that the moral positions he held, rather than laws or governments, would lead to permanent change for Blacks. As opposed to W. E. B. Du Bois, Washington fully subscribed to the familiar quotation by Ben Johnson, "How small, of all that human hearts endure, that part, which laws and kings can cause or cure."[4] A prolific writer on religion, Washington preached to his students that they should be better than the racists surrounding them by taking the moral high road of humility, service, and gratitude, by cultivating the ability to discover the divine in ordinary life. He argued idealistically for African Americans not to allow their humanity to be defined by the mainstream or its Jim Crow laws, but for each individual to build his or her self-determination on a foundation of Christian virtues. Indeed, Washington embraced the very Puritan roots of Lyman Abbott's Congregationalist faith, believing that his talks delivered from the pulpit of the Tuskegee meetinghouse-chapel could lead his flock to rise above and change the darkness of the racist heart. On the one hand, one may interpret this lack of activism as yet another form of accommodationism, a grand failure to use the social and moral power of the Black church to create freedom. On the other hand, it is also possible to find in Washington's religious thoughts a call for independence as a way of pragmatically responding to a racist social and political context and thus a choice to push for personal and communal liberty rather than the freedom of full citizenship.[5] In either case, the Bible and religion are so central to all of Washington's beliefs that they must be examined in order to understand thoroughly his social positions. In Washington's mind, religion sprang from the grassroots of faith and the Bible, never to be untangled in the public sphere from economics, politics, and education.

Recently, an editor for the National Book Foundation asked fifteen of the nation's leading poets, historians, and fiction writers to name the book or books that changed their lives. Only one, Grace Paley, cited the Bible.[6] When asked the same question almost one hundred years earlier by a magazine editor, Booker T. Washington's answer was the Bible, which he claimed had shaped all his "motives and actions." He went on to state, "I very seldom ever write an article for a magazine or paper, or prepare an important speech for the public that I do not find myself quoting directly or indirectly from the Bible."[7] Why? Because, as Washington explained, the Bible's power lay in its practical value for everyday life. He understood the Bible as a book for the here and now, not some transcendent future. From the days of slavery through the present, as they "struggled upward," the Bible had held a special power for African Americans as a way of offering comfort to the masses.[8] Therefore, it would be the Bible, rather than a specific Christian denomination, that Washington advanced as the essential life guide for African Americans.

One of Washington's most poetic uses of the Bible, which is included in this chapter, was a speech he delivered to Tuskegee students at one of his Sunday evening chapel talks in 1906.[9] With Emersonian joy, Washington invites the Tuskegee students to discover how the ordinary natural world is mystically infused with the Holy Spirit. Washington urged his students to develop the ability to find beauty in everything and everywhere. Today's reader may recognize the speech as falling within that long tradition of American optimism that, sometimes with tragic results, believes in the divine power of the individual to conquer all obstacles. Washington emphasized that the Kingdom of God exists in the here and now, not beyond the sun and stars, "The Bible says the Kingdom is right within us."[10] In Washington's mind, to be a modern Christian required a Bible-based faith that enabled one to look on the world with unfettered optimism, bringing daily epiphanies of a divine presence in simple places like the red hills of Macon County, Alabama.

Yet Washington's faith was not without its own mysteries. He grew up as a member of the African Zion Baptist church, a denomination he remained connected to his whole life.[11] After graduating from Hampton Institute in 1875, he briefly found a calling in the Baptist church. For the better part of a year, starting in the fall of 1878, Washington attended Wayland Seminary in Washington, D.C., a small, urban Baptist theology school. This period of Washington's life is both intriguing and transformational. It is intriguing because Washington, a man who usually loved to tell his life story, chose to remain silent his whole life on his experiences at Wayland. According to Louis Harlan, at Wayland, Washington developed his lifelong habit of challenging unlettered preachers, along with a disdain for cities and higher education.[12] Unlike St. Paul's conversion on the road to Damascus, the Washington, D.C., experience seems to have directed Washington to the Bible and away from any religious denomination. As the opportunity arose for a religious training school at Tuskegee, it was a nondenominational Bible school that was built.

Washington's views on religion troubled Whites more than Blacks. A music teacher at the nearby girls school, the Tuskegee Conference Female College, charged that Tuskegee's "Theological Department" was part of Washington's grand scheme to raise money and secretly teach social equality.[13] Washington's religious identity became the subject of a 1902 *Presbyterian Banner* article. The writer saw Washington as an elusive opportunist who somehow convinced Presbyterians that he was one of their own, thus enabling him to raise money from their congregation. Troubled by Washington's tactics, the writer asked, "'Who is Booker T. Washington, and what is his work?' The answer, if given truthfully, would be, He was first a Baptist, then a Congregationalist, afterwards a Unitarian; but now is independent of all denominational control, and accountable to no ecclesiastical body for the use of the funds he gathers in."[14] The breadth of Washington's faith journey is reflected in the variety of Protestant journals in which he published: *Congregationalist, Christian Union, A.M.E. Church Review, Our Day, Missionary Review of the World, Christian Advocate,* and *Methodist Quarterly Review.*

Washington's ability to be a Christian thinker unattached from any particular Protestant tradition provided him with both the freedom to raise money and the ability to develop a curriculum independent from a church governance body. Fund-raising independence allowed him to seek support from several denominations. In addition, it also allowed him to develop at Tuskegee a curriculum based on Christian virtues and character without becoming a religious school controlled by any institution. Christianity formed the basis of many aspects of Tuskegee's spiritual life: the values found in the "correlation" of the curriculum; the Sunday chapel talks, the training offered at the Phelps Hall Bible Training School (opened in 1893); and to the various service activities such as conducting a Sunday services at the Tuskegee county jail.[15]

Unlike recent scholars, Washington's contemporaries found him to be one of the important religious voices of his day. He was frequently called "the Moses of his people." Hampton's principal Hollis Frissell described him as one on the "roll call of heroes of faith."[16] Important Black church leaders of the day, such as Francis Grimké, Daniel Payne, and Bishop Benjamin Tanner, found Washington's religious writings to be compelling. At the core of Washington's faith were simple tenets: love your fellow man, and deeds matter more than faith alone. These tenets were what his friend James Hardy Dillard remembered most about the Tuskegee leader. Dillard, the noted White philanthropic leader of the Jeanes and Slater Funds, Latin professor, and educator (for whom the historically Black university in New Orleans is named), proclaimed Booker T. Washington to be a "Christian philosopher."

In 1925, nearly ten years after Washington died, Dillard told a Tuskegee Founder's Day audience that Washington's moral leadership was based on two "commandments."[17] The first commandment was to believe in the essential goodness of humankind. One finds it frequently expressed as a Christian, turn-the-other-cheek type of love. Perhaps this is what enabled him to see past the dire sufferings of the Jim Crow South and envision the "Kingdom of Heaven" on earth. Washington's second commandment, according to Dillard, was that the so-called race problem would be solved by education, service, and economic exchange. In other words, a Christian life meant action and not faith alone. This would be the path to the eventual harmony bringing together all of God's children. Dillard's assessment describes the nature of a great deal of Washington's writing on the subject of religion.

Although Washington's religious convictions generally inspired positive and encouraging messages, they had on occasion led him to express moral condemnation. The example presented in this chapter was written in 1890 for Lyman Abbott's Congregationalist journal *Christian Union*. It was a fierce attack on the unlettered Black ministry, likely the product of the disillusionment he experienced at Wayland.[18] This diatribe took aim at finding that their excited emotionalism covered for a lack of education. How could an illiterate ministry lead a flock when they are unable to read the Bible? The remedy, which he organized on the Tuskegee campus a few years later, was a Bible school free from denominational control. Its goal was the preparation of a Bible-based ministry bringing racial uplift to a southern agrarian population. His vision, like most of his ideas, was a compromise. He aimed at a middle ground between the unschooled, ecstatic, emotional preacher and the classically trained who was hard-pressed to speak to the working class.

Another religiously inspired writing that stands out from his later work (also included in this chapter) was his calling on people of faith to attack British colonialism in South Africa. In an article in *Our Day*, Washington was outraged at the slaughter of Matabele warriors by heavily armed British troops.[19] In powerful words, he attacked the British for making a mockery out of Christianity, professing the faith but robbing the Africans of life and liberty in their greedy quest for land. This angry cry of injustice stands alone among Washington's religious writings.[20]

Washington's better-known writing on religion drifted from these kinds of attacks and came to focus on the moral character needed to develop a Christian community based on service. His best-known efforts are the four books he developed primarily from his Sunday evening talks to the Tuskegee students: *Daily Resolves* (1896), *Sowing and Reaping* (1900), *Character Building* (1902), and *Putting the Most into Life* (1906).

The basic idea that true faith is manifested through service to one's community comes through loud and clear in these books. In *Sowing and Reaping*, Washington urged his constituents to work hard, not to complain, and to recognize how the entire human family is interconnected. Indeed, Washington believed that we truly are our "brother's keeper."[21] In *Character Building*, Washington told his students to go into the world carrying the "Tuskegee Spirit" of uplift and service. "You must make up your minds in the first place, as I have always said before, that you are going to make some sacrifice, that you are going to live your lives in an unselfish way, in order to help some one."[22]

Washington's later writings on religion recast the theme of community service within the Social Gospel language of economics and religion. *Putting the Most into Life*, included in this chapter, directed people to change the world by first establishing one's own moral compass. "The same people who stand for the most in the educational and commercial world and in the uplifting of the people are in some real way connected with the religious life of the people among whom they reside."[23] Religion is not, he exhorts, merely going to church; the Bible is not merely literature. "Do not mistake denominationalism for reverence and religion . . . The Bible should be read as a daily guide to right living and as a daily incentive to positive Christian service."[24] Washington's involvement with the Young Men's Christian Association (YMCA), for which he gave speeches and his support, led to two important results. The first was his meeting with Julius Rosenwald in 1911. Washington presented the keynote address at a Chicago YMCA dinner celebration. Rosenwald had been deeply moved by reading *Up from Slavery* the year before and looked forward to their meeting.[25] Soon Rosenwald joined Tuskegee as a trustee, supported Black YMCAs, and funded the Rosenwald School program.[26] The second important result of Washington's involvement with the YMCA would be his involvement with the Men and Religion Forward Movement (MRFM). The MRFM, a Social Gospel organization formed from a vast gathering of Protestant groups in 1910, and with YMCA support, seemed tailor-made for Washington. MRFM leaders emphasized the sanctity of the home, the use of efficiency business models, and an antiemotional spirituality. They advocated for a powerful recommitment to the church in response to the rise of the empowerment of women outside their separate sphere.[27] The big event for the MFRM took place in April 1912, when the group organized the Christian Conservation Congress meeting at Carnegie Hall in New York City. Washington's speech at the convention, reproduced in this book, shows the cagey fund-raiser at his best: cajoling, storytelling, patriotic, asking for money while claiming not to be, race proud and yet subservient, and directing his White Christian brothers and potential benefactors where and why to invest.[28]

Finally, in Washington's last talk before the Tuskegee students, published under the title *Team Work*, he challenged students to see the spirit of community and brotherhood as a universal honor code, the results of which could be seen at work in businesses, in a military academy, on sports teams, and at the local YMCA. According to Washington, teamwork had built the Panama Canal and the Standard Oil Company (i.e., the fruits of capitalism). It would now take this universal concept of teamwork, starting within Black spiritual communities, to raise the Black masses up from poverty. His final call for creating the "highest spiritual usefulness" among Tuskegee students best summarizes Washington's views on the need to connect religion and life.[29]

Contents

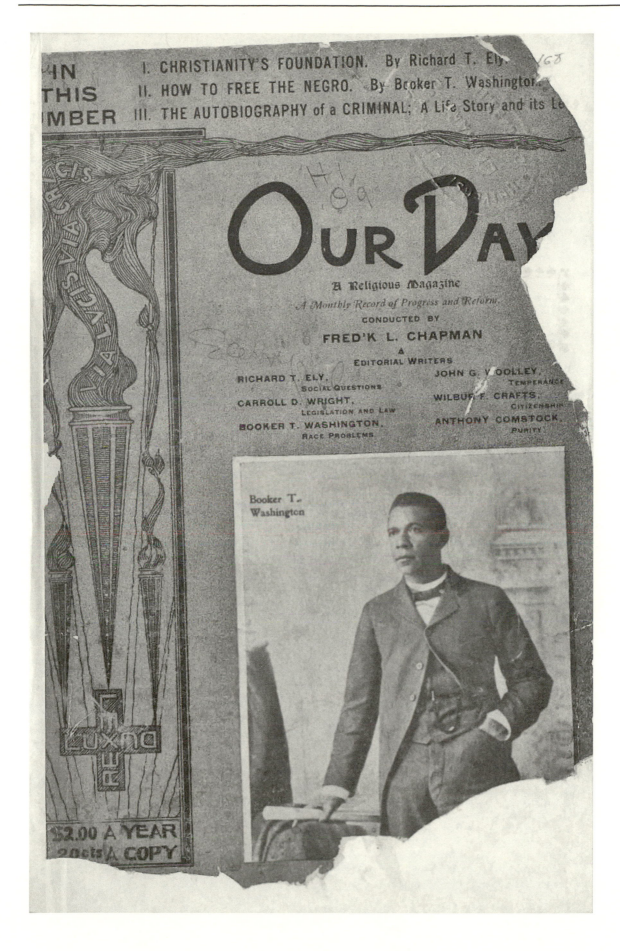

Our Day

government is very largely that—it should be conducted on the best business principles. The office is not for the officer, but the office and the officer are both for society. To make appointments and dismissions on any other basis than fitness and inefficiency, is to sacrifice the interests of society to the selfishness of individuals.

But we shall hardly checkmate the boodler's selfishness by playing against it the taxpayer's selfishness. It can be conquered only from above. We must have not only "a business administration," but also civic patriotism and Christian citizenship.

* * * * * * *

Politics must have nobler ideals than the promise of more profits to the merchant and more wages to the workmen. The writer finds everywhere in his wide travels that young men have little interest in politics because it is but a contest of selfish interests, and he recalls, in contrast, his own boyhood, when rich men sought "protection," not for their own property, but for the slave; and when working men were not in politics for higher wages for themselves, but for the emancipation of their wageless brothers. And in the war it was not bounties and contracts that chiefly interested the people, but the unselfish struggle to save the Union.

* * * * * * *

God has confounded our silver and tariff babel until it would seem impossible to rally the old parties again on these selfish lines. Let us, by all means, learn what is right and wise to do about tariff and currency, but let us also rise out of the party wrecks which such selfish issues have caused with some leading issues more worthy of the close of nineteen Christian centuries, and enter the twentieth century, in which, by correct reckoning, our next presidential election will occur, with such leading aims for the party of progress as divorce reform, purity, industrial justice, the maintenance of the Sabbath, the suppression of gambling and the saloon.

In place of the savage and selfish war cry, "To the victors belong the spoils," let us write that watchword of the true nobility that honors itself in forgetting self.

CHRISTIANIZING AFRICA.

By BOOKER T. WASHINGTON.

BOOKER T. WASHINGTON.

CAPE Town, Aug. 7.—Details have just been received here of the decisive victory won on Wednesday by the seven hundred British troops composing Colonel Plumer's column, over a native force estimated to have numbered from 5,000 to 7,000 men. The latter fought most desperately and bravely, charging up within a few yards of the British rapid fire guns."

"About 500 of the Matabele warriors were slain during the engagement."

"At 6 o'clock on Wednesday morning, a force of about 700 men, whites and natives, cavalry, infantry and artillery, all under British officers, marched to the Umlugu valley.

"But when the screw guns began crashing case-shot into the enemy, tearing wide, bloody gaps in the ranks, and the deadly Maxim rattled its hail of lead into the heaving, serried masses of the rapidly moving impis, the natives wavered in their charge, and a moment later the rush was stopped and they began to give way, leaving heaps of dead and wounded."

The brief extracts quoted above from the press dispatches tell their own story. Such dispatches are nothing unusual. They can be seen almost weekly.

OUR DAY

With such an object lesson before us, why need Christians wonder that Africa is not Christianized faster. What is the crime of these heathen? Why are they thus shot down—mowed down by the acre. Simply because God has given them land that some one else wants to possess—simply because they are ignorant and weak.

On the very day, perhaps at the very hour that the British troops were mowing down those Africans simply because they tried to defend their homes, their wives and their children, hundreds of prayers were being offered up in as many English churches that God might convert the heathen in Africa and bring them to our way of thinking and acting. What mockery!

Have not these Matabele warriors as much right to lay claim to the streets of London, as the English have to claim the native land of these Africans? What England has done every Christian (?) nation in Europe has done.

On one ship a half dozen missionaries go to use the Bible and prayer book—in the next ship go a thousand soldiers to use the rifle.

Can we wonder that the Africans hesitate about exchanging their religion for that of the Anglo-Saxon race?

Booker T. Washington.

THE PSALMIST vs. THE SALOONKEEPER.

By JOHN G. WOOLLEY.

BLESSED is the man that walketh not in the counsel of the ungodly, nor standeth in the way of sinners, nor sitteth in the seat of the scornful, but his delight is in the law of the Lord and in his law doth he meditate day and night. And he shall be like a tree, planted by the meeting of the streams, that bringeth forth his fruit in his season, his leaf also shall not wither and whatsoever he doeth shall prosper."

It has been discovered that David was not the author of the first psalm. It is at least equally certain that he was. It does not much matter, it is not the kind of thing to greatly add to or diminish his fame. Somebody wrote it; it is very old, and so simple, as to both form and substance, that it seems to me that I should have written something very like it myself, if no one else had done it. And the decided weight of opinion is that whoever wrote it did so by the inspiration of God, and I reckon that is so, whatever definition of inspiration be accepted, for it would be hard to find one, learned or simple, who would not put his finger on that stickful of poetic prose and say, "Chance, or law, or miracle, that is right, that is reliable, that is true, that will do to tie to." At any rate, the church imputes to it absolute verity and accepts it unequivocally as the very word of God, and in the most earnest

circles of church work it would greatly detract from one's usefulness, if not destroy it altogether, even to express a doubt upon the subject.

RULE TO VOTE BY.

And so because I prize this hearing, and would set every step of my thought in a sure place today and bar out of this hour any possible personal vagary, I propose to you that, as you have often seen a tailor lay a pattern upon a piece of cloth, we lay this ancient, accepted evident, true, inspired scripture upon our politics and cut it out, and wear it as the toga virilis of our Christian citizenship, wear it, I say, for it matters very little how admirable the cut of one's piety is, if he takes it off in the polling booth, as men take off their overcoats indoor, for fear of not "feeling" them when they come out into the open air.

The question of the liquor traffic is already reduced to a simple equation from which the reduction of a single election day will suffice to give the value of "X"—the cross of Christ upon a free man's ballot slip. An election is an example in division; the voting body is the dividend, the issue is the divisor. If it be single the quotient will be simple and final; if it be a polynomial, the answer will be but another problem, as difficult as the first. The one bright spot

SOWING AND REAPING.

CHAPTER I.

"BE not deceived; God is not mocked; for whatsoever a man soweth that shall he also reap." Again: "He which soweth sparingly shall also reap sparingly; and he which soweth bountifully shall reap also bountifully." (II. Cor. ix. 6.)

These quotations are applicable to man in all the activities of life, both spiritual and material. Our harvest is always in proportion to the amount of earnest labour that we put into our work. A farmer who puts earnest effort into his field work will reap a profitable harvest. The student who puts earnest effort into a lesson will get pleasure and satisfaction from it; he need not, however, be a student only in the closet, but in the great world as well, where practice takes the place of theory. In either case, when he has performed his duty, his conscience will

8   *SOWING AND REAPING.*

be clear; he will be free from any restraint; he will
have courage to face the obligations which confront
all of us in the battle of life. A man gets knowledge and lays the basis of substantial influence in
so far and no farther as he applies himself to the
mastery of the thing to which he is most inclined.

Take, for example, the man engaged in business
pursuits. His profits are always in proportion to
the amount of money, the skill and the labour that
he puts into his business. If he fails to keep his
eyes open to the main chance, if he does not know
when to advance and when to reduce the price of his
goods, he will have no profit; his rivals will get the
best of him, and he may have to go out of business.
And this is true of all the pursuits of life. We get
out of every venture just what we put into it; no
more, no less. To attain success we must put forth
hard and honest labour. At the back of all success
there is hard, persistent labour. There is no royal
road. Those who think there is always fail. No
man ever reaped any success in life who did not sow
wisely. As each man takes up the serious business
of life he must do something, — he must labour and
wait. In order to reap something, something must
be done. Value for value, is the real standard of
life's exchange of benefits.

Show me a man who is always grumbling, always finding fault with his condition, never satisfied with his opportunities, and I will show you a man who does not appreciate the opportunities in the environment in which he is to work out his weal or woe. Hard labour is the key-note to success. One of the wisest things ex-Senator B. K. Bruce ever said was that "luck is a fool." So it is. There is no luck; it is all labour and patience.

And every man who wants to succeed must learn the process of overlapping. That is, no man who wishes to succeed should be afraid of doing just a little more than lies in the direct line of his duty. He must be interested in his work.

No man lives to himself. He is a related creature. He cannot confine himself to himself. He is his brother's keeper, because his brother is his keeper in more ways than one. We lean one upon the other. When we do this we establish a feeling of confidence, of appreciation, of helpfulness, in the estimation of a neighbour, that nothing can destroy. If a person asks us to do a certain thing which is fair and honest, do that thing; not only do that, but do more. Combine your force with his, and win his undivided confidence. This process of overlapping establishes the greatest happiness, since it creates a community

10   *SOWING AND REAPING.*

of feeling and interest, without which no man can hope to succeed.

In every pursuit of life, it may be accepted as an axiom that we get out of every effort just what we put into it of hard, honest labour. That is to say : "Whatsoever a man soweth that shall he also reap."

9

Politics

Booker T. Washington advised, networked, cut deals, made threats, pressured, punished enemies, rewarded friends, greased palms, manipulated the media, signed autographs, read minds with the skill of a master psychologist, strategized, raised money, always knew where the camera was pointing, traveled with an entourage, waved the flag with patriotic speeches, and claimed to have no interest in partisan politics. In other words, he was an artful politician. He was not a lawyer, scholar, college-bred man, or a military hero. But he knew how to use the power of symbolism through the lens of a storyteller. Tuskegee opened on the Fourth of July in an African Methodist Episcopal Zion Church, a mile or so from the present campus. For the institute's gala twenty-fifth-anniversary celebration, he had a replica of the old church-school recreated on the campus grounds alongside the Tuskegee chapel. This overt symbolism of God and patriotism offered visitors, Black and White, both the common ground they shared as Americans and that Booker T. Washington was the right man to bridge the races in progress.[1] Readers familiar with Washington know the considerable body of insightful historical writing devoted to his political positions and strategies.[2] This chapter veers outside of political theory and into literary allusions as a means of understanding Washington's politics because he was a thinker rooted in the Bible and in Shakespeare, a lover of epigrams, a teller of folksy tales, a prodigious writer, and theatrical in his method of inspiring crowds. In the words of his longtime assistant Emmett J. Scott, "As was said of Abraham Lincoln, he [Washington] wrote and spoke his language with literary simplicity."[3] This "literary simplicity" is deceptive because Washington framed his thoughts in literary terms to conjure multivalent messages. The first part of this chapter provides a lens through which to see his leadership style. The second part provides examples of specific political actions.

Washington performed on the world stage as a moral, charismatic leader representing African Americans. Some strongly believe he failed in that role; others believe that he succeeded against the odds. Some believe he was a trickster and self-made man; others firmly believe he was tricked and was a "made-man" by white power brokers. Whatever one's position, it is undeniable that Washington was an influential educational, business, cultural, and political leader. He certainly had all the basics of leadership: a vision, a means of implementing the vision, and the enthusiasm of followers.

Washington's vision, at its simplest, was to build a model educational facility to transform the lives of the "untalented" 90 percent of African Americans by providing the means to prosperity, spiritual fulfillment, and self-sufficiency, which, in turn, would lead to civic, social, and cultural equality: "Tuskegee is sending numerous communities model teachers, model farmers, model masons, model carpenters, model housekeepers. They are able to transform the locality because they become object lessons to their own people."[4] The Bible served as the primary literary source for his vision, which was fitting for a man known as the Moses and Joshua of his people and who preached a turn-the-other-cheek, love-your-enemy philosophy. In *Putting the Most into Life*, Washington linked the struggle of the Jews in the Bible, "a peculiar people," with the special destiny of the Black race.[5] His vision brings to mind the famous line delivered by the priest in Graham Greene's *The Power and the Glory*. Surrounded by poverty and darkness, he finds a trace of divine light to guide the way: "Hate was just a failure of imagination."[6] Washington imagined America beyond lynching, Jim Crow, disfranchisement, and peonage. How that was possible or prudent in the face of his age's White terrorism remains a difficult question to answer.

The means to achieve Washington's vision involved gradualism, economic empowerment, accommodation, ownership of black businesses, the temporary suspension of equal rights, and starting at the bottom. Here is where things get knotty, ambiguous, and, sometimes, troubling. While he appeared to say one thing, he often wore the mask of compliance, choosing deception and subterfuge, convinced that frontal assaults would fail. Did anyone, even Washington, realize the full symbolism in the name he gave his daughter—Portia? Perhaps it was only to signify bourgeois taste and sophistication. Or was it that he admired a character capable of achieving her aims through disguise?[7]

Finally, Washington created enthusiasm for his programs by simultaneously preaching pragmatism and utopian idealism. Included in this chapter is a reproduction titled *Bird's Eye View of Buildings and Grounds of Tuskegee Normal and Industrial Institute*.[8] The print was distributed in a variety of ways, including placement in Washington's books. What is remarkable is that it does not say "proposed" or "future design" but rather states that this is the

campus. The print is part fact and part fiction, just like Washington's pro-
nouncements. While some of the buildings exist, others never did. It miracu-
lously combines town and countryside, lush lawns, filled with bursting foun-
tains, mathematically precise, and perfect in every way.

Washington ingeniously reconciled these polar opposites into a combina-
tion of everyday living maxims and a vision of hope, possibility, and a better
day to come. He made people believe that their honest labor would bear fruit:
"Be not deceived; God is not mocked; for whatsoever a man soweth that he
also reap."[9] On the one hand, he preached that pragmatism and hard work
would eventually change hearts and minds. On the other hand, he believed
that the times required, temporarily, protected and separate Black spheres for
economic, social, and political development. Tuskegee would be a Black utopia, a model community of Black Christian workers living in harmony with
the land. He worked tirelessly to visualize his dream, supplementing his writings with idealized photographs and drawings of self-sufficient Black workers
living in pastoral harmony. Convinced that cities bred corruption, nature constantly appears as a refuge in his writings: "Whenever I want new material for
an address or a magazine article, I follow the plan of getting away from the
artificial surroundings and getting back into the country, where I can sleep
in a log cabin and eat the food of the farmer . . . Many of these seemingly ignorant people, while not educated in the way that we consider education, have
in reality a very high form of education—that which they have gotten out of
contact with nature."[10] A generation of schools soon patterned themselves
after Washington's legendary Tuskegee.[11]

Depending on one's vantage point, Washington's choices were disastrous
and delusional, or lifesaving and necessary. The first, and better-known, position in most historical accounts, is that the naive Washington was painfully
slow to understand the new industrial world, that he grossly miscalculated the
depths of racism, and that, like a Black Esau, he accepted economic handouts
in lieu of equal rights and the full privileges of citizenship in a democracy. The
second, and more controversial reading of Washington's choice, is one in
which he is seen as a separatist and a realist. This reading is based on recognizing that Washington, unlike many other Black leaders of his time, was a
frequent traveler in the Deep South who knew conditions firsthand instead of
in the abstract. Washington was a witness to the violence and racism of Jim
Crow in the Black Belt and lived beside desperate poverty and illiteracy. Because of the paradoxical nature of being both a pragmatic realist and a utopian
separatist, Washington sometimes expressed conflicting and ambiguous positions on issues.

Washington's formula for political empowerment included gaining economic strength while not appearing to rock the political boat. The first part
of the plan, economic growth, was shared by several Black leaders, including
T. Thomas Fortune and the members of the Negro Business League. In their
estimation, political change would happen more quickly with economic lever-
age. They argued for a separate world in which Blacks would buy property,
invest in the Black community, and patronize Black businesses. The second

part of the plan, accommodating the current political system instead of demanding full partnership in democracy, is where Washington equivocated. Poker faced, Washington repeatedly proclaimed that he made it a point to stay clear of politics. This avoidance was amplified by his open disdain for the nation's capital. It is remarkable how many people believed his claim of being apolitical, for nothing could have been further from the truth. Washington was a lifetime Republican, who, during his thirty-plus years as Tuskegee's leader, advised and endorsed both White and Black politicians, paid lobbyists, worked for Black federal appointments, struggled to keep a U.S. post office on the Tuskegee campus, publicly commented on U.S. foreign policy, pushed for funding for Black education, submitted planks for Republican conventions, and worked behind the scenes to fight Jim Crow laws in voting, jury representation, immigration of Africans, lynching, peonage, and segregation on trains.[12] Much of the time, his work was done quite openly, with the exception of fighting Jim Crow laws. In the end, his political position may be described as an indirect resistance that used his charismatic leadership, covert funding of lawsuits, an effective media savvy, and the nationwide Tuskegee machine.

Why all of the posturing to appear apolitical? One reason was money. Washington's campus and national alliances within the Black community needed northern White dollars to function. He never wanted to rock the boat. Another reason lay in this political philosophy. Washington's public distancing from politics serves as a metaphor for his political ideology. In the same way that Washington believed that religion was limited when practiced denominationally, he saw greater possibilities for social and political change outside of party politics.[13] Washington's familiar historical role as W. E. B. Du Bois's rival sometimes leads to his misidentification as a conservative. In a historical context, he was left of center. Historian Jennings Wagoner argues persuasively that Washington was a thinker of the same political stripes as New England liberal Progressives, including such friends as Harvard president Charles W. Eliot.[14] Louis Harlan perceived Washington as a conservative, "political realist."[15] In a historical context, these assessments are not as contradictory as they appear.

Washington developed his coalition of businessmen and professionals, or what became known as the Tuskegee Machine, to mediate artfully brokered deals within a violent, racist South. He threaded his way between his Charybdis and Scylla. On one side were Black-hating racists, such as James Vardaman, Benjamin Tillman, and Thomas Dixon, all of whom saw Washington as anything but a harmless accommodationist. Dixon, writing in the *Saturday Evening Post*, warned that Washington was building "a nation inside a nation" which was "not training his students to be servants and come at the beck and call of any man. He is training them all to be masters of men, to be independent, to own and operate their own industries, plant their own fields, buy and sell and their own goods, and in every shape and form destroy the last vestige of dependence on the white man for anything."[16] As a consequence of this racist vitriol, liberal Whites in the South found that a high cost could be paid for befriending Washington.[17] On the other side were Black activists, such as

Monroe Trotter, W. E. B. Du Bois, and Ida B. Wells, who painted Washington as selling off civil rights for a small measure of economic security. Nevertheless, much of Washington's work was done in a land filled with terror for most Blacks, including himself. Washington traveled the South under open and veiled threats to his life.[18]

Depending on one's view, Washington and his Tuskegee Machine offered either a simple or a simple-minded political philosophy. As with many of his positions, Washington gathered his thoughts on politics and distilled them slowly to a simple, three-part equation. First, like Plato in *The Republic*, Washington's utopian plan begins by developing virtuous citizens.[19] Second, the core virtues, which included thrift, honesty, modesty, service, and a turn-the-cheek attitude toward enemies, would develop knowledge. If this scheme seems idealistic, it should be noted that Washington's personal secretary, Emmett J. Scott, actually quoted Cardinal John Henry Newman at Washington's funeral. Newman, a Roman Catholic theologian and author of the classic *The Idea of the University*, espoused universal knowledge with theology playing a central role in the curriculum. Although Newman describes beauty, utility, and morality in education, only the most imaginative readings of Newman's philosophy of education apply to industrial education.[20] Third, with knowledge firmly built on virtue and character, Black men and women could go forth and build the economic power and social networks required to construct a self-reliant community. The vision would be complete when White men realized that their so-called burden was lifted from their backs. This would be, in Washington's mind, the "natural" path for acquiring equal social rights, the vote, and political power.

With the perspective of a century of hindsight, Washington's single largest failure was his inability to calculate the breadth and depth of southern racism. Washington's most direct early writing on social and political issues may be found in his 1899 *The Future of the American Negro*. Most of Washington's familiar thoughts on politics are found in chapter 6 of that text which is included in this book. The chapter opens by stating that Black voting rights were essentially a losing venture in the South given the current conditions. This loss, he reminds the reader, happened even though Blacks fought patriotically in the American Revolution, the War of 1812, the Civil War, and the Spanish-American War.

Washington argues that the political state of affairs for Blacks had deteriorated because the political process started at the top, not the bottom. He believes change will come from the bottom, starting with Christian character, followed by education, property, and economic clout. Washington then pauses to remind the reader that, though a Republican, he has "always refrained from activity in party politics, and expect to pursue this policy in the future. So in this connection I shall refrain, as I always have done, from entering upon any discussion of mere party politics. What I shall say of politics will bear upon the race problem and the civilisation of the South in the larger sense."[21] This subtle parsing of race politics from party politics is vintage Washington. Here is the master politician claiming to be politically pure, with his issues deftly raised to a level beyond politics. He then turns to the question of why Black political power has diminished. The answer, he believes, is not found in the courts or legislation, for they are no more than an expression of the social and political context that informs them. Southern Whites, most of whom moved to the Democratic Party, were not ready to recognize Black progress. Washington concludes the section with a position predating Du Bois's famous "color line" of 1903, suggesting that "so long as the colour line is the dividing line in politics, so long will there be trouble."[22]

The second half of the chapter shows Washington at his most politically direct. He emphatically states, "I do not favour the Negro's giving up anything which is fundamental and which has been guaranteed to him by the Constitution of the United States. It is not best for him to relinquish any of his rights; nor would his doing so be best for the Southern White man."[23] This statement is followed by one of Washington's best-known open political attacks and an open letter to the Democratic leadership of the state constitutional convention of Louisiana as they actively sought to eliminate Black voters from the state's rolls. Washington's thoughts were printed in the *Picayune* and later by the Tuskegee Institute Press. Rather than attack the restrictions outright, he argued indirectly and claimed that it was in the best interest of Whites. He appealed to fairness by urging that if restrictions on voting eligibility are to be imposed they must apply to both races: "Any law controlling the ballot that is not absolutely just and fair to both races, will work more permanent injury to the white than to the blacks."[24] In a graceful tactical move, he then took a step back from his demands to appeal to the conscience of his White readers. Here he borrows a few lines from his 1895 speech: "You know us. You know that we have cleared your forests, tilled your fields, nursed your children, and protected your families."[25] Trust us, he says. Soon enough, smart tax-paying Black men and smart tax-paying White men will find a common political ground that transcends race.

Washington also worked in 1900 in Alabama and Georgia against efforts to disenfranchise Blacks. In Georgia, he joined forces with more radical leaders, such as Du Bois, in fighting the Hardwick bill. This bill called for a legislative change through an amendment in state law, allowing for a grandfather clause and a form of the literacy test.[26] Washington and others claimed a victory when the bill failed. But as historian Michael Perman has argued, it mattered little since Black voting in Georgia was virtually nonexistent by that date.[27] Washington's argument against the bill, included in this chapter in an interview with the *Atlanta Constitution*, demonstrates his careful challenges to White power. He carefully shows how the bill would harm Whites as well as Blacks, ruining state finances, undermining the Constitution, hurting the poor, and contributing to a rise in crime. He closes the interview by reiterating the idea (perhaps disingenuously) that his was not a political fight but a moral one, about the "principles of citizenship."[28] Reading carefully, one perceives the real Washington, striking subtle but masterful blows: "No form of repression will help matters [in the South]. Spain tried that for 400 years and was the loser. There is one, and but one way out of our present difficulties, and that is the right way."[29] This moral argument carries a veiled threat to those failing to acknowledge the powers of those on the bottom. Readers knew quite well that Spain had just been overthrown in Cuba by a people's revolution two years before.

Washington soon offered a case study of how a bottom-up, gradualist economic formula would lead to successful cooperation between the races. In the 1903 article, "Two Generations under Freedom," Washington used an example from Michigan as evidence of how hard work, economic thrift, property ownership, aesthetic display, and the trust of the White community bore the first fruits of political equality.[30] Embodying the paradox of Washington's utopian pragmatism, Black success in the present and future is expressed in photographs of a Black agrarian world softened into a Pictorialist dream of a bygone era that never existed. On a visit to southwest Michigan, he discovered extraordinary racial harmony (but no "social mingling") and prosperity in small, racially mixed towns in Cass County. With the support of Whites, particularly the local Quaker community, Blacks progressed in every way imaginable. Most impressive for Washington was the acceptance of Blacks in positions of political power. Blacks were members of the County Board of Supervisors and held the offices of director of the school board, town clerks and treasurers, and tax collector. In the end, a little "African colony," such as Calvin, Michigan, offered evidence of how politically savvy Blacks could be successful at self-governance.

Yet Washington's approach was quite different when he met with resistance for the first time. Starting with his disappointment at the failure of the 1898 Louisiana Convention to prevent discrimination at the voting booth, he began a lifetime of activist maneuvering in the shadows. These actions, told by Harlan in "The Secret Life of Booker T. Washington," reveal a political tactician who carefully read the social context and decided whether to attack in the open or with stealth.[31] They also represent the first time, according to Harlan, that Washington's efforts included "secret involvement in a public issue not connected with his institution."[32] When he made public statements, they were ambiguous. Yet for all of his resistance to being pinned down, one thing remained consistent. He never wavered in his belief that meaningful change could not be legislated from the top. Only a Darwinian ascent such as his personal rise from slavery could deliver real progress.

The year 1912 marks another turning point in Washington's career; actually, a turning back, for at that point, he returned to the brief moment of outspokenness during the Spanish American War speech of 1898. The year 1911 had been a terrible year. He had tried and failed to humiliate the newly formed NAACP.[33] He was the center of a national sex scandal and beating.[34] Washington's access to the presidency, which faded under Theodore Roosevelt until it was almost gone under Howard Taft, was nonexistent under the new president, Woodrow Wilson. On certain occasions, Washington would employ an angry voice, attacking social injustices.

Washington's public statements came to the surface in the 1912 essay for *The Century Magazine*, "Is the Negro Having a Fair Chance?" It embodies the

Tuskegee leader's ability to provide conflicting points of view and serves as an example of how he frustrated those who wanted to support him. The article opens and closes by answering the title's question in the affirmative. At both ends of the piece, we learn that there is no doubt that Black Americans have it much better than Blacks elsewhere in the world. Yet the large center of the essay is a litany of problems confronting African Americans. If one took out the first and last pages, clearly the answer to the title's question is absolutely no. Washington clearly outlines the problems for Blacks: lack of employment; unfairness in the criminal justice system; discrimination in hotel accommodations, rail travel, and education; and the outright physical intimidation of lynching. These problems are framed within political structures on regional, state, and federal levels. The result of having "1300 counties in the Southern States is [that each] is a law unto itself. The result is that there are almost as many race problems as there are counties."[35]

Washington even agrees with a Black journalist that Whites, who never read Black newspapers, do not really know anything about African Americans. On the last page of the article is a vivid description of the horrors of lynching, including the false verdicts and the wrath of mobs. A former Alabama governor is quoted as saying that he personally knew of five innocent men lynched during his administration. Washington paints a gruesome picture of a mob grabbing a helpless Black man who had been charged with rape. "Then comes more excitement and more whiskey. Then comes the hanging, the shooting, or the burning of the body."[36] Here, then, is another example of Washington's mixed-message approach to political issues.

The mix of a new degree of outspokenness and the old method of retreat runs through all of Washington's political views after 1912, including the other voting rights' issue of the day—women's suffrage. This proved to be a difficult subject for all Black leaders because of the reluctance of many White women in the movement to support Black rights.[37] For years, Washington allowed that he supported Black women's clubs to deflect questioning about his position on this subject. Moreover, early in his career, he developed a significant relationship with the leadership of the women's rights movement, including Emily Howland, Susan B. Anthony, and Frances Willard.[38] In 1906, he even wrote about Frederick Douglass's advocacy of women's right and the Seneca Falls Convention.[39] But pressure mounted as suffragists sought his endorsement. Washington continually dodged the subject, finally making a statement in the *New York Times* in 1908 largely opposing it.[40] He told readers that women already possessed important influences in many other spheres of public life. But he left the door open to discussion, stating that the question should be left to the "judgment" of women. Not surprisingly, those supporting women's voting rights were disappointed with his stance.

Then, in 1912, certainly in response to this criticism, he clarified his views on suffrage. In a chapter devoted entirely to women in *The Man Farthest Down*, Washington declared that, much to his surprise, he found himself deeply interested in women's issues. The chapter is striking in many ways. First, though no doubt largely informed by his traveling companion, the noted sociologist

Robert Park, the writing tells us what details Washington noticed in his travels. The second aspect of the chapter is how Washington weaves together two basic strands of the women's movement, namely, the vote and temperance. Finally, the chapter allows the viewer to witness Washington trying to solve a problem. Although the remedies are ambiguous (and even perplexing when he claims African American women have advantages over European women), nonetheless he concludes that "in Europe the man farthest down is woman."[41]

In 1915, the last year of his life, Washington's ambiguity evaporated. Realizing that the world was different, the rapidly aging Washington embraced both legal and economic pressures to advance social and political change. World War I had begun in Europe; Woodrow Wilson proved to be no friend of Blacks; and a racist film, *Birth of a Nation*, all helped to bring together the Du Bois and Washington camps. Adding to these national and international setbacks was Washington's personal hardship. His sister died in May 1915. In his last days, a new generation, including Marcus Garvey and Mary McLeod Bethune, sought his counsel. His idealism faded into realism. Only months before he died in 1915, he came out fully endorsing women's suffrage:

To Mary L. Hay, March 6, 1915

Dear Madame:
I write to say that I am altogether in favor of woman suffrage and perfectly willing to have you quote me in the forthcoming suffrage edition of the *Pittsburgh Sun* which is to appear under the auspices of the Equal Franchise Federation of Pittsburgh.

With kindest regards, I am, yours very truly, Booker T. Washington.[42]

Was it all too little too late? He finally signed up for something he was reluctant to do. However, this new stance was never published, and it never made national news, nor did anyone seem to be listening to his late attacks on the failure to fund Black education[43] or the ills of segregation.[44]

Contents

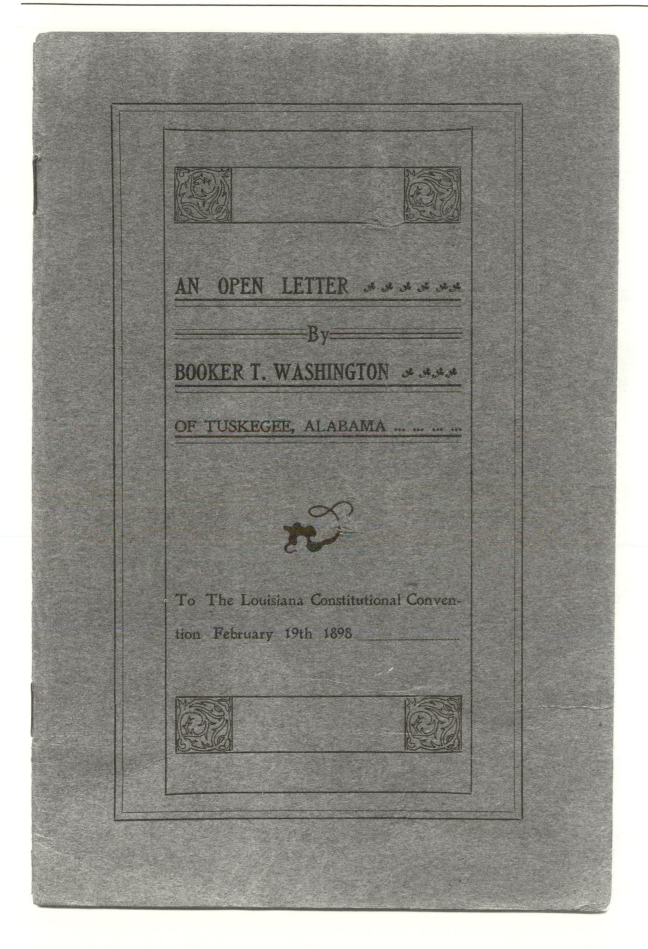

AN OPEN LETTER ❧ ❧ ❧ ❧

By

BOOKER T. WASHINGTON ❧ ❧ ❧

OF TUSKEGEE, ALABAMA ... ...

To The Louisiana Constitutional Convention February 19th 1898

TUSKEGEE, Alabama, Feb. 19, 1898.

To THE LOUISIANA STATE CONSTITUTIONAL CONVENTION

In addressing you this letter, I know that I am running the risk of appearing to meddle with something that does not concern me. But since I know that nothing but sincere love for our beautiful Southland, which I hold as near to my heart as any of you can, and a sincere love for every black and white man within her borders, is the only thing actuating me to write. I am willing to be misjudged, if need be, if I can accomplish a little good.

But I do not believe that you, gentlemen of the Convention, will misinterpret my motives. What I say will, I believe, be considered in the same earnest spirit in which I write.

I am no politician, on the other hand, I have always advised my race to give attention to acquiring property, intelligence and character, as the necessary bases of good citizenship, rather than to mere political agitation. But the question upon which I write is out of the region of ordinary politics; it affects the civilization of two races, not for a day alone, but for a very long time to come; it is up in the region of duty of man to man, of Christian to Christian.

Since the war, no State has had such an opportunity to settle for all time the race question, so far as it concerns politics, as is now given in Louisiana. Will your Convention set an example to the world in this respect? Will Louisiana take such high and just grounds in respect to the Negro that no one can doubt that the South is as good a friend to the Negro as he possesses elsewhere? In all this, gentlemen of the Convention, I am not pleading for the Negro alone, but for the morals, the higher life of the white man as well. For the more I study this question, the more I am convinced that it is not so much a question as to what the white man will do with the Negro, as to what the Negro will do with the white man's civilization.

The Negro agrees with you that it is necessary to the salvation of the South that restriction be put upon the ballot. I know that you have two serious problems before you; ignorant and corrupt government on the one hand, and on the other, a way to restrict the ballot so that control will be in the hands of the intelligent, without regard to race. With the sincerest sympathy with you in your efforts to find a way out of the difficulty, I want to suggest that no State in the South can make a law that will provide an opportunity or temptation for an ignorant white man to

2

vote and withhold the same opportunity from an ignorant colored man, without injuring both men. No State can make a law that can thus be executed, without dwarfing for all time the morals of the white man in the South. Any law controlling the ballot, that is not absolutely just and fair to both races, will work more permanent injury to the whites than to the blacks.

The Negro does not object to an educational or property test, but let the law be so clear that no one clothed with State authority will be tempted to perjure and degrade himself, by putting one interpretation upon it for the white man and another for the black man. Study the history of the South, and you will find that where there has been the most dishonesty in the matter of voting, there you will find to-day the lowest moral condition of both races. First, there was the temptation to act wrongly with the Negro's ballot. From this it was an easy step to dishonesty with the white man's ballot, to the carrying of concealed weapons, to the murder of a Negro, and then to the murder of a white man, and then to lynching. I entreat you not to pass such a law as will prove an eternal millstone about the neck of your children.

No man can have respect for government and officers of the law, when he knows, deep down in his heart, that the exercise of the franchise is tainted with fraud.

The road that the South has been compelled to travel during the last thirty years has been strewn with thorns and thistles. It has been as one groping through long darkness into the light. The time is not distant when the world will begin to appreciate the real character of the burden that was imposed upon the South when 4,500,000 ex-slaves, ignorant and impoverished, were given the franchise. No people had ever been given such a problem to solve. History had blazed no path through the wilderness that could be followed. For thirty years, we wandered in the wilderness. We are beginning to get out. But there is but one road out, and all makeshifts, expedients, "profit and loss calculations," but lead into the swamps, quicksands, quagmires and jungles. There is a highway that will lead both races out into the pure, beautiful sunshine, where there will be nothing to hide and nothing to explain, where both races can grow strong and true and useful in every fibre of their being. I believe that your Convention will find this highway, that it will enact a fundamental law which will be absolutely just and fair to white and black alike.

I beg of you, further, that in the degree that you close the ballot-box against the ignorant, that you open the school house. More than one half of the people of your State are Negroes. No State can long prosper when a large percentage of its citizenship is in ignorance and poverty and has no interest in government. I beg of you that you do not treat us as alien people,

3

We are not aliens. You know us; you know that we have cleared
your forests, tilled your fields, nursed your children and protected
your families. There is an attachment between us that few understand. While I do not presume to be able to advise you, yet
it is in my heart to say that if your Convention would do something that would prevent, for all time, strained relations between
the two races, and would permanently settle the matter of political relations in our Southern States, at least, let the very best
educational opportunities be provided for both races· and add to
this the enactment of an election law that shall be incapable of
unjust discrimination, at the same time providing that in proportion as the ignorant secure education, property and character,
they will be given the right of citizenship. Any other course will
take from one-half your citizens interest in the State, and hope
and ambition to become intelligent producers and taxpayers—to
become useful and virtuous citizens. Any other course will tie
the white citizens of Louisiana to a body of death.

The Negroes are not unmindful of the fact that the white people of your State pay the greater proportion of the school taxes,
and that the poverty of the State prevents it from doing all that
it desires for public education, yet I believe you will agree with
me, that ignorance is more costly to the State than education,
that it will cost Louisiana more not to educate her Negroes than
it will cost to educate them. In connection with a generous provision for public schools, I believe that nothing will so help my
own people in your State as provision at some institution for the
highest academic and normal training, in connection with thorough
training in agriculture, mechanics and domestic economy. The
fact is that 90 per cent. of our people depend upon the common
occupations for their living, and outside of the cities 85 per cent.
depend upon agriculture for support. Notwithstanding this, our
people have been educated since the war in everything else but
the very thing that most of them live by First-class training in
agriculture, horticulture, dairying, stock-raising, the mechanical
arts and domestic economy, will make us intelligent producers,
and not only help us to contribute our proportion as tax-payers,
but will result in retaining much money in the State that now
goes outside for that which can be produced in the State. An institution that will give this training of the hand, along with the
highest mental culture, will soon convince our people that their
salvation is in the ownership of property, industrial and business
development, rather than in mere political agitation.

The highest test of the civilization of any race is in its willingness to extend a helping hand to the less fortunate. A race,
like an individual, lifts itself up by lifting others up. Surely no
people ever had a greater chance to exhibit the highest Christian

4

fortitude and magnanimity than is now presented to the people of Louisiana. It requires little wisdom or statesmanship to repress, to crush out, to retard the hopes and aspirations of a people, but the highest and most profound statesmanship is shown in guiding and stimulating a people so that every fibre in the body, mind and soul shall be made to contribute in the highest degree to the usefulness and nobility of the State. It is along this line that I pray God the thoughts and activities of your Convention be guided. Respectfully submitted,

BOOKER T WASHINGTON

5

AN INTERVIEW ON THE HARDWICK BILL.

The Hardwick Bill was a measure introduced in the Georgia Legislature for the purpose of disfranchising the colored people. While this Bill was before the Legislature, Principal Booker T Washington gave the following interview to The Atlanta Constitution. The Bill was defeated in the Legislature, receiving only 3 votes in its favor in the Lower House where it was introduced, 137 votes being cast against it.

Professor Booker T Washington, the head of the famous industrial school for colored youths at Tuskegee, and probably the foremost man of his race to-day, gave his views on the question of franchise restriction to a representative of The Constitution yesterday Professor Washington spent the day in the city, having come here on business. When asked for an expression on the Hardwick Bill, he said that he did not care to discuss that or any other specific measure, but on the subject of an educational qualification restricting the ballot to the intelligence of the country, he had very decided views. "I dread the idea of seeming to intrude my views too often upon the public," said Professor Washington, "but I feel that I can speak very frankly upon the subject, because I am speaking to the South and Southern people. It has been my experience that when our Southern people are convinced tbat one speaks from the heart and tries to speak that which he feels is for the permanent good of both races, he is always accorded a respectful hearing. No possible influence could tempt me to say that which I thought would tend merely to stir up strife or to induce my own people to return to the old time methods of political agitation, rather than give their time, as most of them are now doing, to the more fundamental principles of citizenship, education, industry and prosperity

DECISION LEFT TO THE SOUTH.

"The question of the rights and elevation of the Negro is now left almost wholly to the South, as it has been long pleaded should be done," added Professor Washington. "The South has over and over said to the North and her representatives have repeated it in Congress, that if the North and the Federal Government would 'hands off,' the South would deal justly and fairly with the Negro. The prayer of the South has been almost wholly answered. The world is watching the South as it has never done before. Not only have the North and the Federal Congress practically agreed to leave the matter of the Negro's citizenship

6

in the hands of the South, but many conservative and intelligent Negroes in recent years have advised the Negro to cast his lot more closely with the Southern white man, and to cease a continued senseless opposition to his interests. This policy has gained ground to such an extent that the white man controls practically every State and every county and township in the South.

VARIOUS ELECTION LAWS.

"There is a feeling of friendship and mutual confidence growing between the two races that is most encouraging. But in the midst of this condition of things, one is surprised and almost astounded at the measures being introduced and passed by the various law-making bodies of the Southern States. What is the object of the election laws? Since there is white domination throughout the South, there can be but one object in the passing of these laws—to disfranchise the Negro. At the present time the South has a great opportunity as well as responsibility Will she shirk this opportunity or will she look matters in the face and grapple with it bravely taking the Negro by the hand and seeking to lift him up to the point where he will be prepared for citizenship? None of the laws passed by any Southern State, or that are now pending, will do this. These new laws will simply change the form of the present bad election system and widen the breach between the two races, when we might, by doing right, cement the friendship between them.

DANGEROUS ALL AROUND.

"To pass an election law with an 'understanding' clause, simply means that some individual will be tempted to perjure his soul and degrade his whole life by deciding in too many cases that the Negro does not 'understand' the constitution and that a white man, even though he be an ignorant white foreigner with recently acquired citizenship, does 'understand' it. In a recent article President Hadley, of Yale University, covers the whole truth when he says 'We cannot make a law which shall allow the right exercise of a discretionary power and prohibit its wrong use.' The 'understanding' clause may serve to keep Negroes from voting, but the time will come when it will also be used to keep white men from voting, if any number of them disagree with the election officer who holds the discretionary power While discussing this matter, it would be unfair to the white people of the South and to my own race, if I were not perfectly frank. What interpretation does the outside world and the Negro put upon these 'understanding' clauses? Either that they are meant to leave a loophole so that the ignorant white man can vote, or to prevent the educated Negro from voting. If this interpretation is correct in either case, the law is unjust. It is unjust

7

to the white man because it takes away from him the incentive to prepare himself to become an intelligent voter. It is unjust to the Negro because it makes him feel that no matter how well he prepares himself in education for voting, he will be refused a vote through the operation of the 'understanding' clause.

IN A FALSE POSITION.

"And what is worse, this treatment will keep alive in the Negro's breast the feeling that he is being wrongfully treated by the Southern white man, and therefore he ought to vote against him, whereas, with just treatment the years will not be many before a large portion of the colored people will be willing to vote with the Southern white people. Then again, I believe that such laws put our Southern white people in a false position. I cannot think that there is any large number of white people in the South who are so ignorant or so poor that they cannot get education and property enough that will enable them to stand the test by the side of the Negro in these respects. I do not believe that these white people want it continually advertised to the world that some special law must be passed by which they will seem to be given an unfair advantage over the Negro by reason of their ignorance or poverty It is unfair to blame the Negro for not preparing himself for citizenship by acquiring intelligence, and then when he does get education and property, to pass a law that can be so operated as to prevent him from being a citizen, even though he may be a large tax-payer. The Southern white people have reached the point where they can afford to be just and generous, where there will be nothing to hide and nothing to explain. It is an easy matter, requiring little thought, generosity or statesmanship to push a weak man down when he is struggling to get up. Any one can do that. Greatness, generosity, statesmanship are shown in stimulating, encouraging every individual in the body politic to make of himself the most useful, intelligent and patriotic citizen possible. Take from the Negro all incentive to make himself and children useful property-holding citizens, and can any one blame him for becoming a beast capable of committing any crime?

REPRESSION WILL FAIL.

"I have the greatest sympathy with the South in its efforts to find a way out of present difficulties, but I do not want to see the South tie itself to a body of death. No form of repression will help matters. Spain tried that for 400 years and was the loser There is one, and but one way out of our present difficulties, and that is the right way All else but right will fail. We must face the fact that the tendency of the world is forward, and not backward. That all civilized countries are growing in the direction of giving liberty to their citizens, not withholding it. Slavery ceased

8

because it was opposed to the progress of both races, and so all forms of repression will fail—must fail—in the long run. Whenever a change is thought necessary to be made in the fundamental law of the States, as Governor Candler says in his recent message 'The man who is virtuous and intelligent, however poor or humble, or of whatever race or color, may be safely intrusted with the ballot.' And as the recent industrial convention at Huntsville, Ala., composed of the best brains of the white South, puts it 'To move the race problem from the domain of politics, where it has so long and seriously vexed the industrial progress of the South, we recommend to the several States of the South the adoption of an intelligent standard of citizenship THAT WILL EQUALLY APPLY TO BLACK AND WHITE ALIKE.' We must depend upon the mental, industrial and moral elevation of all the people to bring relief The history of the world proves that there is no other safe cure. We may find a way to stop the Negro from selling his vote, but what about the conscience of the man who buys his vote? We must go to the bottom of the evil.

SHOULD BE EQUALITY OF TREATMENT.

"Our Southern States cannot afford to have suspicion of evil intention resting upon them. It not only will hurt them morally, but financially In conclusion, let me add that the Southern States owe it to themselves not to pass unfair election laws, because it is against the constitution of the United States, and each State is under a solemn obligation that every citizen, regardless of color, shall be given the full protection of the laws. No State can make a law that can be so interpreted to mean one thing when applied to the black man and another when applied to the white man, without disregarding the constitution of the United States. In the second place, unfair election laws in the long run, I repeat, will injure the white man more than the Negro, such laws will not only disfranchise the Negro, but the white man as well. The history of the country shows that in those States where the election laws are most just, there you will find the most wealth, the most intelligence and the smallest percentage of crime. The best element of white people in the South are not in favor of oppressing the Negro, they want to help him up, but they are sometimes mistaken as to the best method of doing this. While I have spoken very plainly I do not believe that any one will misinterpret my motives. I am not in politics per se, nor do I intend to be, neither would I encourage my people to become mere politicians, but the question I have been discussing strikes at the very fundamental principles of citizenship."—Atlanta Constitution, 1900.

IS THE NEGRO HAVING A
FAIR CHANCE?

BY BOOKER T. WASHINGTON

IF I were asked the simple, direct question, "Does the negro in America have a fair chance?" it would be easy to answer simply, "No," and then refer to instances with which every one is familiar to justify this reply. Such a statement would, however, be misleading to any one who was not intimately acquainted with the actual situation. For that reason I have chosen to make my answer not less candid and direct, I hope, but a little more circumstantial.

THE NEGRO TREATED BETTER IN AMERICA THAN ELSEWHERE

ALTHOUGH I have never visited either Africa or the West Indies to see for myself the condition of the people in these countries, I have had opportunities from time to time, outside of the knowledge I have gained from books, to get some insight into actual conditions there. But I do not intend to assert or even suggest that the condition of the American negro is satisfactory, nor that he has in all things a fair chance. Nevertheless, from all that I can learn I believe I am safe in saying that nowhere are there ten millions of black people who have greater opportunities or are making greater progress than the negroes in America.

I know that few native Africans will agree with me in this statement. For example, we had at Tuskegee a student from the Gold Coast who came to America to study in our Bible Training School and incidentally to learn something of our methods of study and work. He did not approve at all of our course of study. There was not enough theology, and too much work to suit him. As far as he was concerned, he could not see any value in learning to work, and he thought it was a pretty poor sort of country in which the people had to devote so much time to labor. "In my country," he said, "every-

thing grows of itself. We do not have to work. We can devote all our time to the larger life."

LITTLE IMMIGRATION OF NEGROES

IN the last ten years the official records show that 37,000 negroes have left other countries to take residence in the United States. I can find no evidence to show that any considerable number of black people have given up residence in America.

The striking fact is, that negroes from other countries are constantly coming into the United States, and few are going out. This seems in part to answer the question as to whether the negro is having a fair chance in America as compared with any other country in which negroes live in any large numbers.

By far the largest number of negro immigrants come from the West Indies. Even Haiti, a free negro republic, furnishes a considerable number of immigrants every year. In all my experience and observation, however, I cannot recall a single instance in which a negro has left the United States to become a citizen of the Haitian Republic. On the other hand, not a few leaders of thought and action among the negroes in the United States are those who have given up citizenship in the little Black Republic in order to live under the Stars and Stripes. The majority of the colored people who come from the West Indies do so because of the economic opportunities which the United States offers them. Another large group, however, comes to get education. Here at the Tuskegee Institute in Alabama we usually have not far from one hundred students from South America and the various West Indian Islands. In the matter of opportunity to secure the old-fashioned, abstract book education several of the West Indian Islands give negroes a better chance than is afforded them in most of

46

IS THE NEGRO HAVING A FAIR CHANCE? 47

our Southern States, but for industrial and technical education they are compelled to come to the United States.

In the matter of political and civil rights, including protection of life and property and even-handed justice in the courts, negroes in the West Indies have the advantage of negroes in the United States. In the island of Jamaica, for example, there are about 15,000 white people and 600,000 black people, but of the "race problem," in regard to which there is much agitation in this country, one hears almost nothing there. Jamaica has neither mobs, race riots, lynchings, nor burnings, such as disgrace our civilization. In that country there is likewise no bitterness between white man and black man. One reason for this is that the laws are conceived and executed with exact and absolute justice, without regard to race or color

UNEQUAL LAWS THE CAUSE OF RACIAL TROUBLE IN AMERICA

REDUCED to its lowest terms, the fact is that a large part of our racial troubles in the United States grow out of some attempt to pass and execute a law that will make and keep one man superior to another, whether he is intrinsically superior or not. No greater harm can be done to any group of people than to let them feel that a statutory enactment can keep them superior to anybody else. No greater injury can be done to any youth than to let him feel that because he belongs to this or that race, or because of his color, he will be advanced in life regardless of his own merits or efforts.

In what I have said I do not mean to suggest that in the West Indian Islands there is any more social intermingling between whites and blacks than there is in the United States. The trouble in most parts of the United States is that mere civil and legal privileges are confused with social intermingling. The fact that two men ride in the same railway coach does not mean in any country in the world that they are socially equal.

The facts seem to show, however, that after the West Indian negro has carefully weighed his civil and political privileges against the economic and other advantages to be found in the United States, he decides that, all things considered, he has a better chance in the United States than at home. The negro in Haiti votes, but votes have not made that country happy, or have not even made it free, in any true sense of the word. There is one other fact I might add to this comparison nearly all the negro church organizations in the United States have mission churches in the islands, as they have also in Africa.

Does the negro in our country have a fair chance as compared with the native black man in Africa, the home of the negro? In the midst of the preparation of this article, I met Bishop Isaiah B. Scott of the Methodist Episcopal Church, one of the strongest and most intelligent colored men that I know Bishop Scott has spent the greater part of his life in the Southern States, but during the last seven years he has lived in Liberia and traveled extensively on the west coast of Africa, where he has come into contact with all classes of European white people. In answer to my question, Bishop Scott dictated the following sentence, which he authorized me to use:

"The fairest white man that I have met in dealing with the colored man is the American white man. He understands the colored man better because of his contact with him, and he has more respect for the colored man who has accomplished something."

Basing my conclusions largely on conversations which I have had with native Africans, with negro missionaries, and with negro diplomatic officials who have lived in Africa, especially on the west coast and in South Africa, I am led to the conclusion that, all things considered, the negro in the United States has a better chance than he has in Africa.

THE NEGRO AS A DEPENDENT RACE

IN certain directions the negro has had greater opportunities in the States in which he served as a slave than he has had in the States in which he has been for a century or more a free man. This statement is borne out by the fact that in the South the negro rarely has to seek labor, but, on the other hand, labor seeks him. In all my experience in the Southern States, I have rarely seen a negro man or woman seeking labor who did not find it. In the South the negro has business opportunities that he does not have elsewhere.

While in social matters the lines are strictly drawn, the negro is less handicapped in business in the South than any other part of the country. He is sought after as a depositor in banks. If he wishes to borrow money, he gets it from the local bank just as quickly as the white man with the same business standing. If the negro is in the grocery business or in the dry-goods trade, or if he operates a drug store, he gets his goods from the wholesale dealer just as readily and on as good terms as his white competitor If the Southern white man has a dwelling-house, a store-house, factory, school, or court-house to erect, it is natural for him to employ a colored man as builder or contractor to perform that work. What is said to be the finest school building in the city of New Orleans was erected by a colored contractor. In the North a colored man who ran a large grocery store would be looked upon as a curiosity. The Southern white man frequently buys his groceries from a negro merchant.

Fortunately, the greater part of the colored people in the South have remained as farmers on the soil. The late census shows that eighty per cent. of Southern negroes live on the land.

There are few cases where a black man cannot buy and own a farm in the South. It is as a farmer in the Southern States that the masses of my race have economically and industrially the largest opportunity. No one stops to ask before purchasing a bale of cotton or a bushel of corn if it has been produced by a white hand or a black hand.

The negro now owns, as near as I can estimate, 15,000 grocery and dry-goods stores, 300 drug stores, and 63 banks. Negroes pay taxes on between $600,000,000 and $700,000,000 of property of various kinds in the United States. Unless he had had a reasonably fair chance in the South, the negro could not have gained and held this large amount of property, and would not have been able to enter in the commerce of this country to the extent that he has.

SKILLED NEGRO LABOR BETTER TREATED IN THE SOUTH THAN IN THE NORTH

As a skilled laborer, the negro has a better opportunity in the South than in the North. I think it will be found generally true in the South as elsewhere that wherever the negro is strong in numbers and in skill he gets on well with the trades-unions. In these cases the unions seek to get him in, or they leave him alone, and in the latter case do not seek to control him. In the Southern States, where the race enters in large numbers in the trades, the trades-unions have not had any appreciable effect in hindering the progress of the negro as a skilled laborer or as a worker in special industries, such as coal-mining, iron-mining, etc. In border cities, like St. Louis, Washington, and Baltimore, however, the negro rarely finds work in such industries as brick-laying and carpentry One of the saddest examples of this fact that I ever witnessed was in the City of Washington, where on the campus of Howard University, a negro institution, a large brick building was in process of erection. Every man laying brick on this building was white, every man carrying a hod was a negro. The white man, in this instance, was willing to erect a building in which negroes could study Latin, but was not willing to give negroes a chance to lay the bricks in its walls.

Let us consider for a moment the negro in the professions in the Southern States. Aside from school teaching and preaching, into which the racial question enters in only a slight degree, there remain law and medicine. All told, there are not more than 700 colored lawyers in the Southern States, while there are perhaps more than 3000 doctors, dentists, and pharmacists. With few exceptions, colored lawyers feel, as they tell me, that they do not have a fair chance before a white jury when a white lawyer is on the other side of the case. Even in communities where negro lawyers are not discriminated against by juries, their clients feel that there is danger in intrusting cases to a colored lawyer. Mainly for these two reasons, colored lawyers are not numerous in the South; yet, in cases where colored lawyers combine legal practice with trading and real estate, they have in several instances been highly successful.

THE DIFFICULTY OF OBTAINING UNIFORM TREATMENT

HERE again, however, it is difficult to generalize. People speak of the "race

IS THE NEGRO HAVING A FAIR CHANCE? 49

question" in the South, overlooking the fact that each one of the 1300 counties in the Southern States is a law unto itself. The result is that there are almost as many race problems as there are counties. The negro may have a fair chance in one county, and have no chance at all in the adjoining county The Hon. Josiah T Settles, for example, has practised both criminal and civil law for thirty years in Memphis. He tells me that he meets with no discrimination on account of his color either from judges, lawyers, or juries. There are other communities, like New Orleans and Little Rock, where negro lawyers are accorded the same fair treatment, and, I ought to add, that, almost without exception, negro lawyers tell me they are treated fairly by white judges and white lawyers.

The professional man who is making the greatest success in the South is the negro doctor, and I should include the pharmacists and dentists with the physicians and surgeons. Except in a few cities, white doctors are always willing to consult with negro doctors.

The young negro physician in the South soon finds himself with a large and paying practice, and, as a rule, he makes use of this opportunity to improve the health conditions of his race in the community Some of the most prosperous men of my race in the South are negro doctors. Again, the very fact that a negro cannot buy soda-water in a white drug store makes an opportunity for the colored drug store, which often becomes a sort of social center for the colored population.

From an economic point of view, the negro in the North, when compared with the white man, does not have a fair chance. This is the feeling not only of the colored people themselves, but of almost every one who has examined into the conditions under which colored men work. But here also one is likely to form a wrong opinion. There is, to begin with, this general difference between the North and the South, that whereas in the South there is, as I have already suggested, a job looking for every idle man, in the North, on the contrary, there are frequently two or three idle men looking for every job. In some of the large cities of the North there are organizations to secure employment for colored people. For a number of years I have kept in pretty close touch with those at the head of these organizations, and they tell me that in many cases they have been led to believe that the negro has a harder time in finding employment than is actually true. The reason is that those who are out of employment seek these organizations. Those who have steady work, in positions which they have held for years, do not seek them.

As a matter of fact, I have been surprised to find how large a number of colored people there are in Boston, New York, Philadelphia, and Chicago who hold responsible positions in factories, stores, banks, and other places. In regard to these people one hears very little. There is a colored man, for example, in Cleveland who has been for years private secretary to a railway president. In St. Paul there is a colored man who holds a similar position; in Baltimore there is still another colored private secretary to a railway president.

THE SHIFTING OF OCCUPATIONS

IN recent years there has been a great shifting of employment between the races. A few years ago all the rough work in the mines, on the railway, and elsewhere was performed by Irish immigrants. Now this work is done by Poles, Hungarians, and Italians. In cities like New York, Chicago, and Pittsburg one finds to-day fewer colored people employed as hotel waiters, barbers, and porters than twenty years ago. In New York, however, many colored men are employed in the streets and in the subways. In Pittsburg thousands of colored men are employed in the iron mills. In Chicago negroes are employed very largely in the packing-houses. Twenty years ago in these cities there were almost no colored people in these industries. In addition to the changes I have mentioned, many colored people have gone into businesses of various kinds on their own account. It should be remembered, also, that, while in some trades and in some places discrimination is made against the negro, in other trades and in other places this discrimination works in his favor The case in point is the Pullman-car service. I question whether any white man, however efficient, could secure a job as a Pullman-car porter.

BETTER OPPORTUNITY FOR EDUCATION IN THE NORTH

IN the North, as a rule, the negro has the same opportunities for education as his white neighbor When it comes to making use of this education, however, he is frequently driven to a choice between becoming an agitator, who makes his living out of the troubles of his race, or emigrating to the Southern States, where the opportunities for educated colored men are large. One of the greatest sources of bitterness and despondency among colored people in the North grows out of their inability to find a use for their education after they have obtained it. Again, they are seldom sure of just what they may or may not do. If one is a stranger in a city, he does not know in what hotel he will be permitted to stay, he is not certain what seat he may occupy in the theater, or whether he will be able to obtain a meal in a restaurant.

THE UNCERTAINTY OF TREATMENT OF THE RACE IN THE NORTH

THE uncertainty, the constant fear and expectation of rebuff which the colored man experiences in the North, is often more humiliating and more wearing than the frank and impersonal discrimination which he meets in the South. This is all the more true because the colored youth in most of the Northern States, educated as they are in the same schools with white youths, taught by the same teachers, and inspired by the same ideals of American citizenship, are not prepared for the discrimination that meets them when they leave school.

Despite all this, it cannot be denied that the negro has advantages in the North which are denied him in the South. They are the opportunity to vote and to take part, to some extent, in making and administering the laws by which he is governed, the opportunity to obtain an education, and, what is of still greater importance, fair and unbiased treatment in the courts, the protection of the law

I have touched upon conditions North and South, which, whether they affect the negro favorably or adversely, are for the most part so firmly entrenched in custom, prejudice, and human nature that they must perhaps be left to the slow changes of time. There are certain conditions in the South, however, in regard to which colored people feel perhaps more keenly because they believe if they were generally understood they would be remedied. Very frequently the negro people suffer injury and wrong in the South because they have or believe they have no way of making their grievances known. Not only are they not represented in the legislatures, but it is sometimes hard to get a hearing even in the press. On one of my educational campaigns in the South I was accompanied by a colored newspaper man. He was an enterprising sort of chap and at every public meeting we held he would manage in some way to address the audience on the subject of his paper On one occasion, after appealing to the colored people for some time, he turned to the white portion of the audience.

"You white folks," he said, "ought to read our colored papers to find out what colored people are doing. You ought to find out what they are doing and what they are thinking. You don't know anything about us," he added. "Don't you know a colored man can't get his name in a white paper unless he commits a crime?"

I do not know whether the colored newspaper man succeeded in getting any subscriptions by this speech or not, but there was much truth in his statement.

THE GREATEST SOURCE OF DISSATISFACTION TO THE NEGRO IN THE SOUTH

ONE thing that many negroes feel keenly, although they do not say much about it to either black or white people, is the conditions of railway travel in the South.

Now and then the negro is compelled to travel. With few exceptions, the railroads are almost the only great business concerns in the South that pursue the policy of taking just as much money from the black traveler as from the white traveler without feeling that they ought, as a matter of justice and fair play, not as a matter of social equality, to give one man for his money just as much as another man. The failure of most of the roads to do justice to the negro when he travels is the source of more bitterness than any one other matter of which I have any knowledge.

It is strange that the wide-awake men

IS THE NEGRO HAVING A FAIR CHANCE?   51

who control the railroads in the Southern States do not see that, as a matter of dollars and cents, to say nothing of any higher consideration, they ought to encourage, not discourage, the patronage of nine millions of the black race in the South. This is a traveling population that is larger than the whole population of Canada, and yet, with here and there an exception, railway managers do not seem to see that there is any business advantage to them in giving this large portion of the population fair treatment.

What embitters the colored people in regard to railroad travel, I repeat, is not the separation, but the inadequacy of the accommodations. The colored people are given half of a baggage-car or half of a smoking-car In most cases, the negro portion of the car is poorly ventilated, poorly lighted, and, above all, rarely kept clean, and then, to add to the colored man's discomfort, no matter how many colored women may be in the colored end of the car, nor how clean or how well educated these colored women may be, this car is made the headquarters for the newsboy He spreads out his papers, his magazines, his candy, and his cigars over two or three seats. White men are constantly coming into the car and almost invariably light cigars while in the colored coach, so that these women are required to ride in what is virtually a smoking-car

On some of the roads colored men and colored women are forced to use the same toilet-room. This is not true of every Southern railway There are some railways in the South, notably the Western Railway of Alabama, which make a special effort to see that the colored people are given every facility in the day coaches that the white people have, and the colored people show in many ways that they appreciate this consideration.

Here is an experience of R. S. Lovinggood, a colored man of Austin, Texas. I know Mr Lovinggood well. He is neither a bitter nor a foolish man. I will venture to say that there is not a single white man in Austin, Texas, where he lives, who will say that Professor Lovinggood is anything but a conservative, sensible man.

"At one time," he said to me, in speaking of some of his traveling experiences, "I got off at a station almost starved. I begged the keeper of the restaurant to sell me a lunch in a paper and hand it out of the window. He refused, and I had to ride a hundred miles farther before I could get a sandwich.

"At another time I went to a station to purchase my ticket. I was there thirty minutes before the ticket-office was opened. When it did finally open I at once appeared at the window. While the ticket-agent served the white people at one window, I remained there beating the other until the train pulled out. I was compelled to jump aboard the train without my ticket and wire back to get my trunk expressed. Considering the temper of the people, the separate coach law may be the wisest plan for the South, but the statement that the two races have equal accommodations is all bosh. I pay the same money, but I cannot have a chair or a lavatory and rarely a through car. I must crawl out at all times of night, and in all kinds of weather, in order to catch another dirty 'Jim Crow' coach to make my connections. I do not ask to ride with white people. I do ask for equal accommodations for the same money "

LACK OF A "SQUARE DEAL" IN EDUCATION IN THE SOUTH

IN the matter of education, the negro in the South has not had what Colonel Roosevelt calls a "square deal." In the North, not only the Jew, the Slav, the Italian, many of whom are such recent arrivals that they have not yet become citizens and voters, even under the easy terms granted them by the naturalization laws of the Northern States, have all the advantages of education that are granted to every other portion of the population, but in several States an effort is now being made to give immigrant peoples special opportunities for education over and above those given to the average citizen. In some instances, night schools are started for their special benefit. Frequently schools which run nine months in the winter are continued throughout the summer, whenever a sufficient number of people can be induced to attend them. Sometimes, as for example, in New York State, where large numbers of men are employed in digging the Erie Canal and in excavating the Croton Aqueduct, camp schools are started where the men employed on these public works in the day may have an opportunity to learn the English language at night. In some cases a special kind of text-book, written in two or three different languages, has been prepared for use in these immigrant schools, and frequently teachers are specially employed who can teach in the native languages if necessary

While in the North all this effort is being made to provide education for these foreign peoples, many of whom are merely sojourners in this country, and will return in a few months to their homes in Europe, it is only natural that the negro in the South should feel that he is unfairly treated when he has, as is often true in the country districts, either no school at all, or one with a term of no more than four or five months, taught in the wreck of a log-cabin and by a teacher who is paid about half the price of a first-class convict.

This is no mere rhetorical statement. If a negro steals or commits a murderous assault of some kind, he will be tried and imprisoned, and then, if he is classed as a first-class convict, he will be rented out at the rate of $46 per month for twelve months in the year. The negro who does not commit a crime, but prepares himself to serve the State as a first-grade teacher, will receive from the State for that service perhaps $30 per month for a period of not more than six months.

Taking the Southern States as a whole, about $10.23 per capita is spent in educating the average white boy or girl, and the sum of $2.82 per capita in educating the average black child.

Let me take as an illustration one of our Southern farming communities, where the colored population largely outnumbers the white. In Wilcox County, Alabama, there are nearly 11,000 black children and 2000 white children of school age. Last year $3569 of the public school fund went for the education of the black children in that county, and $30,294 for the education of the white children, this notwithstanding that there are five times as many negro children as white. In other words, there was expended for the education of each negro child in Wilcox County thirty-three cents, and for each white child $15. In the six counties surrounding and touch-

ing Wilcox County there are 55,000 negro children of school age. There was appropriated for their education last year from the public school fund $40,000, while for the 19,622 white children in the same counties there was appropriated from the public fund $199,000.

There are few, if any, intelligent white people in the South or anywhere else who will claim that the negro is receiving justice in these counties in the matter of the public school fund. Especially will this seem true when it is borne in mind that the negro is the main dependence for producing the farm products which constitute the chief wealth of that part of Alabama. I say this because I know there are thousands of fair-minded and liberal white men in the South who do not know what is actually going on in their own States.

In the State of Georgia, negroes represent forty-two per cent. of the farmers of the State, and are largely employed as farm laborers on the plantations. Notwithstanding this fact, Georgia has two agricultural colleges and eleven district agricultural high schools for whites, supported at an annual cost to the State of $140,000, while there is only one school where negroes have a chance to study agriculture, and to the support of this the State contributes only $8000 a year When one hears it said that the negro farmer of Georgia is incompetent and inefficient as compared with the white farmer of Minnesota or Wisconsin, can any one say that this is fair to the negro?

Not a few Southern white men see what is needed and are not afraid to say so. A. A. Gunby of Louisiana recently said· "Every one competent to speak and honest enough to be candid knows that education benefits and improves the negro. It makes him a better neighbor and workman, no matter what you put him at."

Every one agrees that a public library in a city tends to make better citizens, keeping people usefully employed instead of spending their time in idleness or in committing crime. Is it fair, as is true of most of the large cities of the South, to take the negro's money in the form of taxes to support a public library, and then to make no provision for the negro using any library? I am glad to say that some of the cities, for instance, Louisville, Kentucky, and Jacksonville, Florida, have

IS THE NEGRO HAVING A FAIR CHANCE?   53

already provided library facilities for their black citizens or are preparing to do so.

One excuse that is frequently made in the South for not giving the negro a fair share of the moneys expended for education is that the negro is poor and does not contribute by his taxes sufficient to support the schools that now exist. True, the negro is poor, but in the North that would be a reason for giving him more opportunities for education, not fewer, because it is recognized that one of the greatest hindrances to progress is ignorance. As far as I know, only two men have ever given thorough consideration to the question as to the amount the negro contributes directly or indirectly toward his own education. Both of these are Southern white men. One of them is W. N Sheats, former Superintendent of Education for the State of Florida. The other is Charles L. Coon, Superintendent of Schools at Wilson, North Carolina, and formerly connected with the Department of Education for that State.

THE NEGRO PAYS MORE THAN HIS SHARE TO EDUCATION IN THE SOUTH

In his annual report for 1900, Mr Sheats made a thorough analysis of the sources of the school fund in Florida, and of the way in which it is distributed between the white and negro schools. In referring to the figures which he obtained, he said.

A glance at the foregoing statistics indicates that the section of the State designated as "Middle Florida" is considerably behind all the rest in all stages of educational progress. The usual plea is that this is due to the intolerable burden of negro education, and a general discouragement and inactivity is ascribed to this cause. The following figures are given to show that the education of the negroes of Middle Florida does not cost the white people of that section one cent. Without discussing the American principle that it is the duty of all property to educate every citizen as a means of protection to the State, and with no reference to what taxes that citizen may pay, it is the purpose of this paragraph to show that the backwardness of education of the white people is in no degree due to the presence of the negro, but that the presence of the negro has been actually contributing to the sustenance of the white schools.

Mr. Sheats shows that the amount paid for negro schools from negro taxes or from a division of other funds to which negroes contribute indirectly with the whites, amounted to $23,984. The actual cost of negro schools, including their pro rata for administration expenses, was $19,467.

"If this is a fair calculation," Mr. Sheats concludes, "the schools for negroes are not only no burden on the white citizens, but $4525 for negro schools contributed from other sources was in some way diverted to the white schools. A further loss to the negro schools is due to the fact that so few polls are collected from negroes by county officials."

Mr Coon, in an address on "Public Taxation and Negro Schools" before the 1909 Conference for Education in the South, at Atlanta, Georgia, said

The South is spending $32,068,851 on her public schools, both white and black, but what part of this sum is devoted to negro public schools, which must serve at least forty per cent. of her school population? It is not possible to answer this question with absolute accuracy, but it is possible from the several State reports to find out the whole amount spent for teachers, and in all the States, except Arkansas, what was spent for white and negro teachers separately The aggregate amount now being spent for public teachers of both races in these eleven States is $23,856,914, or 74.4 per cent. of the whole amount expended. Of this sum not more than $3,818,705 was paid to negro teachers, or twelve per cent. of the total expenditures.

He also brought out the fact that in Virginia, if, in addition to the direct taxes paid by negroes, they had received their proportion of the taxes on corporate property and other special taxes, such as fertilizers, liquor, etc., there would have been expended on the negro schools $18,077 more than was expended; that is, they would have received $507,305 instead of $489,228. In North Carolina there would have been expended $26,539 more than was expended, the negroes receiving $429,197 instead of $402,658. In Georgia there would have been expended on the negro schools $141,682 more than was expended.

In other words, Superintendent Coon

seems to prove that negro schools in the States referred to are not only no burden to the white tax-payers, but that the colored people do not get back all the money for their schools that they themselves pay in taxes. In each case there is a considerable amount taken from the negroes' taxes and spent somewhere else or for other purposes.

CONVICT LABOR A GREAT EVIL IN THE SOUTH

IT would help mightily toward the higher civilization for both races if more white people would apply their religion to the negro in their community, and ask themselves how they would like to be treated if they were in the negro's place. For example, no white man in America would feel that he was being treated with justice if every time he had a case in court, whether civil or criminal, every member of the jury was of some other race. Yet this is true of the negro in nearly all of the Southern States. There are few white lawyers or judges who will not admit privately that it is almost impossible for a negro to get justice when he has a case against a white man and all the members of the jury are white. In these circumstances, when a negro fails to receive justice, the injury to him is temporary, but the injury to the character of the white man on the jury is permanent.

In Alabama eighty-five per cent. of the convicts are negroes. The official records show that last year Alabama had turned into its treasury $1,085,854 from the labor of its convicts. At least $900,000 of this came from negro convicts, who were for the most part rented to the coal-mining companies in the northern part of the State. The result of this policy has been to get as many able-bodied convicts as possible into the mines, so that contractors might increase their profits. Alabama, of course, is not the only State that has yielded to the temptation to make money out of human misery. The point is, however, that while $900,000 is turned into the State treasury from negro-convict labor, to say nothing of negro taxes, there came out of the State treasury, to pay negro teachers, only $357,585.

I speak of this matter as much in the interest of the white man as of the black. Whenever and wherever the white man,

acting as a court officer, feels that he cannot render absolute justice because of public sentiment, that white man is not free. Injustice in the courts makes slaves of two races in the South, the white and the black.

THE BALLOT TO THE INTELLIGENT NEGRO

No influence could ever make me desire to go back to the conditions of Reconstruction days to secure the ballot for the negro. That was an order of things that was bad for the negro and bad for the white man. In most Southern States it is absolutely necessary that some restriction be placed upon the use of the ballot. The actual methods by which this restriction was brought about have been widely advertised, and there is no necessity for me discussing them here. At the time these measures were passed I urged that, whatever law went upon the statute-book in regard to the use of the ballot, it should apply with absolute impartiality to both races. This policy I advocate again in justice to both white man and negro.

Let me illustrate what I mean. In a certain county of Virginia, where the county board had charge of registering those who were to be voters, a colored man, a graduate of Harvard University, who had long been a resident of the county, a quiet, unassuming man, went before the board to register. He was refused on the ground that he was not intelligent enough to vote. Before this colored man left the room a white man came in who was so intoxicated that he could scarcely tell where he lived. This white man was registered, and by a board of intelligent white men who had taken an oath to deal justly in administering the law.

Will any one say that there is wisdom or statesmanship in such a policy as that? In my opinion it is a fatal mistake to teach the young black man and the young white man that the dominance of the white race in the South rests upon any other basis than absolute justice to the weaker man. It is a mistake to cultivate in the mind of any individual or group of individuals the feeling and belief that their happiness rests upon the misery of some one else, or that their intelligence is measured by the ignorance of some one else, or their wealth by the poverty of some one else. I do not advocate that the negro make politics or the holding of office an important thing in

IS THE NEGRO HAVING A FAIR CHANCE?   55

his life. I do urge, in the interest of fair play for everybody, that a negro who prepares himself in property, in intelligence, and in character to cast a ballot, and desires to do so, should have the opportunity.

In these pages I have spoken plainly regarding the South because I love the South as I love no other part of our country, and I want to see her white people equal to any white people on the globe in material wealth, in education, and in intelligence. I am certain, however, that none of these things can be secured and permanently maintained except they are founded on justice.

THE CRIME OF LYNCHING

In most parts of the United States the colored people feel that they suffer more than others as the result of the lynching habit. When he was Governor of Alabama, I heard Governor Jelks say in a public speech that he knew of five cases during his administration of innocent colored people having been lynched. If that many innocent people were known to the governor to have been lynched, it is safe to say that there were other innocent persons lynched whom the governor did not know about. What is true of Alabama in this respect is true of other States. In short, it is safe to say that a large proportion of the colored people lynched are innocent.

A lynching-bee usually has its origin in a report that some crime has been committed. The story flies from mouth to mouth. Excitement spreads. Few take the time to get the facts. A mob forms and fills itself with bad whisky. Some one is captured. In case rape is charged, the culprit is frequently taken before the person said to have been assaulted. In the excitement of the moment, it is natural that the victim should say that the first person brought before her is guilty. Then comes more excitement and more whisky. Then comes the hanging, the shooting, or burning of the body.

Not a few cases have occurred where white people have blackened their faces and committed a crime, knowing that some negro would be suspected and mobbed for it. In other cases it is known that where negroes have committed crimes, innocent men have been lynched and the guilty ones have escaped and gone on committing more crimes.

Within the last twelve months there have been seventy-one cases of lynching, nearly all of colored people. Only seventeen were charged with the crime of rape. Perhaps they are wrong to do so, but colored people in the South do not feel that innocence offers them security against lynching. They do feel, however, that the lynching habit tends to give greater security to the criminal, white or black. When ten millions of people feel that they are not sure of being fairly tried in a court of justice, when charged with crime, is it not natural that they should feel that they have not had a fair chance?

I am aware of the fact that in what I have said in regard to the hardships of the negro in this country I throw myself open to the criticism of doing what I have all my life condemned and everywhere sought to avoid, namely, laying over-emphasis on matters in which the negro race in America has been badly treated, and thereby overlooking those matters in which the negro has been better treated in America than anywhere else in the world.

Despite all any one has said or can say in regard to the injustice and unfair treatment of the people of my race at the hands of the white men in this country, I venture to say that there is no example in history of the people of one race who have had the assistance, the direction, and the sympathy of another race in all its efforts to rise to such an extent as the negro in the United States.

Notwithstanding all the defects in our system of dealing with him, the negro in this country owns more property, lives in better houses, is in a larger measure encouraged in business, wears better clothes, eats better food, has more school-houses and churches, more teachers and ministers, than any similar group of negroes anywhere else in the world.

What has been accomplished in the past years, however, is merely an indication of what can be done in the future.

As white and black learn day by day to adjust, in a spirit of justice and fair play, those interests which are individual and racial, and to see and feel the importance of those fundamental interests which are common, so will both races grow and prosper. In the long run no individual and no race can succeed which sets itself at war against the common good.

PAUL LAURENCE DUNBAR

BY JAMES D CORROTHERS

HE came, a dark youth, singing in the dawn
        Of a new freedom, glowing o'er his lyre,
        Refining, as with great Apollo's fire,
        His people's gift of song.   And, thereupon,
This negro singer, come to Helicon,
        Constrained the masters, listening, to admire,
        And roused a race to wonder and aspire,
        Gazing which way their honest voice was gone,
With ebon face uplit of glory's crest.
        Men marveled at the singer, strong and sweet,
        Who brought the cabin's mirth, the tuneful night,
But faced the morning, beautiful with light,
        To die while shadows yet fell toward the west,
        And leave his laurels at his people's feet.

Dunbar, no poet wears your laurels now,
        None rises, singing, from your race like you,
        Dark melodist, immortal, though the dew
        Fell early on the bays upon your brow,
And tinged with pathos every halcyon vow
        And brave endeavor.   Silence o'er you threw
        Flowerets of love.   Or, if an envious few
        Of your own people brought no garlands, how
Could Malice smite him whom the gods had crowned?
        If, like the meadow-lark, your flight was low,
        Your flooded lyrics half the hilltops drowned,
A wide world heard you, and it loved you so
        It stilled its heart to list the strains you sang,
        And o'er your happy songs its plaudits rang.

THE NEGRO SINGER

BY JAMES D CORROTHERS

O'ER all my song the image of a face
        Lieth, like shadow on the wild, sweet flowers.
        The dream, the ecstasy that prompts my powers;
        The golden lyre's delights bring little grace
To bless the singer of a lowly race.
        Long hath this mocked me·aye, in marvelous hours,
        When Hera's gardens gleamed, or Cynthia's bowers,
        Or Hope's red pylons, in their far, hushed place!
But I shall dig me deeper to the gold,
        Fetch water, dripping, over desert miles,
        From clear Nyanzas and mysterious Niles
Of love; and sing, nor one kind act withhold.
        So shall men know me, and remember long,
        Nor my dark face dishonor any song.

In the Wilstach Gallery, Philadelphia

Engraved on wood by Henry Wolf

THE ANNUNCIATION

PAINTED BY H. O. TANNER

Copyright 1901 Royal Picture Gallery Co,

The above is the handsome gravure representing the RECEPTION and Dinner
given by President Roosevelt to Booker T. Washington, Oct. 19, 1901, exact size
which is 16x20 inches. Being due to the fact that many of our agents have been
stopped from exhibiting or selling this picture, by a prejudiced class, we place it
before you in this manner so as to enable every one to secure one of these pictures.
Sent direct to your home. Price 25 cents prepaid.

Washington Picture Company,

MARINE BUILDING,   CHICAGO, ILLINOIS,

Conclusion

This book aims to reach two different audiences. For those readers experiencing Washington's work for the first time, we hope that you will be inspired to continue with further study on the life and work of one of America's most discussed, polarizing, inspirational, enigmatic, and controversial figures. For those readers familiar with the Washington literature and legacy, this book will be successful if it raises new questions to consider, unsettles some of the established narratives on his life and work, and introduces unfamiliar works to read and reflect on. To achieve these goals, we felt that Washington needed to be considered (1) by a thematic organization of his writings, (2) with his writings in their original formats, and (3) with examples of new, unfamiliar, and difficult to access writings.

The thematic approach demonstrates how Washington evolved on many issues, how he should be considered within new contexts (separate from the familiar positioning opposite W. E. B. Du Bois), how he wrote about subjects that may be unfamiliar to readers, and how the labels assigned to him and his work help both to define and to distort his legacy.

Using original formats, rather than retyping the originals, enables readers to experience Washington's work in the same way his intended audiences received them. We wanted the reader to feel the aura of the original. That impulse spawned bigger questions concerning the nature of originals in conducting research. Does reading a work in its original font and layout and with the original illustrations change the meaning of a work? If so, how? Does seeing the originals help in understanding how a writer spoke to a particular audience? What is an original, especially when different versions exist?

We decided to expand beyond the familiar Washington publications because we felt that much of Washington's scholarship relied on a limited number of works. Anyone familiar with the literature on Washington sees the same books and speeches constantly recycled, partly because of access and partly because a certain analysis has fixed his ideas into place and discouraged further reading. Furthermore, the Washington "canon" was expanded to let readers know that many Washington writings exist beyond those listed in the *Booker T. Washington Papers*. Although we believe that the *Papers* remain the most essential body of materials for conducting research, some readers may not realize that they are a selection. We foresee new discoveries that will continue to expand and change our understanding of Washington. He wrote too much and changed his mind too frequently for us to rely solely on *Up from Slavery* and the Atlanta Cotton States Exposition speech.

When we began this book ten years ago, we wondered whether the world really needed another book on Booker T. Washington. We agreed that his story remains a quintessentially American story, that he remains enigmatic, and that he provides one of the keys to making sense of the Post-Reconstruction era. Washington's is the quintessential, personal story that has it all: slavery, power, greed, celebrity, robber barons, money, ambition, race, violence, heroism, meetings with royalty, global reach, and even a being born in a log cabin. How could Washington be so famous and so obscure? Even with thousands of documents, pictures, and contemporary accounts, no one knows precisely when he was born, who his father was, his real religion, why he left Wayland Seminary, whether he was a Mason, what happened to his fortune, what he was like in private life, and whether he was a help or an impediment to Black progress. As for being the key to the Post-Reconstruction era, how many individuals get an age named after them? That said, when we see in print "The Age of Booker T. Washington," most of us think of issues confronting only Black America. One does not immediately think race when hearing the Age of Andrew Jackson or the Gilded Age.

In 1900, Booker T. Washington was invited to dine with President Theodore Roosevelt in the White House. Washington's physical presence in the White House was controversial, lampooned with cartoons in the press. Even pictures celebrating their meeting caused concern. In 1904, *The Freeman*, an African American newspaper, turned to direct sales when their door-to-door agents selling the picture were blocked by a "prejudiced class" (see the advertisement from *The Freeman* on page 242). We hope that our choices and analysis will open Washington to a new generation of students. We feel he deserves to be examined in a way that appreciates and acknowledges the complexities and uniqueness of his life and work. As our country witnesses the tenure of its first African American president, it is important to remember the journey of those who first won a seat at the table and laid the foundation in our society for the success of another unique and enigmatic figure, Barack Obama.

Notes

INTRODUCTION

1. For an example of a recent essay proposing ideas directly in line with Washington's with respect to rural development, see Oleta Garrett Fitzgerald and Sarah Bobrow-Williams, in *The Covenant with Black America*, ed. Tavis Smiley (Chicago: Third World Press, 2006), 143–161.

2. For an overview of their contrasting approaches, see Jacqueline M. Moore, *Booker T. Washington, W. E. B. Du Bois, and the Struggle for Racial Uplift* (Wilmington, DE: Scholarly Resources, 2003).

3. Louis R. Harlan, *Booker T. Washington: The Wizard of Tuskegee, 1901–1915* (New York: Oxford University Press, 1983), xi. Harlan, *Booker T. Washington: The Making of a Black Leader, 1856–1901* (New York: Oxford University Press, 1972).

4. Ralph Ellison, *Invisible Man* (New York: Vintage, 1995 [1952]), 36.

5. Louis R. Harlan and Raymond W. Smock, eds., *The Booker T. Washington Papers*, 14 vols. (Urbana: University of Illinois, 1972–1989) (hereafter *BTW Papers*). Even this monumental work represents a small fraction of Washington's correspondence and writing. Harlan's edited project is available online at the University of Illinois. Other Washington papers and artifacts are slowly becoming available online. For example, see Documenting the American South and the Internet Archives.

6. Booker T. Washington, "The Story of Tuskegee Institute," *The Nautilus*, February 1912, 44–51. Founded by Elizabeth Towne, the magazine *The Nautilus* was based in Holyoke, Massachusetts. *The Nautilus* expressed the views of the New Thought Movement, a Christian-based religion and philosophy embracing a variety of beliefs, including Emerson's Transcendentalism, pantheism, and Eastern faith traditions. Begun during the 1880s and still active today, the New Thought Movement emphasizes practical spirituality, or what William James called a "religion of healthy-mindedness."

CHAPTER 1: AUTOBIOGRAPHY

1. Rufus White, *A Joshua in the Camp or the Life of Booker T. Washington of Tuskegee, Alabama* (Towson, MD: n.p., 1895).

2. See Donald B. Gibson, "Strategies in Booker T. Washington's Autobiographies," *American Quarterly* 45 (September 1993), 370–393.

3. *BTW Papers*, 14 vols. Volume 1 describes Washington's autobiographies.

4. See Gibson, "Strategies in Booker T. Washington's Autobiographies," 370–393.

5. Booker T. Washington, *The Story of My Life and Work* (Atlanta: J. L. Nichols & Company, 1901). Edgar Webber, a Fisk graduate, was the ghostwriter for the book. Washington expressed his dissatisfaction with Webber's work by dropping his picture from later editions. See *BTW Papers*, xvii–xviii, for a full description of the problems in the working relationship. Harry S. Shepherd, a black photographer based in St. Paul, Minnesota, worked with Washington throughout the 1890s. For more on Shepherd, see Michael S. Bieze, *Booker T. Washington and the Art of Self-Representation* (New York: Peter Lang, 2008), 114–121, and Deborah Willis, *Reflections in Black: A History of Black Photographers, 1840 to the Present* (New York: W. W. Norton, 2000).

6. Booker T. Washington, *Up from Slavery* (New York: Doubleday, Page & Co., 1901). The White journalist was Max Bennett Thrasher, a New Englander, who had written articles for northern White elites before signing on with Washington. Thrasher

died shortly after ghostwriting *Up from Slavery*. Washington expressed his deep sense of loss at Thrasher's death by naming a building at Tuskegee after Thrasher, an honor usually reserved for those, like Andrew Carnegie and John D. Rockefeller, who could buy it. For a complete, contextualized version of *Up from Slavery*, see Hugh Brundage, ed., *Up from Slavery by Booker T. Washington with Related Documents* (New York: Bedford/St. Martin's, 2003). When Washington traveled to New York and sat in Kasebier's Fifth Avenue studio for this portrait, he was being photographed by one of the leading portrait photographers of the era.

7. Washington, *The Story of My Life and Work*, 222–238.

8. Ibid., 228. Northern papers such as the *Chicago Tribune* carried the entire speech, including the reference to "a cancer gnawing at the heart of this republic." "Choice of the Negro," *Chicago Daily Tribune*, October 17, 1898, 2.

9. Washington, *The Story of My Life and Work*, 231.

10. "Miles and Washington Speak," *Chicago Tribune*, October 19, 1898, 4.

11. Washington, *Up from Slavery*, 254–256. Harlan, in one of his few errors, states that Washington included the full text in *Up from Slavery*. Harlan, *Booker T. Washington: The Making of a Black Leader*, 355. In footnote 23 from chapter 12, Harlan writes that a "printed copy of [the Peace Jubilee] address" is included in *Up from Slavery*. In fact, *Up from Slavery* includes only a few passages from what is a five-page speech in *The Story of My Life and Work*.

12. Washington, *Up from Slavery*, 256.

13. Booker T. Washington, "Chapters from My Experience II," *The Worlds' Work*, November 1910, 13627–13640; Washington, *My Larger Education* (New York: Doubleday, Page & Company, 1911).

CHAPTER 2: SPEECHES

1. Major J. B. Pond, "The Eccentricities of Genius," *Saturday Evening Post*, August 19, 1899, 114. Pond served as manager of the speaking tours of Henry Ward Beecher, Henry M. Stanley, Mark Twain, and the Redpath lecture bureau.

2. Max Bennett Thrasher, "Booker T. Washington as a Speaker," *The Ram's Horn*, *Booker T. Washington Papers*, Hampton University Archives.

3. Kelly Miller, "Booker T. Washington Five Years After," copyright Kelly Miller, Washington, D.C., 1921, p. 14.

4. Washington's first wife, Fanny, died in 1884. He married Olivia Davidson in 1885. She died in 1889.

5. "A Negro Talks Sense," *Atlanta Journal*, November 15, 1893. In *BTW Papers*, 3: 371–372.

6. *Indianapolis Freeman*, January 26, 1895.

7. E. Davidson Washington, *Selected Speeches*, Fisk University, Spring 1895. Benjamin Brawley noted in 1921 that Washington delivered an early version of the Atlanta Cotton States Exposition speech at Fisk. "The Atlanta Exposition simply gave him the great occasion that he needed." Brawley, *A Social History of the American Negro* (1921; repr. Mineola, NY: Dover Publications, 2001), 304. The speech is described at length in the opening of chapter 9 of *Story of My Life and Work*. He writes that "90 percent of any race on the globe earns its living at the common occupations of life, and the Negro can be no exception to this rule."

8. Washington, *The Story of My Life and Work*, 113–123. Washington frames an entire chapter in the book on the success of this speech by using positive accounts from the "Southern Press."

9. This printed version of the speech is included in this book because it highlights the original title of the speech (not "Atlanta Compromise").

10. May 20, 1880, speech at Hampton, *BTW Papers*, 3:582.

11. Booker T. Washington, "Taking Advantage of Our Disadvantages," *A.M.E. Church Review*, 10 (April 1894), 478–483. The article is reprinted in the *BTW Papers*, 3:408–413.

12. Booker T. Washington, "Abraham Lincoln," an address delivered before the Republican Club of New York, February 12, 1909, 307–313. In Arthur Charles Fox Davies, ed., *The Book of Public Speaking*, vol. 2 (London: Caxton Publishing Company, 1913).

13. This letter is available in the *BTW Papers*, 13:183.

14. Readers can listen to Washington deliver a portion of the 1895 Atlanta Cotton States Exposition speech through the Library of Congress. This is the only known recorded speech by Washington. It was recorded years after the original speech was given. Few examples of notes from a Washington speech exist. These notes should be compared with extracts from an "Address Delivered at Black Belt Fair, Demopolis, Alabama," September 27, 1912, in *BTW Papers*, 12:15–20.

CHAPTER 3: EDUCATION

1. "Twenty-Five Years of Tuskegee," *The World's Work*, April 1906. For a full discussion of Washington's role in the creation of several education programs beyond traditional schooling, see Virginia Lantz Denton, *Booker T. Washington and the Adult Education Movement* (Gainesville: University Press of Florida, 1993); Louis Harlan, "Booker T. Washington and the White Man's Burden," *American Historical Review*, 61 (January 1966), 441–467; David H. Jackson Jr., *A Chief Lieutenant of the Tuskegee Machine: Charles Banks of Mississippi* (Gainesville: University Press of Florida, 2002); Jackson, *Booker T. Washington and the Fight against White Supremacy: The Southern Educational Tours, 1908–1912* (New York: Palgrave Macmillan, 2009); Andrew Zimmerman, *Alabama in Africa: Booker T. Washington, the German Empire, and the Globalization of the New South* (Princeton, NJ: Princeton University Press, 2010).

2. Booker T. Washington, "Among Negro Students," *The Youth's Companion*, September 2, 1902, 423.

3. The Settlement House Movement, begun in London in the late nineteenth century, offered "uplift" to the urban poor. Among the American pioneers of this social reform movement, Jane Addams's Hull House in Chicago (founded 1889) is among the best known. Soon after, African American women began forming "clubs" to organize Black women to battle race issues and offer social support in local neighborhoods. Margaret Murray Washington and twelve women cofounded the Tuskegee's Women's Club (1895) to assist the rural poor in life skills, child care, advice on health care and diet, and a variety of other concerns facing families. See also Deborah Gray White, *Too Heavy a Load: Black Women in Defense of Themselves, 1894–1994* (New York: W. W. Norton & Co, 1999).

4. For example, Harvard graduates Leslie Pinckney Hill, Clement Richardson, and Henry Kempton Craft, as well as Minnie Kelley, probably the first Black woman to graduate from the Art Institute of Chicago. However, as Willard B. Gatewood points out, their tenure was usually very brief. See Gatewood, *Aristocrats of Color: The Black Elite, 1880–1920* (Fayetteville: University of Arkansas Press, 1990), 313.

5. "Twenty Five Years of Tuskegee," 7433. Washington admired African Methodist Episcopal church leaders, but few others. Washington created his own bible school.

6. NEA speech, July 1884, Harlan, *BTW Papers*, 2:257.

7. *Eighteenth Annual Report of the Principal of the Tuskegee Normal and Industrial Institute, 1899.*

8. Booker T. Washington, "'The Story of Tobe Jones,'" *New England Magazine*, January 22, 1898, 143.

9. For example, it was the motto of Livingstone College in Salisbury, North Carolina. See Glenda Elizabeth Gilmore, *Gender and Jim Crow* (Chapel Hill: University of North Carolina Press, 1996), 40.

10. W. M. Beardshear, "The Three H's in Education," *The World Today*, August 1902. Many liberal arts schools, both Black and White, offered industrial classes.

11. "A Speech of Mr. Booker T. Washington," *Southern Workman*, June 1893, v–vi.

12. Booker T. Washington, "Problems in Education," *Cosmopolitan*, September 1902, 511.

13. "Getting Down to Business," *The Fra*, December 1909, 83.

CHAPTER 4: WORK

1. Examples include E. Franklin Frazier, *Black Bourgeoisie* (New York: The Free Press, 1957), 68. Frazier offers quotes from the Atlanta speech containing the phrase. Leon Litwack, *Trouble in Mind: Black Southerners in the Age of Jim Crow* (New York: Vintage Books, 1999), 79–80. Litwack directly connects Washington's use of the phrase "dignity of labor" with one of the Tuskegee trustees, Long Island Railroad president William Henry Baldwin. Richard Wormser, *The Rise and Fall of Jim Crow* (New York: St. Martin's Press, 2003), 47. Wormser writes, "His [Washington's] goal was to teach them the dignity of labor."

2. William Allan Neilson, ed., *Charles W. Eliot: The Man and His Beliefs* (New York: Harper & Brother, 1926), 192. From an address delivered to the National Education Association, July 6, 1903, titled "The New Definition of the Cultivated Man."

3. Donald Spivey, *Schooling for the New Slavery: Black Industrial Education, 1868–1915* (Westport, CT: Greenwood Press, 1978), 20. Spivey describes how Armstrong, who believed Blacks to be inferior to Whites, pushed manual labor as a form of teaching virtues. Spivey writes: "It was hoped that this sort of training instilled in them the dignity of labor."

4. Quoted from the 1895 Atlanta Cotton States Exposition speech, Booker T. Washington, *Up from Slavery* (New York: Doubleday, Page & Co., 1901), 220. In ca. 1906 (the exact year is disputed), Booker T. Washington recorded an excerpt from his 1895 speech at the Cotton States Exposition in Atlanta.

5. "An Interview in the St. Paul *Dispatch*," January 14, 1896, in *BTW Papers*, 4:101–102.

6. Booker T. Washington, "The Awakening of the Negro," *Atlantic Monthly*, 1896.

7. Booker T. Washington, "The Successful Training of the Negro," *The World's Work*, 1903.

8. *Basic Writings of Neitzsche*, with an introduction by Peter Gay (New York: The Modern Library, 2000), 111. Nietzsche writes: "Let us mark this well: the Alexandrian culture, to be able to exist permanently, requires a slave class . . . when its beautifully seductive and tranquillizing utterances about the 'dignity of man' and the 'dignity of labor' are no longer effective, it gradually drifts toward a dreadful destruction." Originally appeared in *The Birth of Tragedy* (1871). Earle Labor, ed., *The Portable Jack London* (New York: Penguin Books, 1994), 459. London writes, "I hope I have made it clear that I was proud to be one of Nature's strong-armed

noblemen. The dignity of labor was to me the most impressive thing in the world. Without having read Carlyle, or Kipling, I formulated a gospel of work which put theirs in the shade."

9. The Working Men's Party marched through the streets of San Francisco, California, in 1877 behind a huge banner with the words, "The Dignity of Labor."

10. C. M. Woodward, *The Manual Training School* (Boston: D. C. Heath & Co., 1887; repr., New York: Arno Press, and *The New York Times*, 1969), 6. Woodward writes, "One great value of the school is education to foster a higher appreciation of the THE VALUE AND DIGNITY OF INTELLIGENT LABOR, and the worth and respectability of laboring men. A boy sees nothing in manual labor but mere brute force, despised both labor and the laborer."

11. Patricia M. Amburgy, "Culture for the Masses: Art Education and Progressive Reforms, 1880–1917," in *Framing the Past: Essays on Art Education*, ed. Donald Doucy and Ann Stankiewicz (Reston, VA: National Art Education Association, 1990), 108–110.

12. John Dewey, *Democracy and Education* (New York: Macmillan, 1916; repr., New York: The Free Press, 1966), 256. Dewey writes: "It [the classical Greek concept of education] is not secured by a change in sentiment regarding the dignity of labor, and the superiority of a life of service to that of an aloof self-sufficing independence."

13. Several writings demonstrate the connection. For example, in Mrs. N. F. Mosells's *The Work of Afro-American Women* (Philadelphia: Geo. S. Ferguson Company, 1894), "work" refers to published African American writings as a means of inspiring "race pride" and gender pride (pp. 9–10).

14. For example, see Horace Bumstead, "The Kind of University Most Needed in the South," *American Missionary*, June 1882, 164. Bumstead was Atlanta University's president at the time.

15. In "The Significance of the Niagara Movement," *Voice of the Negro*, August 1905, 600.

16. Booker T. Washington, "Why Should Negro Business Men Go South?," *Charities*, October 7, 1905.

17. Booker T. Washington, *The Negro in Business* (Boston: Hertel, Jenkins and Co. 1907).

18. Pensacola was already in demise as a model city for race relations when Washington stopped by during his Florida tour of 1912. See David H. Jackson Jr., "Booker T. Washington's Tour of the Sunshine State, March 1912," *Florida Historical Quarterly*, Winter 2003, 263.

19. Booker T. Washington, "What Can the White Man Do to Help the Black Man?," *Home Herald*, June 24, 1908.

20. Booker T. Washington, "The Negro Doctor in the South," *The Independent*, July 11, 1907, 89.

21. Booker T. Washington, *The Man Farthest Down* (Garden City, NY: Doubleday, Page & Co.), 338–340. The book was co-written with the noted sociologist Robert Park.

22. Ibid., 390.

CHAPTER 5: PHILANTHROPY

1. The fault line running through Washington scholarship, which sees him as a submissive partner with northern industrialist money, begins with Du Bois. In 1903, Du Bois charges that the north "cannot salve her conscience by plastering it [the so-called

Negro problem] with gold." W. E. B. Du Bois, *The Souls of Black Folk* (New York: Signet Classic, 1982), 94. For thorough examinations of Washington and philanthropy from this perspective, see James D. Anderson, *The Education of Blacks in the South, 1860–1935* (Chapel Hill: University of North Carolina Press, 1988), and William H. Watkins, *The White Architects of Black Education* (New York: Teachers College, 2001).

2. See Marybeth Gasman and Katherine V. Sedgwick, *Uplifting a People* (New York: Peter Lang, 2005).

3. See Michael Bieze, "Booker T. Washington: Philanthropy and Aesthetics," in *Uplifting a People*.

4. Washington could, on occasion, tell questionable jokes or shift into vernacular voice to perform in what he perceived to be a humorous role. In the introduction to volume 4 of the *BTW Papers*, Louis Harlan writes that, after the 1895 speech, "all over the country [Washington] spoke to overflow audiences of both races, using a conversational tone, conventional ideas, and humor, amusing listeners with Negro, chicken, and mule stories that often offended other blacks." Later in life, Washington discouraged such humor.

5. Booker T. Washington, "The Tuskegee Normal and Industrial Institute," *The World To-day*, August 1902, 1727.

6. Booker T. Washington to Emily Howland, November 21, 1898, *BTW Papers*, 4:516–517. Emily Howland Papers, Swarthmore College Archives.

7. *BTW Papers*, Reel 324. Burrell's Press Clippings Bureau, May 27, 1915. When Benson was fired as president of Kowaliga in 1915 by the stock company controlling the school's finances, Washington was immediately suspected of being behind it.

8. W. E. B. Du Bois, "Benson," *The Crisis*, December 1915, 79–80. In this obituary, Du Bois describes Benson as a friend of twenty years, handsome as a god, whose great "Tragedy" was receiving the "great Denial." The "great Denial" was Du Bois's way of assigning Benson's demise to Washington's lack of support. Du Bois continued to attack Washington's unwillingness to steer philanthropists and capitalists toward Kowaliga in *Dusk of Dawn*. Even late in Du Bois's life, in the novel *Mansart Builds a School*, Washington is denounced for misusing his ties to philanthropy.

9. Emmett J. Scott, "The Tuskegee Negro Conference," *Voice of the Negro*, May 1904, 180.

10. Booker T. Washington, "Negro Self-Help," *The Independent*, November 23, 1905, 1207–1208. The article details the support by Black churches and individuals for Black schools.

11. Henry O. Tanner is the best-known artist supported by Washington. For example, in 1904 Washington wrote to Robert Ogden asking for assistance in making Ogden's network of industrialist friends aware of Tanner's paintings for possible purchase. Booker T. Washington to Robert Odgen, February 19, 1904, *BTW Papers*, 255. Washington, a longtime friend of Bishop Tanner, helped by hiring Tanner's daughter Hallie and by writing essays in support of Henry O. Tanner's paintings. He initially tried to develop an interest in the Black community for buying photographic reproductions of Tanner's paintings. See the *Colored American*, July 22, 1899, 2. In 1902, he wrote an essay for the Congregationalist. Ogden eventually bought Henry O. Tanner's famous *Banjo Lesson* that hangs in Hampton University Museum.

12. Mary Weston Fordham, *Magnolia Leaves* (Charleston, SC: Walker, Evans & Cogswell, 1897).

13. Booker T. Washington to G. Addison Turner, February 12, 1906, *BTW Papers*, Reel 274. Washington tells Turner that he will arrive with Whitfield McKinley, a prominent Black businessman active in Washington, D.C., politics for the Republican Party.

14. The Arts and Crafts movement, shaped largely by the ideas of John Ruskin and William Morris in England, offered handcrafted, functional forms as a challenge to the negative effects of industrialization, especially the alienated worker. The movement, which inspired a number of schools and communities in the United States, supported the idea of a community of artist-workers creating forms based on nature.

15. Photograph by A. P. Bedou, one of Washington's personal photographers.

16. For another example, see Washington's 1903 article for *The Outlook*, "Two Generations under Freedom," in which he chronicles the success story of towns in Cass County, Michigan, a region noted for its prominent role in the Underground Railroad.

17. Booker T. Washington, "Chicken, Pigs, and People," *The Outlook*, June 1, 1901, 294.

CHAPTER 6: AESTHETICS

1. James A. Porter, *Modern Negro Art* (New York: Arno, 1969), reprint of the 1943 original, p. 82.

2. For example, see Romare Bearden and Harry Henderson, *African-American Art: From 1792 to the Present* (New York: Pantheon Books, 1993).

3. Booker T. Washington, *The Story of the Negro* (New York: Doubleday, Page, Company, 1909), 1:46–47.

4. Lisa E. Farrington, *Creating Their Own Image: The History of African American Women Artists* (New York: Oxford University Press, 2005), 21.

5. Booker T. Washington, Letter to the Editor, *The Colored American Magazine*, September 1907, 191.

6. Washington, *Story of the Negro*, 1:8–9.

7. *Tuskegee Student*, 12 (May 5, 1900), 2, *BTW Papers*, 5:500.

8. W. E. B. Du Bois to Booker T. Washington, April 10, 1900, *BTW Papers*, 5:480.

9. George Washington Carver to Booker T. Washington, November 4, 1903, *BTW Papers*, LC Reel 7.

10. Booker T. Washington to Thomas J. Calloway, April 17, 1907, *BTW Papers*, LC Reel 277. Washington stated that the reason Tuskegee did not participate was the great costs incurred when hosting their twenty-fifth anniversary celebration in 1906.

11. Washington, *Up from Slavery*, 220, 224. The speech is remarkably rich in references to the arts, comparable to John Dewey.

12. Booker T. Washington, "Problems in Education," *The Cosmopolitan*, September 1902, 514.

13. Found on the walls of Tuskegee could be a variety of high-art prints, including works by Raphael Jules Breton. Washington negotiated with prominent galleries, such as Knoedler in New York, for donations of art works.

14. Michael Bieze, "Ruskin in the Black Belt: Booker T. Washington, Arts and Crafts, and the New Negro," *Notes in the History of Art*, Summer 2005, 24–34.

15. Without citing the painting by name, Washington compared the struggling Black worker just after slavery to the famous image of Jean-Francois Millet's *Man with a Hoe*. While Millet's work appears today as Romantic and sentimental, in the nineteenth century, his work carried a political charge and dangerous associations with socialism. Washington and Hubbard admired each other. They shared the "head, heart and hand" philosophy, were promoters and businessman, rose from rags to riches, oversaw publications, and never tired of homey epigrams to their ideology. Hubbard found Tuskegee's curriculum pointing the way toward the "Ideal City" of education (Hubbard, "A Little Journey to Tuskegee," *The Philistine*, July 1904, 51).

Among Washington's possessions that his family has kept over the generations is an inscribed copy of Hubbard's *Little Journeys* from Hubbard and his wife, Alice, to Washington after the Tuskegee principal visited Roycroft in 1909. It is inscribed, "To Booker T. Washington with love and blessing for his masterly address, & because he is what he is. July 11, 1909." For more on Hubbard and Washington, see Bieze, "Ruskin in the Black Belt."

16. Booker T. Washington, "Signs of Progress among the Negroes," *The Century Magazine*, January 1900, 475, 478.

17. Booker T. Washington, "Industrial Education for the Negro," in *The Negro Problem* (New York: James Pott & Company, 1903), 19. Washington, who frequently reused his favorite sayings, repeated this from an earlier speech delivered to an African American audience. Booker T. Washington, "The Storm before the Calm: Extracts from Speech Delivered by Booker T. Washington before A.M.E. Conference, May 23, 1900," *The Colored American*, 1, no. 4 (September 1900), 205.

18. Emmett J. Scott, "Present Achievements and Governing Ideals," in *Tuskegee and Its People*, ed. Booker T. Washington (New York: D. Appleton and Company, 1906), 30.

19. Shortly after Washington's death, a photography department under C. M. Battey was established. It was taught next to architecture in Trades Building A.

20. See Michael Bieze, *Booker T. Washington and the Art of Self-Representation* (New York: Peter Lang, 2008).

21. Booker T. Washington, "Negro Homes," *The Colored American Magazine*, 5 (September 1902), 378–379.

22. Booker T. Washington, "Negro Homes," *The Century Magazine*, May 1908, 71–78.

23. Booker T. Washington, Letter to the Editor, *Washington Colored American*, June 1899, *BTW Papers*, 5:141–144.

24. Mary Weston Fordham, *Magnolia Leaves*, with an introduction by Booker T. Washington (Charleston, SC: Walker, Evans & Cogswell, 1897).

25. Paul Laurence Dunbar to Booker T. Washington, January 23, 1902, *BTW Papers*, 6:380–381. See letter for an insight into Washington and Dunbar's aesthetic debate over the Tuskegee song.

26. *Twenty-Four Negro Melodies Transcribed by S. Coleridge-Taylor*, with a preface by Booker T. Washington (Boston: Oliver Ditson Co., 1905). Coleridge-Taylor, a supporter of Booker T. Washington, initially approached Washington to help him with the marketing of his first tour of the United States. See Coleridge-Taylor to Booker T. Washington, June 10, 1904, *BTW Papers*, 7:527–529.

27. Emmett J. Scott to C. M. Battey, March 23, 1912, *BTW Papers*, LC Reel 336.

28. The goal of gaining recognition from the mainstream press extended to the Du Bois's camp. Du Bois[?], "A Photographer," *The Crisis*, May 1917, 31. The author, probably Du Bois, wrote a short biography of Battey, noting his portraits of elites in the White world as well as his ability to get a work published in *Everybody's Magazine* in November 1910.

29. Tanner to BTW, May 7, 1904, *BTW Papers*, 7:497. Other Washington supporters, such as White philanthropist Robert Ogden, bought Tanner's famous *Banjo Lesson*.

30. Booker T. Washington, "Tuskegee: A Retrospect and Prospect," *North American Review*, April 1906, 523.

31. Washington, *The Story of the Negro*, 12.

32. Ibid., 48.

33. Washington, *My Larger Education*, 284.

34. Although he was not opposed to higher education, the practical-minded Washing-

ton frequently offered representations of what he considered to be the decadent branch of college learning. A favorite symbol for Washington of wasted knowledge, or that which was not applied, was of a young Black man studying French outside a deteriorating cabin. For an example, see the opening lines of "The Awakening of the Negro," *Atlantic Monthly*, September 1896, 322.

35. Booker T. Washington, "Plantation Melodies, Their Value," *Musical Courier*, 71, no. 25 (December 23, 1915), 47.

CHAPTER 7: RACE

1. The phrase *New Negro* is often associated with the Harlem Renaissance of the 1920s. However, it first reached a national level for Black leadership at the Cotton States and International Exposition held in Atlanta in 1895. The phrase was used repeatedly throughout 1895 to describe a willingness to forego political agitation and instead push for material advancement framed within a spirit of Christian racial uplift.

2. "Booker T. Washington," *The Advance*, March 7, 1895, 798.

3. Social Darwinism is a complex phrase with a wide variety of understandings. All share an acceptance of racial inequality and some hierarchical scale marking the uncivilized to the civilized races. At one end, it overlaps with scientific racism, eugenics, and a political dimension characterized by restrictions on immigration and fear of miscegenation. Works such as Madison Grant's infamous *The Passing of the Great Race* represent its aims and beliefs. At the other end, benevolent White businessmen believed, as enlightened leaders of the civilized ruling class, in lifting the poor up through their philanthropic efforts. In this case, Andrew Carnegie's *Gospel of Wealth* comes to mind. For further reading on social Darwinism and education, see William H. Watkins, *The White Architects of Black Education: Ideology and Power in America, 1865–1954* (New York: Teachers College Press, 2001).

4. Leon Litwack, *Trouble in Mind* (New York: Vintage, 1998), 184.

5. Booker T. Washington, "Our Solution of the Negro Problem," *The Advance*, March 7, 1895, 800.

6. *Address of Booker T. Washington Delivered at the Alumni Dinner of Harvard University, Cambridge, Mass., June 24, 1896* (Tuskegee, AL: Tuskegee Steam Press, 1901), 6.

7. Tommy Shelby, *We Who Are Dark: The Philosophical Foundations of Black Solidarity* (Cambridge, MA: Harvard University Press, 2005), 30.

8. Booker T. Washington, "Heroes in Black Skins," *The Century Magazine*, September 1903, 724–729.

9. *Twenty-Four Negro Melodies: Transcribed by S. Coleridge-Taylor*, preface by Booker T. Washington (Boston: Oliver Ditson Company, 1905).

10. Booker T. Washington, *The Story of the Negro* (New York: Doubleday, Page and Co., 1909), 1:16.

11. Washington, *The Story of the Negro*, 14.

12. Sir Harry Johnston, *The Negro in the New World* (New York: Macmillan, 1910). Booker T. Washington, "The Negro in the New World," *Journal of the African Society*, January 1911, 173–178.

13. A speech at Western University, March 4, 1914, *BTW Papers*, vol. 12.

14. Greenwood was a model community designed on the aesthetics of a New England village. Washington's ill-fated Hilton Head project, which only lasted a few years, has yet to be fully explored.

15. Booker T. Washington, "A Town Owned by Negroes: Mound Bayou, Miss., An Example of Thrift and Self-Government," *The World's Work*, July 1907, 9125–9134.

CHAPTER 8: RELIGION

1. Washington wrote articles for Abbott's *Christian Union* and *Outlook*. Abbott and his wife were present for the dedication of Phelps Bible School in 1893. Abbott deeply admired Washington.

2. The Social Gospel, a Progressive era movement, carries a range of meanings. For most of its adherents, though, the Social Gospel meant the Christian moral and social reform led by Protestant clergy such as Walter Rauschenbusch. It was often seen as being in opposition to social Darwinism (though they certainly overlapped at some points). Social Gospel supporters believed in applying Christian ethics to social issues, conducting missionary work with the poor, social justice, and work with settlement house, the YMCA, and churches to work directly with the impoverished. For further reading, see Ralph E. Luker, *The Social Gospel in Black and White: American Racial Reform, 1885–1912* (Chapel Hill: University of North Carolina Press, 1991), and Nina Mjagkij, *Light in the Darkness: African Americans and the YMCA, 1852–1946* (Lexington: University Press of Kentucky, 1994).

3. Clifford Taulburt, *Eight Habits of the Heart* (New York: Penguin Books, 1997).

4. Ben Johnson's famous quotation as found in Oliver Goldsmiths' *The Traveller*, 1764.

5. This distinction follows the one delineated by David Hackett Fischer as liberty meaning "unbound, unrestricted, and released from restraint," and freedom referring to "ties of kinship and rights of belonging." As opposed to Du Bois, Washington seems to have believed that, for Blacks, liberty needed to be established before freedom was possible. David Hackett Fischer, *Liberty and Freedom* (New York: Oxford University Press, 2004), 5.

6. Diane Osen, ed., *The Book That Changed My Life* (New York: The Modern Library, 2002).

7. Booker T. Washington, "To the Editor of *The Delineator*," February 20, 1909, *BTW Papers*, 10:44. The letter was never published.

8. Booker T. Washington, "A Statement on the Bible: What the Bible Has Been to Me," April 6, 1911, *BTW Papers*, 88–89.

9. Booker T. Washington, "The Kingdom of God," *Tuskegee Student*, October 13, 1906.

10. Ibid.

11. According to older Tuskegee residents and Margaret Washington Clifford, Booker T. Washington occasionally attended Mt. Olive Baptist Church in Tuskegee.

12. Louis Harlan, *Booker T. Washington: The Making of a Black Leader, 1856–1901* (New York: Oxford University Press, 1972), 96–97.

13. S. Becker Von Grabill, *Letters from Tuskegee, Being the Confessions of a Yankee*, 2nd ed. (Birmingham, AL: Roberts and Son, 1905), 31–36. The author claimed that all of Washington's efforts were but a series of well-crafted lies aimed at raising money to build a school covertly advocating social equality.

14. A.B.I.M., "Booker T. Washington—Where Does He Belong? *The Presbyterian Banner*, April 10, 1902, 2.

15. Max Bennett Thrasher, *Tuskegee: Its Story and Its Work* (Boston: Small, Maynard & Company, 1901), 126.

16. Hollis Burke Frissell, "A Man of Faith," in *The Freedman's Friend*, January to March 1916 (Cambria, VA: Christianburg Industrial Institute Press, 1916), 23–26.

17. James Hardy Dillard, *Booker T. Washington: A Christian Philosopher: Founder's Day Address Delivered at Tuskegee Institute, April 5, 1925* (Tuskegee, AL: Tuskegee Institute, 1925).

18. Booker T. Washington, "The Colored Ministry; Its Defects and Needs," *Christian Union*, August 14, 1890, 199–200. This article is the only one in which Washington specifically recounted in *Up from Slavery* (1901), 230–232.

19. Booker T. Washington, "Christianizing Africa," *Our Day*, December, 674–675.

20. *Our Day* was a Boston-based, bimonthly, reform-minded journal begun in 1888, which merged with the *Altruistic Review*.

21. Booker T. Washington, *Sowing and Reaping* (New York: H. M. Caldwell Co., 1900), 9.

22. Booker T. Washington, *Character Building* (New York: Doubleday, Page & Co., 1903), 287.

23. Booker T. Washington, *Putting the Most in Life* (New York: Thomas Crowell & Co., 1906), 24–25.

24. Ibid., 25–26. Washington first articulated this theme in "The Religious Life of the Negro," *North American Review*, July 1905, 20–23.

25. Peter M. Ascoli, *Julius Rosenwald: The Man Who Built Sears, Roebuck and Advanced the Cause of Black Education in the American South* (Bloomington: Indiana University Press, 2006). Louis Harlan, "Booker T. Washington's Discovery of the Jews," in *Booker T. Washington in Perspective*, ed. Raymond W. Smock (Jackson: University Press of Mississippi, 1988).

26. Mary S. Hoffschwelle, *The Rosenwald Schools of the American South* (Gainesville: University Press of Florida, 2006). Among other projects, Rosenwald contributed the last $25,000 needed to complete the Colored Men's Branch of the YMCA in Washington, D.C., designed by Washington's son-in-law, William Sidney Pittman.

27. L. Dean Allen, *Rise Up, O Man of God* (Macon, GA: Mercer University Press, 1992).

28. Booker T. Washington, "The Church and the Negro Problem," in *Messages of the Men and Religion Movement: Congress Addresses* (New York: Funk & Wagnalls Company, 1912), 1:143–151.

29. Booker T. Washington, *Team Work: Dr. Washington's Last Sunday Evening Talk to Teachers and Students, delivered in the Institute Chapel, Sunday Evening, October 17, 1915* (Tuskegee, AL: Tuskegee Institute, 1915), 14.

CHAPTER 9: POLITICS

1. The most complete account of the event is found in the *Tuskegee Student*, April 28, 1906. It contains full text of the speeches delivered by many of the speakers, including Washington, Robert Ogden, Lyman Abbott, Andrew Carnegie, and Charles W. Eliot. Washington's address opened, "And Jesus said, I will make you fishers of men." Secretary of War William H. Taft stated, "A great leader of a people is one who sees their primary need and their pathway to a higher life and by action turns their steps into that pathway. This is what Booker T. Washington has done for the Negroes of America" (unnumbered, p. 13).

2. Examples, in chronological order include, Louis Harlan, "Booker T. Washington and the Politics of Accommodation," in *Black Leaders of the Twentieth Century*, ed. John Hope Franklin and August Meier (Urbana: University of Illinois Press, 1982), 1–18; Cary D. Wintz, ed. *African American Political Thought, 1890–1930* (Armonk, NY: M. E. Sharpe, 1996); and Raymond W. Smock, *Booker T. Washington: Black Leadership in the Age of Jim Crow* (Chicago: Ivan R. Dee, 2009).

3. Emmett J. Scott, *Twenty Years After: An Appraisal of Booker T. Washington*" (privately printed, n.d.), reprinted from the *Journal of Negro Education*, October 1936.

4. Booker T. Washington, *Black Belt Diamonds* (New York: Greenwood Press, 1998), 101.

5. Booker T. Washington, *Putting the Most in Life* (New York: Thomas Crowell & Co., 1906), 31.

6. Graham Greene, *The Power and the Glory* (1940; repr. New York: Penguin Classics, 2003), 131.

7. Ruth Ann Stewart, *Portia* (New York: Doubleday & Company, Inc. 1977). Portia's biographer tells us that the *Merchant of Venice* was one of Washington's favorite plays (p. 18).

8. *Bird's Eye View of Buildings and Grounds of Tuskegee Normal and Industrial Institute*, Tuskegee Alabama ca.1900. The print can be found in *The Story of My Life and Work* (Atlanta: J. L. Nichols & Co., 1901), p. 117, and *Working with the Hands* (New York: Doubleday, Page & Co., 1904), between pages 244 and 245.

9. Booker T. Washington, *Sowing and Reaping* (New York: H. M. Caldwell Co., 1900), 9.

10. Booker T. Washington and W. E. B. Du Bois, *The Negro in the South: His Economic Progress in Relation to His Moral and Religious Development, Being the William Levi Bull Lectures for the Year 1907*, introduction by Herbert Aptheker (New York: Citadel Press, 1970), 52.

11. Many schools were patterned after Tuskegee. To give some sense of their geographic diversity, these include Snow Hill Normal & Industrial Institute in Alabama (one of the so-called Little Tuskegees founded by a Tuskegee graduate), the Fargo School in Arkansas, the Topeka Industrial & Educational Institute in Kansas (known as the "Western Tuskegee), Robert Hungerford Industrial School in Florida (founded by a Tuskegee graduate), Christianburg Normal & Industrial Institute in Virginia, and the Bordentown School in New Jersey (known as the "Northern Tuskegee").

12. For an example of a strong stance maintaining a progressive policy on African immigration, see "Fair Play for Negro Aliens," *New York World*, January 6, 1915, 8. *Booker T. Washington Papers*, 13:209–210. At the same time, Washington was a supporter of European colonialism in Africa.

13. One of Washington's strongest justifications for not entering politics is found in "Colonel Roosevelt and What I Have Learned from Him," in *My Larger Education* (New York: Doubleday, Page & Company, 1911), 158–182.

14. Jennings L. Wagoner, Jr., "The American Compromise: Charles W. Eliot, Black Education, and the New South," in *The History of Higher Education*, ASHE Reader Series, 2nd ed. (Needham Heights, MA: Simon & Shuster Custom Publishing, 1997), 459–472.

15. Louis Harlan, "Washington and the Politics of Accommodation," in *Booker T. Washington in Perspective* (Jackson: University Press of Mississippi, 1988), 179.

16. Thomas Dixon, "Booker T. Washington and the Negro: Some Dangerous Aspects of the Work of Tuskegee," *Saturday Evening Post*, August 19, 1905, 1–2.

17. For example, noted Trinity College (today Duke University) professor John Spencer Bassett's support of Washington led to a famous academic freedom debate.

18. For an introduction to the threats facing Washington, see Robert J. Norrell, "Understanding the Wizard," in *Booker T. Washington: Up from Slavery 100 Years Later*, ed. W. Fitzhugh Brundage (Gainesville: University of Florida Press, 2003), 58–80.

19. Washington quoted Socrates and Plato on education on more than one occasion. He actually delivered a talk, "Some Lessons from Socrates," to the Literary Society of Tuskegee in 1887.

20. John Henry Newman, *The Idea of the University* (New Haven, CT: Yale University Press).

21. Booker T. Washington, *The Future of the American Negro* (Boston: Small Maynard, 1889), 131.

22. Ibid., 138.

23. Ibid., 141.

24. *An Open Letter by Booker T. Washington of Tuskegee, Alabama, to the Louisiana Convention, February 19th, 1898* (privately printed, n.d.), 4. The speech first printed in the *New Orleans Picayune*, February 21, 1898.

25. *An Open Letter by Booker T. Washington of Tuskegee to the Louisiana Constitutional Convention, February 19th 1898* (Tuskegee, AL: Steam Press, ca. 1901), 3.

26. Many tactics were employed by Whites to prevent Black participation in voting, including the use of the grandfather clause, literacy tests, and poll taxes. For a comprehensive account, see Michael Perman, *Struggle for Mastery: Disfranchisement in the South 1888–1908* (Chapel Hill: University of North Carolina Press, 2001).

27. Ibid.

28. "An Interview on the Hardwick Bill," an *Atlanta Constitution* interview from 1900 in *An Open Letter by Booker T. Washington*, 8.

29. Ibid., 7.

30. Booker T. Washington, "Two Generations under Freedom," *Outlook*, February 7, 1903, 292–305.

31. Louis Harlan, "The Secret Life of Booker T. Washington," *Journal of Southern History*, 37 (August 1971), 393–416.

32. Louis Harlan, *Booker T. Washington: The Making of a Black Leader, 1856–1901* (New York: Oxford University Press, 1975), 298.

33. For more on Washington and the NAACP, see Louis R. Harlan, *Booker T. Washington: The Wizard of Tuskegee, 1901–1915* (New York: Oxford University Press, 1983), 359–378.

34. In 1911, the aging Booker T. Washington made front-page news for alleged drunkenness and making sexual advances toward a White woman in an "easy morals" section of New York. He was assaulted by the woman's husband, Henry Ulrich. For a full description, see Harlan, *The Wizard of Tuskegee*. The chapter on the Ulrich affair is titled "Night of Violence."

35. Booker T. Washington, "Is the Negro Having a Fair Chance?" *Century Magazine*, November 1912, 49.

36. Ibid., 55.

37. He could point to the fact that the Tuskegee Women's Club, founded 1895, had a Department of Woman Suffrage and a Temperance Division. In the club's tenth annual report, the group "given a full report or statement of the life and work of Frances E. Willard." *BTW Papers*, 8:478. For the women's movement and race, see Louise Michele Newman, *White Women's Rights: The Racial Origins of Feminism in the United States* (Oxford: Oxford University Press, 1999).

38. Emily Howland was a longtime supporter of Tuskegee; Susan B. Anthony corresponded with Washington and delivered an address at Tuskegee, and Washington offered one of the tributes to Willard in Anna A. Gordon, *The Beautiful Life of Frances E. Willard, Memorial Edition* (Chicago: Woman's Temperance Publishing Association, 1898), 387.

39. Booker T. Washington, *Frederick Douglass* (New York: George W. Jacobs & Company, 1906), 135–137.

40. "Booker T. Washington Questions Benefits to Women," *New York Times*, December 20, 1908, 5.

41. Booker T. Washington, *The Man Farthest Down* (New York: Doubleday, Page & Company, 1912), 318.

42. BTW to Mary L. Hay, March 6, 1915, *Booker T. Washington Papers*, 249–250.

43. Booker T. Washington, "An Address before the American Missionary Association and National Council of Congregational Churches, New Haven, Conn., October 25, 1915," in *Selected Speeches of Booker T. Washington*, ed. E. Davidson Washington (Garden City, NY: Doubleday, Doran & Company, 1932), 277–283.

44. Booker T. Washington, "My View of Segregation Laws," *The New Republic*, September 13, 1915, 113–114.

Index

Page numbers in italics refer to facsimiles.